The Dragon, the Eagle, and the Private Sector

The governments of China and the United States – despite profound differences in history, culture, economic structure, and political ideology – both engage the private sector in the pursuit of public value. This book employs the term collaborative governance to describe relationships where neither the public nor private party is fully in control, arguing that such shared discretion is needed to deliver value to citizens. This concept is exemplified across a wide range of policy arenas, such as constructing high speed rail, hosting the Olympics, building human capital, and managing the healthcare system. This book will help decision-makers apply the principles of collaborative governance to effectively serve the public, and will enable China and the United States to learn from each other's experiences. It will empower public decision-makers to more wisely engage the private sector. The book's overarching conclusion is that transparency is the key to the legitimate growth of collaborative governance.

Karen Eggleston is Senior Fellow at the Freeman Spogli Institute for International Studies and Director of the Asia Health Policy Program in the Shorenstein Asia-Pacific Research Center at Stanford University.

John D. Donahue is Faculty Chair for the Master's in Public Policy program at the Harvard Kennedy School.

Richard J. Zeckhauser is the Frank Ramsey Professor of Political Economy at the Harvard Kennedy School.

The Dragon, the Eagle, and the Private Sector

Public–Private Collaboration in China and the United States

KAREN EGGLESTON
Stanford University

JOHN D. DONAHUE
Harvard University

RICHARD J. ZECKHAUSER
Harvard University

CAMBRIDGE
UNIVERSITY PRESS

CAMBRIDGE
UNIVERSITY PRESS

University Printing House, Cambridge CB2 8BS, United Kingdom

One Liberty Plaza, 20th Floor, New York, NY 10006, USA

477 Williamstown Road, Port Melbourne, VIC 3207, Australia

314–321, 3rd Floor, Plot 3, Splendor Forum, Jasola District Centre, New Delhi – 110025, India

79 Anson Road, #06–04/06, Singapore 079906

Cambridge University Press is part of the University of Cambridge.

It furthers the University's mission by disseminating knowledge in the pursuit of education, learning, and research at the highest international levels of excellence.

www.cambridge.org
Information on this title: www.cambridge.org/9781108837071
DOI: 10.1017/9781108938167

© Cambridge University Press 2021

First published 2021

A catalogue record for this publication is available from the British Library.

ISBN 978-1-108-83707-1 Hardback

Contents

Figures

Tables

Acknowledgments

We acknowledge with deep gratitude the very useful discussions with, and comments and suggestions received from, Alain Enthoven, Victor Fuchs, Yijia Jing, Elizabeth Linos, Prashant Loyalka, Barry Naughton, Michael O'Hare, Fengqiao Yan, and Lei Zhang for various chapters. Many others provided insights informally. We thank Annie Chang, Helen Chen, Karissa Xinyue Dong, Xiaochen Fu, Yingtian He, Lynn Huanmin Hu, Karry Jiao, Lily Zimeng Liu, Yanghe Sha, Rebecca Spencer, Yuzhou Wang, Nancy Hanzhuo Zhang, Shirley Zhao and Sen Zhou for excellent research assistance. For fieldwork and research assistance, we gratefully acknowledge financial support from the Ash Center for Democratic Governance and Innovation of Harvard Kennedy School, the Harvard China Fund, and a Stanford Asia-Pacific Research Center (APARC) faculty research award. We also thank Robert Dreesen and two anonymous reviewers for their perceptive and constructive feedback.

Abbreviations

AADA	analyze, assign, design, and assess
AARP	American Association of Retired People (US)
ACA	Affordable Care Act (US)
ACO	accountable care organization
AI	artificial intelligence
BID	business improvement district (US)
BOCOG	Beijing Organizing Committee for the Olympic Games
BOCWOG	Beijing Organizing Committee for the 2022 Olympic and Paralympic Winter Games
BRI	Belt and Road Initiative (PRC)
CEO	chief executive officer
CG	collaborative governance
CHC	community health center
CITIC	China International Trust and Investment Company (PRC)
COVID-19	coronavirus disease 2019 caused by the SARS-CoV-2 coronavirus
CPC/CCP	Communist Party of China or Chinese Communist Party
CRH	cheap rental housing (*lian zu fang*, PRC)
DPT	diphtheria, pertussis, and tetanus (vaccine)
ECH	economical and comfortable housing (*jingji shiyong fang*, PRC)
FDA	Food and Drug Administration (US)
FDI	foreign direct investment
FDR	Franklin Delano Roosevelt
FQHC	Federally Qualified Health Center (US)
GDP	gross domestic product
GNP	gross national product
GNGO	government-organized nongovernment organization
HPF	Housing Provident Fund (PRC)

HUD	Department of Housing and Urban Development (US)
Hukou	Household registration (PRC)
ICC	Interstate Commerce Commission (US)
IOC	International Olympic Committee
IT	information technology
JV	joint venture
K-12	kindergarten through 12th grade (US)
MACRA	Medicare Access and CHIP Reauthorization Act of 2015 (US)
MHRSS	Ministry of Human Resources and Social Security (PRC)
Minban	"people-run" (PRC)
MTR	Mass Transit Railway Corporation (Hong Kong)
NCMS	New Cooperative Medical Scheme (PRC)
NGO	nongovernment organization
NIH	National Institutes of Health (US)
OECD	Organization for Economic Co-operation and Development
PBoC	People's Bank of China (PRC)
PRH	public rental housing (*gong zu fang*, PRC)
R&D	research and development
SARS	severe acute respiratory syndrome
SASAC	State-owned Assets Supervision and Administration Commission (PRC)
SEZ	special economic zone
Shehui zuzhi	social organizations (PRC)
SLOC	Salt Lake Olympics Committee
SOE	state-owned enterprise
PPP	public–private partnership (or purchasing power parity, Figure 7.1)
UEBMI	Urban Employees Basic Medical Insurance (PRC)
URBMI	Urban Residents Basic Medical Insurance (PRC)
WHO	World Health Organization

PART I

THE FRAMEWORK

Private Roles for Public Goals in China and the United States

Dragons – as befits a mythical species – are diverse. In the Western tradition, unlike the East, dragons are terrifying, fire-breathing brutes. Even within the West they differ, particularly in size. In virtually every self-respecting European city there is an art museum with some version of a medieval St. George and the Dragon. The saint tends to be pretty similar from country to country. But the dragon's scale dwindles dramatically from the south to the north of Europe, ranging from whale-sized in Spain or Portugal to something more like a middling Doberman Pinscher in Norway or Sweden. The Chinese dragon is a different beast altogether – sinuous, intelligent, dangerous to be sure but not without a quotient of benevolence. In ancient mythology dragons bring the life-giving rain; droughts result when dragons aren't properly respected. As China surged to renewed global prominence in the late twentieth and early twenty-first centuries, it at times resembled the Western dragon with its intimidating roars and the latent risk of conflagration. As it becomes more confident in its leading role, at the same time accommodating to a less ferocious growth rate, the Chinese dragon is reverting to the wise Eastern version.

The eagle – specifically the bald eagle – is America's symbol. The bald eagle is blessed with majestic strength and the ability to soar to amazing heights. The United States' leadership of the world for several decades following World War II made the metaphor seem especially appropriate. But the noble bird flirted with extinction in the late twentieth century. And the nation it symbolized hit hard times as well: the erosion of its manufacturing sector, a financial and economic meltdown in 2008–2009, and, most recently, a poisonous political environment compounded by a devastatingly bungled pandemic response. Since flirting with extinction the bald eagle has rebounded, and that is a trajectory that American patriots should surely take as a hopeful omen for their nation's fortunes.

China and the United States appear destined to lead the world over the next several decades. Only as history plays itself out will their respective roles and the precise blend of warmth and antagonism, interdependence and rivalry, in their bilateral relationship be revealed. This book explores an important, and perhaps surprising, shared feature of their efforts to forge successful futures for their citizens: public–private collaboration to accomplish some of each society's most vital collective purposes. Our goals are twofold: first, to offer definitions, principles, and prescriptions that can help decision-makers understand, and wisely use, this special model for getting things done for the public; and, second, to examine the evolution of public–private collaboration in the United States and China across five policy domains offering a rich spectrum of options and choices for public–private interaction.

Although the two countries we choose to examine account for a large share of humanity and of the global economy, comparing them may require some additional justification. Indeed, in many ways – including some of the most obvious ways – they are utterly different. Despite rising inequality, America is a rich country with a per capita income of about $59,000 (as of 2017). And despite spectacular progress in raising a substantial share of the world's population from poverty in just a few decades, China remains a relatively low-income country, with the 2017 per capita GDP barely past $8,800.[1] It too is plagued by inequality. Comparative prosperity is not the only striking difference. The whole planet knows that China is dramatically on the rise; America sometimes seems to be resting on its laurels, or even flirting with decline. China officially remains a communist state; America enshrines free enterprise.

Political structure is probably the most salient difference for accomplishing public goals. China operates under the disciplined control of a single party, whose members comprise but 6 percent of her population (although their number equals a quarter of America's entire population). The Communist Party of China (CPC or CCP) has been in power since 1949, a period spanning seven decades. Long-term single-party leadership brings both massive advantages and disadvantages. Policy shifts are relatively easy to come by. China's government mobilized over 10 percent of GDP within a few months during the 2008–2009 global financial crisis. And the current administration has marshaled resources equivalent to several percentage points of GDP for ambitious programs such as Made in China 2025, the Strategic Emerging Industries initiative, and the Belt and Road Initiative (BRI) – what Barry Naughton (2019) calls "grand steerage" and Nicholas Lardy (2019) characterizes as a resurgent role of the state.[2] In crafting

---

[1] Per capita GDP figures in US dollars for both countries are from the World Bank, http://data.worldbank.org/indicator/NY.GDP.PCAP.CD, accessed October 2018.
[2] Barry Naughton, "Grand Steerage: The Temptation of the Plan," in Thomas Fingar and Jean C. Oi, eds., *Fateful Decisions: Choices That Will Shape China's Future.* Stanford University Press, 2020: 51; and Nicholas R. Lardy, *The State Strikes Back: The End of Economic Reform in China?* Peterson Institute for International Economics, 2019.

and implementing these policies, the preferences of the vast majority of the population may go unheard, private property rights may go unprotected,[3] and whistleblowers may go unheeded.[4] Crises tempt governments to expand control. In fighting COVID-19, China's government quarantined millions, deployed surveillance technologies at will, and collaborated with firms to accelerate the development of vaccines. While its aggressive response was by no means costless, China suffered far fewer deaths per million population than did many higher-income economies.

The United States is raucously democratic. In those same seven decades that define the CPC's rule in China, America's two major parties have repeatedly gained and lost control of the presidency and the two legislative chambers. The government has been divided – no party in control of all three power centers – more often than united. Divided government balances power, a prized feature in America, but it also hampers policy progress in all but the most extreme circumstances. These differences are dramatic. Yet the two global giants also display a surprisingly large, if sometimes subtle, set of similarities that will be explored in more depth in the chapters that follow. Despite stark disparities in pro forma economic dogma and de facto rule of law, both in practice have economies powered by entrepreneurialism.[5] Both have displayed throughout their histories a pragmatic eclecticism when it comes to the organizational means for accomplishing a particular goal. Most pertinent to this book, China and the United States alike have public needs that far outstrip the abilities of their governments to deliver. For both countries, reasonable public goals are limitless; resources are tightly circumscribed. Neither society can afford to rule out any element of a plausible repertoire for advancing public goals. Thus, both have sought innovative ways to create public value by sharing responsibility and discretion with the private sector, a process that we label "collaborative governance." The eagle and the dragon are very different creatures. But the

---

[3] China's Premier Li Keqiang acknowledged that one factor in China's relative economic slowdown and reason for decline in private investment was "weak protection of property rights and other factors" in March 2018 at the close of the National People's Congress (quoted in Lardy 2019, p. 21).

[4] "Internet Mourns the Death of Wuhan Whistleblower Doctor," www.caixinglobal.com /2020–02–07/caixin-china-biz-roundup-internet-mourns-the-death-of-wuhan-whistleblower-doctor-101512868.html, accessed February 7, 2020.

[5] For example, entrepreneurs like Jack Ma have out-competed many traditional firms, and innovation proxied by patent numbers has risen dramatically in China. One careful empirical study reveals that patent quality is also improving (e.g., patents granted in China soared from 45,064 in 1995 to 1,302,687 in 2014, while patents granted to Chinese firms by the US Patent and Trademark Office grew by 38 percent per year from 2005 to 2014); the authors conclude "the data on Chinese patents, both from a quantity and quality perspective, appear encouraging ... about China's prospects for successful transition to a more innovation-based growth model" (Shang-Jin Wei, Zhuan Xie, and Xiaobo Zhang, 2017, "From 'Made in China' to 'Innovated in China': Necessity, Prospect, and Challenges," *Journal of Economic Perspectives*, 31(1), 49–70; quote on page 68).

differences don't negate the case for a careful, serious look at the areas of overlap in purpose, structure, and function.

DEFINITIONS AND DISTINCTIONS

Our term "collaborative governance" has a reasonably specific definition: private engagement in public tasks on terms where the two sectors share discretion. It occupies the crucial middle ground on the spectrum of public–private interactions, a spectrum with strict government control at one end, and private volunteerism at the other. This definition will be elucidated at length shortly, because other authors have used the same or similar term with less precision. It is essential to start with some basic understandings with respect to terms and definitions. Indeed, it may be helpful at the outset to explicitly designate some important elements of the political and institutional landscape that fall largely or entirely outside our domain.

For starters, our comparative assessment is not about the relative scale of the public and private sectors within the overall economy. China has substantially dismantled central planning in favor of a market-based economy, but it retains a distinctive government role with renewed emphasis on government-owned firms in crucial segments of the economy (see Chapter 2). Perhaps surprisingly, using official definitions government spending as a share of GDP is roughly the same in the two countries, as we discuss in more detail later. However, the definitions of "public" and "private" differ so starkly between the two countries, and are so rapidly in flux within China, that it would be difficult to come up with any method for comparing the scales of the sectors that didn't attract a whole host of entirely reasonable objections. For the analyses that follow, we embrace definitions of "public" and "private" that allow for shades of gray – with government agencies and public service organizations (*shiye danwei* such as public schools) clearly "public"; and "private" encompassing non-state actors running the gamut from corporatized state-owned enterprises (SOEs) to social organizations (*shehui zuzhi*) and other not-for-profit entities, not just for-profit private firms.[6]

More broadly, the appropriate balance between public and private organization depends on such a long and interconnected list of considerations about values, preferences, and competencies that even in the absence of formidable conceptual and empirical impediments it is impossible to reach any meaningful conclusions as to which country will come closer to the "right" answer, just judging for itself. While we steer clear of questions about

---

[6] Following Lardy (2019) and others, "private" includes any firm with a sole, majority, or dominant owner that is not the central or local government or village collective, as well as the "third sector" of nongovernmental organizations (NGOs) and social organizations; and "public" usually refers to traditional and corporatized SOEs in which the state is the dominant shareholder (sometimes including fifty-fifty joint ventures). We depart from this only in the degree to which corporatized SOEs are considered closer to the "private" end of the ownership spectrum than traditional SOEs, distinguishing them from government ministries or agencies.

the *absolute* size of the public or private sector, we deal quite extensively with issues of "comparative advantage" – how high or how low a particular function should be on the list of candidates for public-sector or private-sector responsibility, however far down the list a particular society decides to go in practice (see Chapter 2).

Nor does collaborative governance pertain exclusively or even primarily to contractual outsourcing of public services to private providers, though this form of public–private interaction is addressed episodically throughout the book. Outsourcing contracts that are incomplete may involve de facto sharing of discretion, and such arrangements may evolve into relationships that actively embrace shared discretion. The outsourcing of governmental services is extensive in both countries – relatively static at a high level for America and rapidly growing from a low base for China. As of the start of the twenty-first century, privately delivered services accounted for a little over 40 percent of all governmental service spending if Medicare and Medicaid are included, and a little over 30 percent if these huge, heavily outsourced programs are excluded.[7] Following the same opportunistic measurement strategy by which US service outsourcing is estimated, researchers have found that China's public service outsourcing has grown quickly and now accounts for approximately a third of government service expenditures.[8] Remarkably, it seems that the two countries have converged on roughly the same level of service contracting, despite starting from radically different places.

Chinese authorities have also promoted "public–private partnership" (PPP) models – similar but not identical to our notion of collaborative governance for resources – to address financing needs for basic infrastructure, sewage disposal, energy supply, environmental protection, and other domains. These projects draw on a long legacy of promotion by various stakeholders, including the World Bank.[9] According to China's own tally, they totaled 11,000 by the end of 2016, with substantial regional variation in quantity and effectiveness.[10] PPPs

---

[7] Minicucci and Donahue 2004, esp. Table 5, p. 505. S. Minicucci and J. D. Donahue, 2004, "A Simple Estimation Method for Aggregate Government Outsourcing," *Journal of Policy Analysis and Management*, 23(3), 489–507.

[8] Yijia Jing, 2008, "Outsourcing in China: An Exploratory Assessment," *Public Administration and Development: The International Journal of Management Research and Practice*, 28(2), 119–128; D. H. Rosenbloom and T. Gong, 2013, "Coproducing 'Clean' Collaborative Governance: Examples from the United States and China," *Public Performance & Management Review*, 36(4), 544–561.

[9] For background, see www.worldbank.org/en/topic/publicprivatepartnerships, accessed August 14, 2020.

[10] See, for example, Zhirong Jerry Zhao, Guocan Su, and Dan Li, "The Rise of Public-Private Partnerships in China," chapter 29 in Jianxing Yu and Sujian Guo, eds., *The Palgrave Handbook of Local Governance in Contemporary China*. Palgrave Macmillan, 2019: 617–636; and the performance indices developed by Tsinghua university researchers based on measures of governmental management capacity, financial support, and other metrics, as detailed, for example,

as conventionally understood represent one particular form of collaborative governance arrangement, one designed to supplement government spending with private-sector resources, which we term "collaboration for resources" (see Section "Resources" later).[11]

Collaborative governance and service contracting are certainly related, but more like cousins than siblings. Both embody government's ambition to tap the efficiency advantages that the private sector often enjoys for broad classes of activities. Both depend on the diverse, vibrant private economy that America has long possessed and that has blossomed, with startling speed, in China. Both require a well-elaborated system of law and ownership rights so that obligations and entitlements can be specified and secured. If either form of delegation to the private sector is to be effective – in what seems a paradox only when shallowly considered – it absolutely depends upon a high level of governmental competency. If government lacks the personnel with the skills to structure and manage relationships with private providers (whether contractors or collaborators), then delegation – at least delegation that is efficient and accountable – is off the table. And we want to be very clear that both contracting and collaboration have their place. In many circumstances (as we will discuss in multiple chapters of this book), the simpler approach of contracting is superior to collaboration.

The key difference between the two hinges on the defining feature of *discretion*. Contracting – at least when it works as it should – is a matter of government issuing clear instructions to its private agent and holding that agent tightly accountable for following those instructions. The private provider does what it is told (and is paid) to do with little or no discretion. Collaborative governance, conversely and by definition, involves a meaningful degree of discretion exercised by both public and private parties. Such discretion might apply to choices about inputs, processes, or outcomes.

Finally, to complete this effort to clarify collaborative governance by exclusion, by specifying what it is *not*, we are not putting the term forward to include volunteer activity, philanthropy, or corporate social responsibility. This is not because we see public-minded action undertaken at the initiative of private actors to be rare, unimportant, or undesirable. To the contrary, private volunteer activity, which for our purposes can be defined broadly to include both philanthropy and corporate social responsibility, is a vast and vital category of collective action. Our point is merely that volunteer activity is fundamentally *different* from collaborative governance. With contracting, the

in the report *2017niandu Zhongguo Chengshi PPP Fazhan Huanjing Zhishu* ("Chinese cities PPP development environment indexes in 2017") available at www.ppp.tsinghua.edu.cn/chengguo/results/0468724f-98b8-4c91-8dde-c13faf5e45b6.html, accessed January 28, 2019.

[11] For example, one definition states "public-private partnership (P3) projects [are those] where businesses supplement public investment in return for reaping rewards such as tolls and fees." Elyse Maltin, "What Successful Public-Private Partnerships Do," *Harvard Business Review*, January 8, 2019, https://hbr.org/2019/01/what-successful-public-private-partnerships-do.

public party monopolizes discretion (or nearly does so); with volunteer activity the private party dominates discretion. With collaborative governance, discretion is shared.

In contrast to contracting, where the United States and China seem to be converging, the two countries remain very far apart on the role that volunteer activity plays within their economies and societies. Observers from de Tocqueville onward have remarked upon Americans' penchant for organizing themselves in ways that depend on neither government direction nor the profit motive. This tradition thrives today, and the United States continues to lead the world in its use. Between 1988 and 2015 the number of 501(c)(3) entities – the religious or charitable organizations that comprise the biggest category, though by no means all, of American "civil society" – grew from about 124,000 to about 209,000, and their total assets went from about half a trillion dollars to almost 4 trillion dollars.[12]

Here the China of yesterday and today provides a stark contrast. Neither in its ancient nor in its modern versions has China shared the United States' aversion to government. That reason alone would dramatically reduce the pressures for a consequential nonprofit sector, equivalent to what is seen in America, as we discuss in Chapter 2. However, the role for Chinese nonprofits is limited, and not merely because there is less room for a new species given the space occupied by and respect afforded to the government. The Chinese government actively discourages volunteer and civic activities in some realms, no doubt in part to discourage entities that might challenge the Communist Party. Chinese authorities have not only allowed but encouraged the establishment of private nonprofit organizations in health care and education, while actively restricting community-based collective action on sensitive policy areas. Moreover, while social organizations and charitable activity have grown in China, including innovations in venture philanthropy, a large contrast with US civil society remains (see Chapter 2). Consider, for example, social organization ownership per 10,000 population, which in China grew from 2.7 to 5.1 between 2006 and 2016, whereas the figure stood at 67.8 in the United States.[13] Over the same period, charitable giving in China grew rapidly from 0.05 percent to 0.16 percent of GDP, but remained considerably below the 0.6 percent of GDP spent on charitable giving in the United States.[14]

---

[12] From IRS website, www.irs.gov/uac/SOI-Tax-Stats-Charities-and-Other-Tax-Exempt-Organizations-Statistics, Form 990 Data, Tables 1 and 3, accessed October 2018.

[13] See p. 253 of Ming Wang and Shuoyan Li, "The Development of Charitable Organizations in China Since Reform and Opening-Up and a New Layout for State-Society Relations," chapter 12 in Jianxing Yu and Sujian Guo, eds., *The Palgrave Handbook of Local Governance in Contemporary China.* Palgrave Macmillan, 2019: 245–266.

[14] Social donations represent an even larger share of GDP for some other countries, such as Israel and the United Kingdom (Wang and Li 2019, p. 253).

As noted, collaborative governance – in contrast to contractual outsourcing at the one extreme and volunteer activity at the other – occupies the crucial middle ground where the government and the private sector *share* discretion. Both the public and the private collaborators have a significant say in how the task is pursued and, in many cases as well, in the details of how the task is defined. Collaborative governance is not some new, uniformly superior replacement for direct governmental action or, when the private sector is already on scene, for contracting or for volunteerism and philanthropy. To begin, it is not new; as will become clear in chapters to come, public–private collaboration in terms of shared discretion has a very long history. Rather than replacing other forms of public–private interaction, it adds to the menu and well deserves its distinctive name. There will always be tasks for which conventional governmental action will be the right approach, and others where simple contracting or volunteer activity is appropriate. But there are also public purposes – including some of the most important ones – where the two sectors should collaborate in determining what should be done and in what ways. And this is increasingly true in China as well as in America, our dragon and eagle.

As we demonstrate at length in the pages to follow, collaborative governance is a major player in both countries, but in neither has it received much study relative to its current significance and (to an even greater extent) relative to its potential. Not surprisingly, the central prescriptions that emerge from such study have often not been implemented. Hence, some activities are not delegated to the private sector when they should be, while others are delegated when they should not be. Still others are rightly delegated, but in an ineffective or inappropriate fashion – using contractual models where volunteer activity makes more sense or inviting hands-off philanthropy where accountability demands that government retain some control.

And when collaborative governance is directly employed, government not infrequently shares discretion haphazardly rather than strategically; if so, needless costs are incurred.[15] Some costs always threaten when discretion is shared, as defined in more detail in Chapter 2. They take two primary forms. "Payoff discretion" arises when private collaborators divert payoffs to themselves from the public at large. Corruption is a prominent example. "Preference discretion" occurs when private collaborators substitute their own preferences for those of the overall community.

We shall not discuss whether the politically polarized United States or centralized authoritarian China does better, on balance, at designating the right public goals. Rather, we will take specific public purposes as given (be they

---

[15] For example, of nine PPPs reviewed in a recent European Union report, seven were late and over budget. For other European and US cases, see, for example, Maltin "What Successful Public-Private Partnerships Do."

educating youth, housing the poor, or hosting the Olympics) and discuss choices of contracting, collaboration, or pure delegation in achieving those goals (see Chapter 2). We argue that through a more deliberate application of the collaborative model, and more strategic choices among the different forms of public–private interaction, a more favorable balance between the benefits and costs of allowing private discretion can be achieved.

This book develops and illustrates five broad themes, some specific to our chosen two countries, and others more generally applicable to the analysis of public–private interactions in any nation:

- China and the United States differ dramatically in their societies, economies, and governments, yet both draw heavily upon the private sector in their pursuit of public goals.
- The *form* of public–private interaction matters at least as much as the *degree*.
- Collaborative governance is a special form of undertaking between the public and private sectors. It is distinguishable from more familiar models where the two sectors interact, such as contracting and volunteer activity.
- Both countries are experimenting regularly with collaborative governance. Yet neither is fully examining its distinctive features or understanding its strengths and challenges.
- Careful definitions, illustrations, and prescriptions – starting with those in this book – can help decision-makers in both countries, or indeed in other countries, make more extensive, appropriate, and successful use of this special strategy for creating public value.

WHY COLLABORATIVE GOVERNANCE?

There are four chief justifications for collaborative governance – that is, for engaging the private sector, and doing so under terms that allow shared discretion, rather than through direct government action on one hand, or through volunteer activity on the other. These four justifications are private-sector advantages in *productivity, information, legitimacy,* and *resources* that can advance public-sector missions. An important further condition is that these advantages can only be fully and effectively activated when discretion is shared. Each of these justifications will be introduced briefly here and illustrated through cases throughout the book.

Productivity The most common justification for collaborative governance is the private sector's advantage in productivity – an advantage that is far from universal but both very common and widely acknowledged. Productivity plays a role in many of the cases in the US-focused book on collaborative governance that two of us wrote not many years ago. One notable example, in chapter 4 of that book, deals with the management of the US Space Shuttle, in which the US government capitalized on the productivity of the American aerospace industry.[16] In China, the extraordinarily active area of real estate development also illustrates collaboration for productivity (Chapter 5). Such a collaborative approach is essential, given that the government lacks both the expertise and the deftness required for most real estate development, even though it technically owns all of the nation's land and holds responsibility for managing the nation's rapid and massive urbanization. The private sector has demonstrated a strong productivity advantage in developing urban land, in the context of an increasing diversity of land-use rights. Unfortunately, numerous scandals involving Chinese land use, including confiscatory acquisitions of farmland to exploit for urban development and economic development more generally, plague these arrangements, and numerous real estate firms are thought to be over-leveraged. In addition, the central government's goal of increasing affordable housing requires aligning the incentives of both local governments (which could obtain much higher revenues if they allocate land to commercial use) and private developers (whose profit margins are capped for affordable housing construction, but who often seek good will and legitimacy by participating in low-income housing developments). Our discussion analyzes how this sector exemplifies "collaborative governance, Chinese style,"[17] such as how contracting may take the form of de facto collaboration under highly imperfect or incomplete contracts. Our conceptual framework elucidates how China, as well as other countries, might be able to gain even more of the benefits from private involvement in this area while lowering the costs, risks, and adverse effects.

Information Beyond productivity advantages, the private sector frequently has much better information about an activity than does the government, whether in China or America. The cost of getting pertinent information may be high for the government in many contexts, and the private sector may refuse to divulge some critical information that it possesses. Or information may be so deeply embedded in a private organization that it is hard to provide or interpret outside its context. If so, even a cooperative private player cannot fully and credibly share it with the government. For example, how will a messenger RNA-based vaccine compare to an adenovirus vector vaccine for Disease X in population Y in terms of safety, efficacy, and cost? Governments in both nations have a strong motive to collaborate with their better-informed private-sector counterparts to answer such questions.

The recognition that the private sector has more information and expertise in an area than the government drives many collaborative arrangements. In the

---

[16] Today that chapter would be notably expanded, since brilliant entrepreneurs Jeff Bezos and Elon Musk have both launched major space-exploration companies, which work in collaboration with NASA, and which have major facilities at Cape Kennedy.

[17] The epithets "Chinese style" or "with Chinese characteristics" pervade policy documents and social science discourses on China, illustrating a parallel: both the United States and China consider themselves sui generis.

United States, governments often employ a collaborative approach in worker training, workplace safety, and other domains given the private sector's superior access to relevant information. Similarly, China uses collaborative strategies for some areas of human capital development (see Chapter 6) as well as for dealing with technological and environmental challenges. For example, the government has recruited top private firms such as Baidu, Tencent, and Alibaba to its "national artificial intelligence team." As we shall discuss in more detail in Chapter 2, SOEs and firms derived from previous government research agencies play a prominent role in such collaborative undertakings. For example, the manager of one government-designated partner in the artificial intelligence (AI) initiative said: "I was not aware of this advantage until I founded CloudWalk. ... Obviously the state-owned banks and public security departments have more faith in our technologies and products because we come from the Chinese Academy of Sciences."[18] Unsurprisingly, China's aggressive embrace of specific private-sector collaborators for industrial policies has aroused significant complaints by foreign nations about support for companies engaged in international trade. Trade policy falls outside the scope of this book. Our focus, rather, is the extent to which collaboration for information can further specific public goals such as education and population health.

A prime example is the collaborative approach China employed for successful development of vaccines for COVID-19 and earlier for Ebola (see Chapter 7). As Yin Weidong, CEO of Sinovac Biotech, commented regarding their plans to produce and distribute a vaccine for COVID-19, "the government has given us tremendous support. Integrating us in the larger strategic layout and development [of Beijing], the Beijing Municipal government released to us nearly 70, 000 square meters of land...We have carried out clinical research while simultaneously preparing for mass production with our manufacturing workshop under construction 24/7."[19] This case illustrates how China's local governments share resources such as land in collaborating for information and productivity to address collective challenges such as coping with public health crises.

Legitimacy Legitimacy is in the eyes of the beholder. Beholders in the United States tend to view the private sector as holding greater legitimacy, given that nation's long-standing reverence for private enterprise and characteristically jaundiced view of collectivism. The United States is an international outlier in this regard. In policy arenas from foreign aid to health care to financing college

---

[18] Tony Peng (April 20, 2018). China's "National AI Team" Gets Busy. Retrieved from https://syncedreview.com/2018/04/20/what-is-chinas-national-ai-team/.

[19] Li, Yukun, "Interview with Yin Weidong, C.E.O. of Sinovac: Inactivated COVID-19 Virus Vaccine Entering Test Production in July [zhuanfang Kexing dongshizhang Yin Weidong: xinguan bingdu miehuo yimiao 7-yuefen shi shengchan]," Beijing News, May 10 2020, http://www.bjnews.com.cn/news/2020/05/10/725904.html.

education, a private role has been built into governmental undertakings as a ploy to make them more politically palatable. Private involvement has happened even absent practical advantages from private engagement in some arenas, and sometimes entailing sacrifices in efficiency or accountability.

China's beholders have a more jaundiced view of private sector legitimacy. Indeed, in China, private firms may gain legitimacy from collaborating with government.[20] What is distinctly similar between the two nations is that there are many legitimacy-motivated collaborative arrangements in each, implying that there are opportunities to exchange lessons.

Resources Partnership with the private sector can augment a government's own resources with those of the private partners who have an interest in a particular public interest undertaking. That interest may be commercial (as with pharmaceutical firms that contribute user fees to speed up the US government regulators' review process for new drugs) or community-minded (as with wealthy American citizens who offer financial support to charter schools). Resources can take many forms beyond financial resources, including relevant human capital and technical expertise that may be lacking in a given locality.

A noteworthy American example of collaboration for resources, visible to any visitor who ventures to New York City, involves the resurrection of the city's Central Park in the last two decades of the twentieth century. City government, strapped for cash, secured substantial private resources by granting discretion to a private group, the Central Park Conservancy. Now the Conservancy essentially runs the park, with modest oversight and contributions from the City. Various environmental and green growth initiatives in China somewhat resemble this case.

In China, local governments draw on non-state actors to access many kinds of resources. Localities vary tremendously in levels of economic development: per capita income was 4.5 times higher in Beijing than in Gansu (the poorest province in 2017). Moreover, since local finance accounts for approximately 80 percent of fiscal expenditures,[21] neither central government transfers nor the still small charitable giving in China fill the gap for poorer localities. Collaboration for resources can sometimes help.

Education might well illustrate another promising arena for such resource-motivated collaboration. Indeed, this is the arena where Jack Ma of Alibaba

---

[20] Indeed, "enhanced organizational reputation and brand" was ranked above other reasons, such as funding, by 116 non-profit organizations in Shanghai that received contracts from the Shanghai Municipal Government. Jing, Yijia, and Bin Chen, 2012, "Is Competitive Contracting Really Competitive? Exploring Government-Nonprofit Collaboration in China," *International Public Management Journal*, 15(4), 405–428.

[21] Christine Wong, 2019, "Public Policy for a Modernising China: The Challenge of Providing Universal Access to Education under Fiscal Decentralisation," in Kim, J. and S. Dougherty eds., *Fiscal Decentralisation and Inclusive Growth in Asia*, OECD Publishing, Paris, https://doi.org /10.1787/68248dec-en.

professes the greatest interest in devoting his time and treasure after stepping down from Alibaba, and many firms, such as US-based Coursera, play a role in the technology-driven educational system of the twenty-first century in both countries. In a rough parallel with Ma's intended efforts, philanthropy has already sharply augmented the resources available for charter schools in some parts of the United States and for addressing disparities in online learning during the coronavirus pandemic. In China, *minban* ("people-run") schools have a long tradition as a form of collaboration for resources, even as early as the Mao era, and more recently the development of private schools and universities in China, with some contributions from philanthropists, also bring significant new resources to education (see Chapter 6).

Of course, these motivations need not be mutually exclusive. Arguably all four spur some collaborative arrangements, such as both countries' efforts to control the COVID-19 pandemic through development and distribution of vaccines. In such collaborations, the risks of payoff discretion need to be carefully managed. The summer 2018 vaccine scandal in China illustrates the dangers (see Chapter 7).

TWO COUNTRIES, TWO (VERY DIFFERENT) SYSTEMS

We do not want to overstate the theme of similarities. Collaborative governance tends to manifest itself quite differently in China than in the United States. While both countries rely on public–private collaboration, the differences in governmental structures and political cultures are stark, with implications for collaborative structures. In the pursuit of public goals in general, the Chinese government is much more likely to choose agencies affiliated with the state. For example, in China, higher education and health-care provision are overwhelmingly government activities, whereas in the United States they are primarily delivered by private entities. Competition is enshrined as a virtue in the United States, much less so in China.

When it does collaborate with the private sector, the Chinese government typically retains more power than does its American counterpart. As noted, China generally turns the American legitimacy argument – private involvement boosts the legitimacy of a public task – on its head. Private firms in China often gain legitimacy by working with the government. The overwhelmingly dominant position of the government in China's society creates opportunities, but it also brings hazards. In collaborations for resources, private Chinese organizations are often induced to serve public purposes as a means to gain connections with government agencies. Conversely, unclear property rights and the dominance of the executive over the judicial and legislative branches of the Chinese government deprive private organizations of legal recourse should conflicts arise. Hence, private organizations in China may have *less* incentive than their American counterparts to risk providing resources for public purposes, even though arguably more of Chinese government motivation for collaboration stems from seeking private resources to supplement those of government.

Moreover, China's approach to the private sector reflects its position as a middle-income country recently transitioned from central planning to a market-based economy. Though the market controls most of the territory, the government retains the "commanding heights." Naturally many facets of China's policies contrast with those of the United States, a high-income country with a long-established capitalist tradition. State-owned enterprises play a major role in China and a minuscule role in the United States. Private corporations are important in both countries. Though their role is relatively larger in officially capitalistic America, it has greatly increased in China since the reform policies instituted in 1978. Nonprofits are massively more important in America than in China, where they constitute a growing but still minor force.

China and the United States also differ in their emphases on the justifications for collaborative governance. Collaboration for productivity and information is critical in both nations. However, China arguably undertakes more collaborations for resources, especially in less-developed regions, and almost certainly far fewer for legitimacy. In addition, as we argue in companion research with Yijia Jing, some public purposes, such as the provision of social services, will probably shift from collaboration for resources to collaboration for information and productivity as time moves forward, with differences in approach driven largely by differences in local government capacity[22]:

Evidence from a survey of 17 medium-sized cities in China suggests an "uneven tendency for private involvement in social services to be somewhat higher for both low-income *and* high-income locales and somewhat lower in the middle. One possible interpretation is that in less-developed cities, 'delegation by default' occurs when the government lacks the necessary resources. At the other extreme ... local governments in more-developed areas delegate with conscious strategic intent, and have rich ecologies of private counterparts and the institutional capacities to oversee their effort, so as to permit experimentation with collaborative governance, in both simple and complex forms, as well as simple outsourcing. This theory that collaborative governance in China comes in two models, basic and sophisticated, may ultimately prove to be the driving force for today's pattern. Whether or not, a high degree of diversity in the earlier stages of policy development can pay dividends down the road. Best practices advance when the most promising approaches expand and proliferate, while less effective models wither. ... [Moreover, collaborative approaches may be especially important for social services because] contractual outsourcing, where government retains discretion and private agents simply do what they're paid to do, is constrained by the difficulty of writing sufficiently specified contracts for many social services. Voluntary philanthropy, where private parties advance the public good as they define it with little discretion for

[22] Jack Donahue, Karen Eggleston, Yijia Jing, and Richard J. Zeckhauser, "Private Roles for Public Goals in China's Social Services," chapter 12 in Karen Eggleston ed., *Healthy Aging in Asia*, Stanford University Walter H. Shorenstein Asia-Pacific Research Center series with Brookings Institution Press, 2020: 199–215.

government, is constrained by the underdevelopment of the non-profit sector in general and philanthropy in particular. Thus we expect China to become a laboratory for that middle ground of collaborative governance, where the public and private sectors experiment with models of shared discretion for the delivery of social services. And the world will watch and learn."[23]

It is important to recognize the real differences between the two countries, without letting them obscure the large and growing roles for collaborative governance in both.

Although some of China's distinctive features inhibit US-style public–private collaboration, it also has some special characteristics that favor collaborative governance. Perhaps foremost among them is that collaborative governance – as distinct from related approaches like social entrepreneurship or corporate social responsibility – preserves for government a privileged role in defining the public purposes to be pursued. This assumption resonates with Chinese history and with China's top leadership.

China has long relied on experimentation and pilot reforms to test policies prior to bringing them to scale, as it did with the Special Economic Zones set up at the beginning of the reform period. Since then, official policy has called for bold experimentation to find solutions to the immense, innumerable, and often seemingly intractable challenges facing China. Since China's public and private institutions remain works in progress, shared discretion may bring greater risks than it does in the United States, but it may also offer far greater potential rewards.

Let us be specific about what we mean by the term "collaborative governance" in the Chinese context. The term does not refer to the existing policy of welcoming entrepreneurs into the CPC; nor does it refer to efforts by specific individuals or agencies to co-opt and control business associations, to establish state corporatism, or to collude in what has been labeled "crony communism." These are all issues amply explored by political scientists studying public–private relations in China. They are also far less promising as means to bringing China public value. Instead, our focus is on how the government does and could harness private capabilities to the pursuit of specific public missions.

China and the United States, like many countries and despite their vast differences, face a common challenge: they must find innovative and sustainable ways to provide for the welfare of their citizens. The resources and capabilities of their respective governments are simply too limited to complete this task alone. Thus both nations are likely to call increasingly upon the private sector, and to share discretion – knowingly or unknowingly, strategically or accidentally, to good effect or ill – when doing so. In both countries, the understanding of collaborative governance is limited, which has

[23] Donahue, Eggleston, Jing, and Zeckhauser 2020, pp. 211–212.

contributed to an under-recognition of its current role. Finally, a failure to recognize its distinction from both contracting and volunteer activity often leads to avoidably poor performance.

Here, we aim to add a fresh perspective to other research. This book first lays out a general conceptual framework about how to identify the appropriate use of collaborative governance. It then documents the parallel institutional evolution of collaborative governance in these two very different countries. Thus, it assesses examples from China and interprets American experience to illuminate the shared opportunities and challenges of enlarging these two great nations' repertoires for creating value for their citizens. To do so, we do not adhere to strictly parallel time periods of analysis, but rather focus on developmental phases that shaped the path-dependent evolution of each country's current approach and potential lessons for each other as well as for other countries.[24]

A TOUR OF THE BOOK

Chapter 2, "Concepts and Context," lays out in greater depth our conceptual framework and the institutional context shaping contracting and collaborative approaches in each country. It largely follows the steps of our "delegation decision tree" in discussing how to identify when collaborative governance can out-perform other ways to pursue public goals. Each branch of that tree answers a key question. Starting from the left of the tree, those questions are: Should a given mission or service involve government at all, rather than being left to individuals? If the answer is "yes," should the government produce the service itself, or should it delegate some or all of production to the private sector? If delegating, should the delegation take the form of completely prescribed contracting or fully flexible volunteerism (including philanthropy), or should it feature shared discretion between the government and the private entity, the form we term collaborative governance? If collaborative, should the private partner be for-profit or nonprofit? After laying out this decision-tree framework, we delve into the more granular tactics for implementing collaboration, highlighting our four-step cycle of analyze, assign, design, and assess. This analytic framework applies quite generally, and we expect that the lessons distilled from its application to the United States and China would apply to many other countries that take a pragmatic approach to the production of public value.

[24] We are far from the first to do so. For example, Ming Wang and Shuoyan Li argue that "there are striking similarities between the present-day vigorous growth in public services and charity works in China and the related upsurge at the beginning of the twentieth century in the United States" (p. 252 of Ming Wang and Shuoyan Li, "The Development of Charitable Organizations in China since Reform and Opening-Up and a New Layout for State-Society Relations," chapter 12 in Jianxing Yu and Sujian Guo, eds., *The Palgrave Handbook of Local Governance in Contemporary China*. Palgrave Macmillan, 2019: 245–266).

The second part of Chapter 2 lays the foundation for our application of this general conceptual framework to the development of public–private interaction across five specific policy domains in two consequential countries, the United States and China. To do so, we briefly overview the players in the process before turning to specific aspects of the context in each country, such as the role of civil society and private nonprofits in the United States, and the central roles of regional heterogeneity, local bureaucrats, and SOEs in China. The chapter concludes by mapping the most important risks and downsides of the collaborative approach to governance in any country.

The second, and central, part of the book focuses on five specific public purposes. We compare and contrast the historical development and current status of private roles in rail transportation, real estate development, hosting the Olympics, education, and health care.

Chapter 3 tells the story of public–private collaboration in American and Chinese rail. Three distinctive features of railroads – the costly capital investment required up front coupled with low marginal costs of carrying freight or passengers, their need to secure rights of way, and their intricate connection to economic development – militate against simple laissez-faire, even in America. The US history of rail development is a tale of extensive collaboration between the public and private sectors. Both successes and failures are abundant. In China, railway development illustrates how key sectors considered the "commanding heights" of the economy (including iron and steel, utilities, and telecommunications), once completely dominated by direct government provision, developed into sectors dominated by corporatized SOEs with separate regulatory structures, and later embraced elements of contracting out to domestic private firms and, for a few specific projects, collaborating with shared discretion.

Railways represent an interesting parallel institutional ecology in the United States and China, with SOEs and hybrid organizations. Amtrak and Conrail constitute rare SOEs for the United States, necessitated by the rescue phase, whereas in China, SOEs are often the private counterpart for contracting and collaborating with government agencies, emblematic of initial private engagement and tentative steps toward greater sharing of discretion. The chapter discusses China's development of subways as well, including Beijing subway Line 16 and the metro system in Hong Kong (one of the best operated metro companies in the world), as well as the world's largest high-speed rail network, all constructed within the first two decades of the twenty-first century.

We turn in Chapter 4 to real estate development, a domain with extensive public–private collaboration. The chapter starts with a high-level overview of real estate in the United States, organized by three broad sub-categories: owner-occupied housing, rental housing (especially subsidized low-income rentals), and commercial (office, retail, hotels, and industrial) real estate. It then segues to cover the parallel story in China, where the government and village collectives own all the land and urbanization rapidly moved and is moving hundreds of millions of people from rural areas to cities. Once dominated by direct provision, China's system now prominently features private engagement and aspects of collaborative governance in providing affordable housing and commercial real estate development. Home ownership in China is extraordinarily high (about 90 percent, and higher in rural than urban areas), with an unprecedented housing boom that makes the recent US housing gyrations look "stable and dull"[25] by comparison. Overall, real estate development projects exhibit collaboration for resources, information, and productivity. In China, one could say that collaboration for legitimacy also plays a role, since local government leaders gain legitimacy as promoters of local economic development, and private firms gain legitimacy and access to coveted resources such as land if chosen for development projects. In 2020, Chinese authorities deployed real estate policies in their fiscal stimulus designed to counteract the devastating economic impact of the efforts to control the COVID-19 pandemic.

From these classic collaborative contexts of ongoing infrastructure development, in Chapter 5 we turn to a major event that involves statecraft and national image, while requiring efficient infrastructure and logistical management: hosting the Olympic Games. We discuss the US approach to hosting the 1984 Los Angeles Summer Games, the 1996 Atlanta Summer Games, and the 2002 Salt Lake City Winter Games, with significant involvement of business, nonprofits, and civil society. The analysis then turns to Beijing, which will be the first city in modern times to host both the Summer (2008) and the Winter (2022) Games. While the government almost single-handedly managed the 2008 Games, the approach of the Beijing Organizing Committee for the 2022 Olympic and Paralympic Winter Games appears to be more collaborative, an approach that may expand in other areas of governance as China becomes more comfortable with its complex features and its great potential to yield high payoffs when well managed.

Chapters 6 and 7 explore the role for collaboration in two aspects of human capital development: education and health. In the all-important arena of education and training, the United States and China display both meaningful similarities and striking differences in approach. After briefly touching upon the role of race and ethnicity in US human capital disparities, Chapter 6 offers a high-level overview of the public, private, and mixed models that have been employed in elementary and secondary schooling for children and youth (including US charter schools and *minban* schools in China); in higher education for young adults, a heralded strength with prominent public and private (largely nonprofit) universities in the United States, and dramatic recent expansion in China, mostly with public universities; and finally in postsecondary worker training. Education in the United States displays a rich ecology of different institutional forms. In China, public schools dominate most levels of the education system, although the private

[25] Glaeser, E., Huang, W., Ma, Y., and Shleifer, A., 2017, "A Real Estate Boom with Chinese Characteristics," *The Journal of Economic Perspectives, 31*(1), 93–116.

share has grown. By 2016, about 8 percent of primary school students, 12 percent of secondary school students, and 15 percent of college students were enrolled in private schools and universities. Chapter 6 shows that both nations have much room for improvement in bolstering quality and securing better value for money in their collaborative projects for education and job training. Complexities render it difficult to identify and implement desirable arrangements, heightening the need for making contracting and collaboration accountable. Effectively harnessing private-sector contributions to human capital development requires government to take on new, often unfamiliar, roles in contracting and management to assure that public value is maximized.

We then turn to the health sector. Chapter 7 first discusses some conceptual issues important for understanding collaborative challenges in the financing and delivery of health-care services, and then discusses the United States and Chinese health systems. The US system, most observers agree, produces a mediocre outcome at extraordinary expense – utilizing more than one-sixth of GDP. The approach is collaborative; public funds pay for roughly half of medical services, while a mixed ecology of public and private delivery extends back to the nineteenth century, with direct government delivery declining and private nonprofits playing a dominant role. We discuss how the US government has partnered to leverage private strengths for a range of health system goals, such as hospital construction, coverage through private insurance plans (Medicare Advantage and Part D pharmaceutical coverage), monitoring drug safety through the FDA's Sentinel Initiative, or increasing access for the most vulnerable patients through the nation's network of community health centers. We then turn to how China achieved universal health coverage at a modest benefit level through social insurance reforms starting in the early twenty-first century, infusing a large amount of government financing and welcoming private sector delivery for some services. By 2018, about one in four hospital beds was private (slightly more for-profit than nonprofit), and the private share was larger for many nonhospital services. Several of the fundamental tensions that plague the health sector in the United States plague China as well. Health expenditures absorb only 6 percent of GDP in China at present, but they are increasing rapidly, while economic growth is slowing and the population is aging. Both countries will need to improve and strengthen their management of collaborative governance in this sector to meet their citizens' expectations for safe, quality, innovative yet affordable health services.

We conclude – in Part III and Chapter 8 – by stepping back from sector-by-sector comparisons. The chapter instead offers more general perspectives on private roles for public goals in both countries by turning a critical eye on the issue of transparency, conventionally viewed as a defense against the defects of direct governmental action. We argue that transparency is indispensable as well for any delegation of public purposes, and perhaps especially so for effective collaborative governance. Performance monitoring, outcome metrics, media oversight, financial audits, and other tools of transparency can be powerful tools against inefficiency, unresponsiveness, and outright corruption. The chapter concludes by offering some observations about "collaborative governance, Chinese style" and the general themes emerging from our exploration of how officials in each country engage the private sector to better meet specific public goals.

Throughout this book we aim to establish both the payoffs and the perils of collaboration with the private sector in the service of the public good. Appropriately targeted and adroitly managed, collaborative governance can bolster the impact, efficiency, and precision of collective undertakings. It can also widen the circle of social actors with stakes and expertise in the common weal. But when applied in settings to which it is ill-suited, or clumsily implemented, public–private collaboration can undermine efficiency, tarnish legitimacy, and invite corruption. Our goal, accordingly, is to equip public leaders in China and the United States, and any other pragmatic public servants, to engage their private counterparts in ways that foster public value. We aim to put a little intellectual wind under the wings of the dragon and the eagle alike.

2

Concepts and Context

Collaborative governance (CG) can outperform other ways to pursue public goals in important circumstances. The conceptual framework developed in this chapter identifies those circumstances and defines the principles and design features required for success.[1] The chapter then examines some salient elements of the Chinese and US contexts that shape adoption of the collaborative approach in each country.

Five straightforward diagnostic questions define where and how CG should operate. First, should some missions involve government at all, rather than being left to private parties? If the answer is "no," then we're done – at least for the purposes of this book. Second, if the answer is "yes," should the government produce the service itself, or should it delegate production (in whole or in part) to the private sector?[2] Third, for functions that *should* be delegated, *how* should that delegation take place?

Delegation can take any of three fundamental forms. As briefly noted in Chapter 1, they are distinguished by the allocation of discretion. Contracting (for example, hiring a firm to pave a highway) is at the extreme of minimal private discretion. Philanthropy resides at the opposite end: the donor has complete freedom to choose how to spend the time and money she or he

---

[1] For alternative conceptual frameworks regarding collaborative governance, see C. Ansell, and A. Gash, 2008, "Collaborative Governance in Theory and Practice," *Journal of Public Administration Research and Theory*, 18(4), 543–571; and K. Emerson, T. Nabatchi, and S. Balogh, 2012, "An Integrative Framework for Collaborative Governance," *Journal of Public Administration Research and Theory*, 22(1), 1–29.

[2] As noted in Chapter 1, when CG is motivated by collaboration for resources (as opposed to, for example, collaboration for productivity), the shared discretion involves financing as well as production. For clarity of exposition, we focus in this chapter on choices about delegation of production. This summary and the accompanying decision tree (though not other parts of the book) set aside some of the complexities that collaboration introduces when government takes less than full responsibility for financing some undertaking.

devotes to her or his own vision of the common good. Collaborative governance is the in-between case: the government and the private entity share discretion.

In addition to the question of *what kind of delegation*, a fourth fundamental decision concerns delegation *to whom* – should a for-profit or nonprofit private entity[3] undertake production? Then, the fifth and final question arises: How should the collaboration be designed?

This series of diagnostic questions is arrayed in the delegation decision tree shown in Figure 2.1.

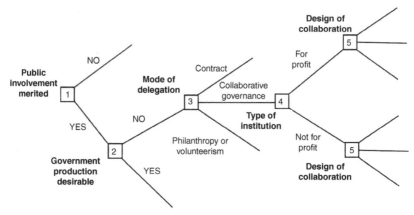

FIGURE 2.1 The delegation decision tree

We don't kid ourselves that real-world collaborative undertakings always, or even usually, stem from such a conscious and conscientious decision process. Some undertakings are relics of times gone by, maintained by inertia, whatever their current merits. Others reflect powerful interests pushing for structures that favor their goals. And still others arose and endure at least partly due to chance. But acknowledging the limited role of rational analysis doesn't mean endorsing that limit. In this book (and generally), we are unabashed cheerleaders for making collective choices through the disciplined application of evidence and analysis.

This chapter roughly tracks our delegation decision tree. It first discusses – in a necessarily very abbreviated way – the justifications for any government role. Next, it addresses the decision of whether government should produce directly or delegate to the private sector. It then takes up the three basic types of delegation and explores when and why shared discretion makes sense. Following this it moves on from broad strategy to more granular tactics for the concrete implementation of collaboration, highlighting our four-step cycle for structuring, conducting, and continually refining the collaborative process.

---

[3] This binary choice between two pure forms is an oversimplification. For example, some non-profits, such as major hospitals, may be highly profitable. The effective constraint is that they cannot distribute those profits to individuals, such as trustees or managers, or to corporations.

The chapter concludes by mapping the most important risks and downsides of the collaborative approach to governance.

THE DECISION PATH TO COLLABORATIVE GOVERNANCE

The Justifications for a Government Role Before addressing any issues of delegation, the first task is to determine what goods and services should be a public responsibility in the first place. Philosophers, pundits, and politicians have addressed this foundational topic at length and in depth. But the debate has narrowed since the collapse of the Soviet Union and its particular version of communism. Virtually no one today would propose that the government should take responsibility for equipping citizens with smartphones. At the other extreme, virtually no one would propose that the government wash its hands of responsibility for national defense. Most would likewise agree that macroeconomic stability is largely the government's job. Other goals – health care, education, environmental protection, economic development – also tend to be high on the list of governmental duties, but individuals and cultures differ on the right balance between individual and collective responsibility for financing and producing them.

Fifty years ago, the justifications for a government role would have been far different in China than in the United States. China's government held responsibility for virtually all production. Ever since Deng Xiaoping boldly initiated economic reforms in the late 1970s, China has shifted away from central planning. Today it vests the vast portion of its economy in the private sector as it strives to reach the goal of building a "moderately prosperous society" based on "market socialism" as part of "socialism with Chinese characteristics for a new era."[4] China still tilts more toward government than does the United States, though not by much; the public proportion of gross domestic product (GDP), broadly defined, is a little more than a third in both countries.[5] The key difference is the mixture of public financing, as well as state control. Compared to the United States, China's government devotes one-third fewer percentage points of GDP to health-care financing, but directly controls the "commanding heights" of the economy through key state-owned enterprises (SOEs) and significant industrial policy initiatives (both discussed more later).

Government has a role where the market functions poorly. That is the case with "public goods," such as national defense, roads, and basic research. The

---

[4] See for example Xi Jinping, "Secure a Decisive Victory in Building a Moderately Prosperous Society in All Respects and Strive for the Great Success of Socialism with Chinese Characteristics for a New Era," Report to the 19th Party Congress, October 18, 2017, www.xinhuanet.com /english/special/2017–11/03/c_136725942.htm.
[5] See Naughton 2017 and https://tradingeconomics.com/united-states/government-spending-to-gdp.

benefit that an individual gets from such a good does not depend upon his financial contribution to it. Moreover, his consumption in no way detracts from the consumption of others. (Both these "non-exclusion" and "non-rival" conditions, to be sure, range in practice from absolute and obvious to complex and partial). "Externalities" arise when one person's economic choices affect another person's wellbeing. Here too a governmental role can be justified, since left alone the outcome will be suboptimal. Governments require vaccinations, control levels of pollution, and employ tolls to dampen congestion. Information that does not flow freely can hamper markets. Governments often attempt to remedy flaws in the quantity or quality of information. For example, interventions such as quality regulation enable individuals to consume food or drugs with confidence. "Merit goods" are determined (by whomever in a society has standing to make such determinations) to be those that individuals should be able to consume even if they would not pay their full price. They constitute a major component of governments' responsibilities. Health care and education are perhaps the best examples.

Finally, the redistribution of income justifies government involvement in many areas. In concept, a less unequal income distribution can be framed as a special case of a "public good." Given its prominence as a concern in twenty-first century China and the United States, economic inequality deserves its own category. According to the widely cited measure of income inequality known as the Gini coefficient, inequality in both China and the United States is higher than in most developed countries.[6] Indeed, despite China's extraordinary success in lifting hundreds of millions out of poverty, contemporary inequality is such a salient issue that in tackling the question "Is China Socialist?" Naughton (2017) offers the following answer:

> The Chinese government has direct or indirect control over 38 percent of GDP in 2015. … While the Chinese government owns a relatively small share of overall productive assets, the assets that it owns often give it a monopoly position (land, natural resources, transport, and communication). … The value of government assets in China, relative to GDP [306% of GDP, table 1], is much higher than in other countries. … It seems broadly fair to view China as moving towards a version of "socialism" … that is authoritarian and top-down, but with a market economy based primarily on private ownership. … [However] in my opinion, China cannot be considered a socialist country until it makes much greater progress fulfilling its own declared policy objectives of universal social security, modest income redistribution, and amelioration of environmental problems. … the system may continue to evolve in the direction of stronger

---

[6] This standard metric is, unfortunately, not very intuitive to non-economists. Basically lower is better. In both China and the United States it now exceeds .4, though in China it is down from .5 as recently as 2008–2010. See Barry Naughton, 2017, "Is China Socialist?" *Journal of Economic Perspectives*, 31(1), 3–24; and Ravi Kanbur, Yue Wang and Xiaobo Zhang, "The Great Chinese Inequality Turnaround," BOFIT Discussion Papers 6/2017, www.bofit.fi/en.

"socialist" and redistributive institutions. As that happens, the mix of attributes will change, and a "Chinese model" of socialism may begin to emerge.[7]

On a purely theoretical basis, it would be better to conduct redistribution through the tax and transfer system.[8] But politics often shunts action against inequality off into many other domains. The tax and transfer system often ends up being less progressive than would be desirable. As a strategic response, the poor and their supporters knock on a great variety of policy doors; they get some redistributive resources in return.

Public goods, externalities, information failures, merit goods, and inequality: Now that we have identified the most prominent landmarks in this vast terrain of collective responsibility, we will turn to the conduct of CG. We note that any number of excellent texts in public finance provide in-depth guidance on "in which realms" and "how much,"[9] but they neglect, or devote less time to addressing, the question of "how." That "how" question is the focus of this book.

Should the Government Produce Directly? Public services differ dramatically in how well-suited they are for private production. Though we have mercifully eschewed the use of equations in this book, we believe that economic theory is quite useful in determining which entities should play which roles in producing public value. Economic concepts – including incomplete contracting and principal-agent theory in the context of public goods and externalities – provide insights about the strengths and weaknesses of CG for accomplishing public goals.

Comparative Advantage As a framework for discussing the merits of alternative ways of accomplishing public purposes, we employ the concept of comparative advantage as developed in Zeckhauser and Eggleston (2002).[10] And here we stand on the shoulders of David Ricardo, the brilliant nineteenth century British political economist, who is generally identified as the discoverer of comparative advantage. Ricardo showed that England might well be better off having Portugal produce wine and England produce wool, even if England had an *absolute* advantage in producing both goods – that is, could produce either more cheaply than could Portugal.

The process we are proposing is related but somewhat more subtle. Following the international trade analogy, our variant is more in the spirit of twenty-first century supply chains for sophisticated products such as the Apple

[7] Naughton, "Is China Socialist?".

[8] Aanund Hylland and Richard Zeckhauser, 1979, "Distributional Objectives Should Affect Taxes But Not Program Choice or Design," *Scandinavian Journal of Economics*, 81(2), 264–284.

[9] See, for example, Jonathan Gruber, *Public Finance and Public Policy*. Worth Publishers, 2005.

[10] Karen Eggleston and Richard Zeckhauser, "Government Contracting for Health Care," chapter 2 in John D. Donahue and Joseph S. Nye Jr., eds., *Market-Based Governance: Supply Side, Demand Side, Upside and Downside*, Brookings Institution Press, 2002: 29–65.

iPhone. That product is labeled as "designed in California." But it is manufactured with components from a great many countries. Apple coordinates all of this, assesses how the process is performing, and decides which new products to produce and how.

We emphasize the notion of *comparative* advantage for a reason: Everybody should be able to have a productive discussion on which functions are relatively better and worse suited for government to handle, even if we differ dramatically on the right size of government overall. Consider the American health-care system – the perennial focus of fierce partisan debates about bigger versus smaller government. But even democratic socialists are basically onboard with private companies producing pharmaceuticals (albeit with government regulation on safety). And all but the most fervent of free-market fundamentalists would grant government a role in the control of epidemics (though with those pharma companies making the vaccines.) There's even a reasonable degree of consensus across the political spectrum that the nonprofit model should predominate among hospitals.

Public providers have a comparative advantage for goods and services that possess some combination of the following characteristics. They are: (a) difficult to contract; (b) involve pure public goods or significant externalities; (c) not easily monitored by pupils, patients, or households in the sense that they can discern distortions in quality; and (d) highly susceptible to inefficient sorting of students or patients. Examples in the health sector would include regulating public goods vital for health, such as clean air and water; population-based health initiatives and other services conveying large positive externalities (e.g., control of infectious disease); and services plagued by asymmetry of information and inability of the recipient to assess quality or exercise effective choice, such as care for the severely mentally ill and long-term care for frail elderly.

It is certainly more difficult for consumers to judge the quality of an educational institution than that of a restaurant or retail store. For-profit suppliers' incentives may be the same in both realms, but they cannot profitably chisel on quality where consumers can spot poor quality and sanction it by "voting with their feet." Where feet-voting will work, as with restaurants at a beach or lodging in public parks, efficiency advantages tilt the scales strongly toward private production.

More generally, private providers have a comparative advantage for goods and services that combine one or more of the following features: (a) readily contractible; (b) quality readily monitored by consumers such as students, parents, and patients (directly or through the reputation of the supplier); (c) susceptible to competition; (d) not amenable to the dumping of unprofitable clients (e.g., special-need students, unprofitable patients), or for which the risk adjustment of payment is feasible and reasonably accurate; and (e) incentives for rapid quality innovation are more valuable than incentives for cost control that will damage quality. Examples include most aspects of job training that are specific to firms; elective surgery and most dental care, as well as the provision of drugs and many aspects of primary health care. A murkier middle ground covers services with redistributive concerns and economic spillovers, and areas where selection and dumping of unprofitable students and patients could be addressed in part through public financing rather than direct delivery (e.g., government funding for K-12 education and basic medical insurance).

For many important undertakings aimed at creating public value, only one sector needs to be involved. Government can go it alone on foreign policy. The for-profit private sector can handle the production of television sets. (Yes, we understand that entertainment for the citizenry does promote the public interest, and that diplomacy does not spread its benefits and costs perfectly evenly. "Close enough" is the best we can shoot for in parsing these kinds of choices.)

But often a collective undertaking works best if it involves more than one sector, enabling it to capitalize on the best capabilities of each. Consider the progress of pharmaceutical drugs in the United States. The government heavily supports fundamental research. Most of that research is done by private nonprofits, but significant amounts are done as well by the highly regarded government-run National Institutes of Health. Applied research is predominantly the responsibility of for-profit pharmaceutical companies. However, there's seldom a bright line between basic and applied research; hence, for-profits inevitably do some of the former and nonprofits some of the latter. The government through the FDA bears final responsibility in determining whether a drug is efficacious and safe enough to be permitted in the market. The drug is then sold to consumers, with support from insurance plans and health-care providers run by each of the three sectors, at costs that are often subsidized, at times heavily, by the government. And if this intricate multi-sector collaboration at times gives rise to an opioid epidemic, or underinvestment in pandemic preparedness, or slow response to scaling up testing for a new virus, the government – at the central, state and local levels – bears responsibility for redressing the payoff and preference discretion underlying those deviations from public value.

PRINCIPAL–AGENT THEORY: CONTRACTING, COLLABORATION, DELEGATION

When private sector engagement seems promising in principle, the task remains of choosing what kind of private role will work best in practice. And this involves finding the right point on a spectrum from pure contracting to complete delegation.[11] All such arrangements involve a principal–agent relationship.

---

[11] Contracting out need not be confined to traditional sectors such as infrastructure; in China, it includes contracting with private services for policing social media. For example, Qin et al. (2017) estimate that China social media features about 600,000 government-affiliated accounts, posting 4 percent of all posts on Sina Weibo about political/economic topics (p. 119); and that

Whether through contracting or collaboration, the governmental principal must monitor and motivate the private agent. To the extent that contracts can fully describe desired outputs or outcomes, and their delivery can be monitored and enforced, there is no role for the sharing of discretion, and its associated transaction costs.[12] When contracts must inevitably be incomplete, however – the normal case, not the exception – much depends on who has control.[13]

The distinguishing feature of CG is that control is explicitly and deliberately shared. Such sharing introduces an unavoidable degree of both analytic and managerial complexity. Intentional engineering of institutional relationships is a prerequisite for establishing an accountable CG structure. Public managers need to develop the skills of orchestrating collaborative arrangements. In choosing between straightforward contracts and shared discretion, for example, Bruce et al. (2018) find that US agencies with relevant technical capabilities are more likely to adopt cooperative agreements and thus secure the associated benefits. In the twenty-first century, skillful government leaders will increasingly be those who master the art and science of collaboration. We invoke the metaphor of the collaborating government official as a circus ringmaster that was set forth in our previous work (Donahue and Zeckhauser 2011, chapter 8). As this top-hatted figure, the official orchestrates a performance and keeps all the players on their toes as circumstances shift.

For China, by contrast, a different circus metaphor, favored by sociologist Xueguang Zhou et al. (2013, p. 146), is of the local official as an acrobat on a high wire. She or he is actively adjusting her balance ("muddling through") in pursuit of a public goal:

The logic of meeting targets dictates that a Chinese government bureaucrat focuses on reaching the goal set by higher authorities. In this sense, the bureaucrat, like the acrobat, is rational and goal-directed. However, in the course of reaching the goal, the bureaucrat needs to make constant adjustments in response to pressures from other logics—maintaining political coalitions and providing incentives—that pull or push in different directions. The key to survival in the Chinese bureaucracy involves maintaining a balance between these different pressures while moving toward the goal, and this results in behaviors characteristic of muddling through.[14]

"in practice, censorship is implemented largely by private service providers who are registered in Beijing" (p.121). Qin, Bei, David Strömberg, and Yanhui Wu, 2017, "Why Does China Allow Freer Social Media? Protests versus Surveillance and Propaganda," *Journal of Economic Perspectives*, 31(1), 117–140.

[12] See Paul Milgrom and John Roberts, *Economics, Organization, and Management*, (Englewood Cliffs, NJ: Prentice-Hall, 1992), and John W. Pratt and Richard J. Zeckhauser, eds., *Principals and Agents: The Structure of Business*, (Boston: Harvard Business School Press, 1991)

[13] O. Hart, 2017. "Incomplete Contracts and Control," *American Economic Review*, 107(7), 1731–1752; K. Eggleston, E. A. Posner, and R. Zeckhauser, 2000, "The Design and Interpretation of Contracts: Why Complexity Matters," *Northwestern University Law Review*, 95, 91.

[14] Zhou, Xueguang, Hong Lian, Leonard Ortolano, and Yinyu Ye, 2013, "A Behavioral Model of 'Muddling through' in the Chinese Bureaucracy: The Case of Environmental Protection," *China Journal*, 70, 120–147.

The metaphors differ with the details of task and context, but a general lesson for any effort to create public value through private capabilities – whether in China, the United States, or elsewhere – is that the government must take on new, often unfamiliar roles. Public managers need to be able to choose appropriate collaborative partners and foster shared discretion, while maintaining a regulatory framework that stays one step ahead of the ways private actors seek to reap gains through downgrading quality,[15] manipulation of shrouded attributes,[16] or other opportunistic abuse. Meaningful monitoring can take many forms, and incentives need to be well-tailored. Local government officials, like individual consumers, must be aware that markets and firms only imperfectly catch and discipline misconduct, and indeed some firms may specialize in misconduct[17] and prey on unsophisticated consumers.[18]

Contracts and agreements are almost inevitably incomplete, with the need to fill in gaps or adjust to new circumstances as the relationship unfolds.[19] This incompleteness gives rise to de facto collaborative approaches that share discretion between the contracting parties. This form of collaboration may be more frequent with local governments, particularly those in poorer regions. Such governments are more likely to lack the information, experience, and skills to delegate service contracting with any specificity or effective enforcement. In China, for example, such de facto collaborative approaches arise more frequently in poorer and/or western regions, and less often in the coastal megacities. Indeed, such heterogeneity in local government constitutes an integral part of what we characterize as "collaborative governance, Chinese-style."

---

[15] O. Hart, A. Shleifer, and R. W. Vishny, 1997, "The Proper Scope of Government: Theory and an Application to Prisons," *The Quarterly Journal of Economics*, 112(4), 1127–1161.

[16] Gabaix, Xavier, and David Laibson, 2006, "Shrouded Attributes, Consumer Myopia, and Information Suppression in Competitive Markets," *The Quarterly Journal of Economics*, 121 (2), 505–540.

[17] See for example Egan, Mark and Matvos, Gregor and Seru, Amit, 2019, "The Market for Financial Adviser Misconduct," *Journal of Political Economy*, 127(1), 233–295.

[18] Akerlof and Shiller provide many compelling examples in their book. (Akerlof, George A. and Robert J. Shiller. *Phishing for Phools: The Economics of Manipulation and Deception*. Princeton University Press, 2015). They do not apply their economic analysis of deception to differences in ownership. However, since the presumption is that profit-seeking underlies the incentive for "phishing" opportunities, their arguments reinforce our point that nonprofits have a comparative advantage in muting those incentives where they are powerful.

[19] As alluded to previously, Nobel prize-winning economist Oliver Hart developed the property rights theory of ownership based on a theory of incomplete contracts. In such cases, it matters which party has residual control rights in the non-contracted circumstances, and adopting "guiding principles" and/or engaging in constructive communication may help to overcome the dangers of contractual incompleteness. Principal among them are the self-serving biases of the parties, or what we term payoff and preference discretion. See Frydlinger, David, and Oliver Hart, 2019, "Overcoming Contractual Incompleteness: The Role of Guiding Principles." National Bureau of Economic Research working paper #26245.

Few studies quantify the net public value of collaborative arrangements – that is, the public value of outcomes, net of the associated transaction costs of governance complexity inherent in a collaborative approach. The few studies undertaken, to date, suggest that these are fruitful areas for future research to guide policy innovation. Scott (2015) studied local arrangements for managing watersheds, finding that collaborative groups produced gains in water quality and in-stream habitat relative to arrangements without collaborative discretion. The complexity of collaborative arrangements was justified.[20]

The comparative advantage of CG may be especially salient for fostering innovation. As one recent empirical study of more than 4,000 US government R&D contracts demonstrates, agencies choose cooperative agreements – in which government employees have substantial decision rights (what we term discretion) – over grants for earlier-stage, more uncertain projects. That was especially true when they had the domain-specific technical expertise; and such cooperative agreements performed better than grants in terms of patents generated.[21]

Analyze, Assign, Design, and Assess

However wisely collaborative arrangements are chosen at the outset, conditions change. Some of the changes are external: demands from the environment, technology, and the tasks that need to be accomplished. Other changes develop within the collaboration itself: personnel turnover; interests and goals of the collaborating parties change; those parties create conditions to secure private payoffs or to promote private values. External to the collaboration, political views evolve, and ruling coalitions shift. Collaborative governance should not be a one-time decision. It should involve a continual process of analytic and managerial work to define and refine relationships.[22]

We identify four key elements that comprise a continuous cycle of review: analyze, assign, design, and assess.[23] This cycle shares insights with other well-known management and design processes, such as Deming's famous

---

[20] Scott, Tyler, 2015, "Does Collaboration Make Any Difference? Linking Collaborative Governance to Environmental Outcomes," *Journal of Policy Analysis and Management*, 34 (3), 537–566.

[21] Bruce, Joshua Robert, John M. De Figueiredo, and Brian Silverman, "Public Contracting for Private Innovation." *Academy of Management Proceedings*. Vol. 2018. No. 1. Briarcliff Manor, NY 10510: Academy of Management, 2018.

[22] Participants in effective collaborative projects often credit such a process with undergirding project success. For example, see Maltin, Elyse. "What Successful Public-Private Partnerships Do." *Harvard Business Review*. January 8, 2019. https://hbr.org/2019/01/what-successful-public-private-partnerships-do.

[23] See, Donahue and Zeckhauser 2011, Figure 8.1 The Cycle of Collaboration.

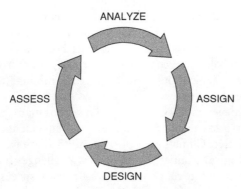

ANALYZE

ASSESS

ASSIGN

DESIGN

FIGURE 2.2 The analyze, assign, design, and assess (AADA) cycle

plan-do-study-act cycle, or the "design thinking" process as modified for policy analysis by Fukuyama and Weinstein.[24]

Collaboration starts with sound *analysis* of the specific goals that are sought, as well as the menu of stakeholders and potential private collaborators. Next, the manager must *assign* appropriate responsibilities to collaborators or contract counterparties. The third task is the *design* of the contract – what is allowed and expected of each party, and their respective incentives and accountability – or, with more complexity, design of the collaborative relationship and the parameters of shared discretion. Having analyzed alignment of interests and chosen counterparts accordingly, the design phase builds in appropriate incentives to guide discretion toward the shared public purpose. Most collaborations will endure for a length of time and require *assessment* and reanalysis to make sure that they still maximize public value. Sometimes only minor tweaks are needed; at other times, a wholesale overhaul of the design is warranted to adapt to new realities. It is even possible that CG no longer provides the best avenue for achieving that specific public goal.

This cycle is illustrated in Figure 2.2. We shall sometimes refer to it by the acronym AADA.

Collaborative arrangements, once established, can be difficult to dismantle or reinvent, because the beneficiaries of even a poor collaborative arrangement gain at the expense of the public. Collaboration requires continuous assessment

---

[24] See, for example, the plan-do-study-act (PDSA or Shewhart) cycle discussed in chapter 6 of Deming, William Edwards. *The New Economics: For Industry, Government, Education.* MIT Press, 1993; the Stanford d.school materials on design thinking (e.g. https://dschool.stanford.edu/resources-collections/a-virtual-crash-course-in-design-thinking); Fukuyama and Weinstein's "engineering policy change" cycle (problem identification, solutions development, implementation: reframe, prototype, iterate) within the Stanford University Master's in International Policy Program, see https://fsi.stanford.edu/masters-degree and https://fsi.stanford.edu/masters-degree/content/mip-practicum; and Burnett, William, and David John Evans, *Designing Your Life: How to Build a Well-lived, Joyful Life.* Knopf, 2016.

and periodic renewal to remain relevant for current circumstances. For example, as Akerlof and Shiller point out in *Phishing for Phools*, the disastrous 2008 financial crisis resulted in part because the regulators of the US financial system failed to recognize that formerly solid institutions had been undermined. Some organizations were "reputation mining" to the detriment of the broader financial system.

In an economy developing as rapidly and facing as many pressing challenges as today's China, reassessment of collaborative arrangements through this four-step cycle is imperative. China's pace of economic growth will slow as it reaches the global technological frontier, entailing new challenges for value-producing interaction across a broad range of sectors. China's success in CG over the decades to come will depend on its skill, discipline, and honesty in the *analysis* of policy challenges and opportunities; the *assignment* of appropriate collaborators; the *design* of collaborative relationships; and the capacity to *adjust* in the light of information about the benefits reaped from production discretion net of the costs incurred from payoff and preference discretion.

EXISTENCE DOES NOT IMPLY DESIRABILITY

The natural selection metaphor has power over our minds. When we observe a characteristic in some living creature, such as spots on a Dalmatian, we immediately assume that it plays a useful role. The metaphor then gets extended to ecosystems, where we assume that the species that are present enable the system to maintain its balance. The next intellectual step is to the economy. Absent impediments, we assume that gas stations will locate where drivers will need to fuel up, that restaurants will set up shop where people will realize they are hungry, and so on. Each step in this extrapolation process involves a small intellectual leap, and a modest set of assumptions.

It may seem tempting to take the next step and assume that the mix of public programs, the blend of sectors that produce them, and the discretion that each sector enjoys in that production, all make sense. But that conclusion may be a leap too far. One obvious indicator that current arrangements aren't necessarily optimal is that reasonable observers frequently disagree on who should be producing what. Even more telling, there are cases where any dispassionate critic would agree that there has to be a better way. (We'll nominate, for starters, the bizarre, mixed ecology of the public postal service and for-profit delivery companies in the United States.) A final piece of evidence is that within both China and the United States, different locales employ very different modes for treating the sick, teaching the children, and maintaining the parks. These differences are explained mainly by the forces of politics and path dependence, not by any reasoned analysis of who should do what.

There is simply no process of natural selection that guarantees, or even makes it highly likely, that an agency or a country will gravitate toward the right means for pursuing some public end. Delivery models often prove sticky, and interests become both powerful and vested. Those who are profiting do not mind blocking even urgently needed adaptation. Scholars have long recognized this problem and put forward wise proposals.[25] Those proposals are, at best, unevenly adopted.[26]

If context, history, and private interests matter as much as or more than evidence and logic in shaping delivery models for public missions, it is all the more reason for analysts to take account of the distinctive contexts in the United States and China. The American history with railroads illustrates a recurring theme in this book. A public policy challenge arises. All parties recognize that neither the government nor the private sector can, or perhaps should, handle it on its own. Some reasonably pragmatic collaborative approaches are then developed – call them "muddling through" if you wish, or employ Deng Xiaoping's justly famous phrase of "crossing the river by groping for stones." But rarely has there been sufficient attention to collaborative structures. Often that inattention is deliberately engineered by parties grabbing personal value or power while the public has not yet focused its attention. A second contributing factor, which we hope we can, to some degree, mitigate in these pages, is the lack of a clear conceptual framework for how collaboration should be conducted.

The historical, social, and economic differences between the United States and China are many and deep and, for the most part, their full description is well beyond the scope of this book. We also avoid, as noted in the introduction, judgments about the relative virtues and liabilities of the dramatically different political systems in China and the United States. But, it is important to undertake at least a brief overview of the players in the process before turning to specific aspects of the context in each country.

THE PLAYERS

Most of our analysis focuses on policies, programs, and institutional structures. But since policies and programs are designed and implemented by human beings, and since institutions are mechanisms made up of human beings, we mention briefly here the main players in both countries. However cynical or self-interested government officials or private sector players might be, they would probably agree that the purpose of collaborative processes is to enhance the welfare of the people. Whether in a rough-and-tumble democracy or an

---

[25] Olson calls for policymakers to create institutional structures flexible enough to accommodate transitions to new ways of producing goods and services when economic justifications change. Olson, Mancur, 1982, *The Rise and Decline of Nations: Economic Growth, Stagflation, and Social Rigidities*. Yale University Press.

[26] Douglass North has argued that institutions adapt to improve economic performance best when alternative policies can be tried and ineffective policies can be eliminated; "adaptive efficiency evolves only after a relatively long period of evolving informal norms and we know of no shortcut to this process." North, Douglass C. *Understanding the Process of Economic Change*. Vol. 32. Princeton University Press, 2010, p.163.

authoritarian state, the people, through political processes, will be the ultimate judges of the goods and services produced.

In both China and the United States, it is natural to focus on the national governments, and those who lead them at the top. Here the pictures differ dramatically across the two countries. In China, only one party has ruled since 1949. The current General Secretary of the CCP, Xi Jinping – also the President – is the most powerful leader in recent memory. In the United States, by contrast, the Democrats and Republicans have rotated the Presidency nine times from Harry Truman till Donald Trump. Though reelection has been common, given the advantages of incumbency, only once has a President's party been able to elect its successor. (George H. W. Bush succeeded as a one-term President after Ronald Reagan.)

It would be understandable if our Chinese readers inferred that the in-and-out pattern of national politics in the United States reflects chronic dissatisfaction with public goods and services. (Goods are minor in most governmental production, so we mostly just refer to public services in this section and later). Otherwise, why should voters so often reject the party in power? The logic does not follow, for two main reasons: First Congress, not the President, writes the laws governing what government delivers and how. Second, the overwhelming majority of public services in the United States are delivered at the state and local levels.

To understand the political dimensions of public service delivery, one must delve into judgments of mayors and governors, city councils, and state legislatures, and other sub-national decision-makers, such as school boards and county health officers. Matters are much the same in China, not surprisingly, given that it is a more populous country with greater regional heterogeneity in levels of economic development and highly decentralized fiscal expenditures. Though directives often come from the central government, the real action tends to be at the provincial, prefectural, and municipal or county level. For example, China has universal health coverage through insurance programs that are administered at the municipal or county level, and a health service delivery system dominated by locally controlled public hospitals and clinics. So, specifics of health service contracting and the degree of collaboration with the private sector differ substantially from one locale to another. Education policy arguably features an even greater degree of local finance and control.

China's system is distinct from conventional categories of unitary or federalist polities in several ways, including the prominent role for local government. For example,

although the central government has supreme authority and unlimited intervention rights, the share of central fiscal expenditures over the total fiscal expenditures has been 15–30% in the past 30 years, which is much lower than in Western developed countries (where the proportion is usually 50–60%). ... The central contribution towards fiscal expenditures on education, health-care, environmental protection and social security is remarkably low compared with those in developed countries.[27]

Collaborative governance in China is employed most frequently well below the national level. It involves three parties: the government, the private producer, and the citizenry. And, however much control the first two parties possess, it is the citizens' interests that should be served. Citizens should get good value for the resources that they put up, whether through taxes, payments for services, or through the power that they have ceded implicitly or explicitly to the government. Good public officials, in China as well as in the United States, recognize this truth. It might be construed as central to Xi Jinping's declaration that the new "main contradiction" China's leaders must focus on is that "between unbalanced and inadequate development and the people's ever-growing needs for a better life."[28]

In the United States, elections, however imperfect, are the ultimate instrument for enforcing accountability on arrangements for producing public value, although authorities also must respond to its active civil society and to protests, such as those that erupted in 2020 against police brutality and anti-Black racism. In China, where competitive elections rarely are held above the village level, officials must be concerned both with discipline from above for poor performance, and dissatisfaction from below, as was evident during the response to COVID-19.[29] Protests and civil disturbances in reaction to disappointing public services are something that officials seek to avoid at all costs. Where they do erupt, discipline from above can be expected.

US CIVIL SOCIETY AND THE ROLE OF PRIVATE NONPROFITS

Civic Associations and Civil Society A civic association is defined as a voluntary organization that aims to represent the interests of a community. Such associations can be political, environmental, educational, recreational, or can represent some ethnic group, religion, or geographic community. Civil society is basically the aggregate of these civic associations. Civil society has a long and

---

[27] P. 49, L. A. Zhou, 2016, "The Administrative Subcontract: Significance, Relevance and Implications for Intergovernmental Relations in China," *Chinese Journal of Sociology*, 2(1), 34–74.

[28] See discussion in Alice Miller, "Xi Jinping and the Evolution of Chinese Leadership Politics," chapter 1 in Thomas Fingar and Jean C. Oi, eds., *Fateful Decisions: Choices That Will Shape China's Future*, Stanford University Press, 2020.

[29] "Xi demanded more understanding and tolerance for people in Hubei and Wuhan if some vent their feelings for long time under self-quarantine, as well as efforts to ensure the supply of their life necessities. . . . Calling the response to the virus a "test" for China's system and capacity for governance, which has brought both experience and lessons, Xi demanded efforts to fix the shortcomings and weak links as soon as possible." "'Turning the tide' – Xi leads anti-virus war toward victory" *People's Daily*, March 11, 2020. http://en.people.cn/n3/2020/0311/c90000-9666845.html [accessed March 12, 2020].

vibrant historical record in the United States. Alexis de Tocqueville, the Frenchman who toured the United States as a young man and chronicled his findings in *Democracy in America* (1835, 1840), was struck by the prominence of American civic associations by contrast to statist Europe.

"[Americans] are forever forming associations. There are not only commercial and industrial associations in which all take part, but others of a thousand different types–religious, moral, serious, futile, very general and very limited, immensely large and very minute. .... Nothing, in my view, deserves more attention than the intellectual and moral associations in America."

He was equally impressed by the role such associations played in enabling democracy to flourish.

"Americans group together to hold fêtes, found seminaries, build inns, construct churches, distribute books, dispatch missionaries to the antipodes. They establish hospitals, prisons, schools by the same method. Finally, if they wish to highlight a truth or develop an opinion by the encouragement of a great example, they form an association."[30]

Though hardly his objective, Tocqueville anticipated, by over a century, key findings on the economics of information. He recognized the importance of transmitting private information, and the role of information and ideas in promoting technological advance in society.

"In the United States, as soon as several inhabitants have taken an opinion or an idea they wish to promote in society, they seek each other out and unite together once they have made contact. From that moment, they are no longer isolated but have become a power seen from afar whose activities serve as an example and whose words are heeded."[31]
    "It might be said that, in the United States, there is no limit to the inventiveness of man to discover ways of increasing wealth and to satisfy the public's needs. The most enlightened inhabitants of each district constantly use their knowledge to make new discoveries to increase the general prosperity, which, when made, they pass eagerly to the mass of the people."[32]

Institutional development in the United States has always involved some public element, to be sure. The individual states regulated which organizations could adopt the corporate form to accumulate resources with the benefit of limited liability. Prior to the twentieth-century, states "systematically withheld such valuable associational rights from groups that challenged the social order in some fundamental way – for example, by opposing the institution of slavery, advocating political rights for women, or even seeking a better deal for labor."[33] Yet civic associations have successfully pushed social reform. Soup

---

[30] De Tocqueville 2003, p. 596.   [31] De Tocqueville 2003, p. 599.
[32] De Tocqueville 2003, p. 594.
[33] P.17 of N. R. Lamoreaux, and J. J. Wallis, eds., *Organizations, Civil Society, and the Roots of Development*. University of Chicago Press, 2017.

kitchens and charity hospitals have long been undertakings of religiously affiliated groups. In Philadelphia and elsewhere, social clubs for prominent women successfully promoted public baths and laundries for the poor.[34] Religious leaders of many faiths played a profound, indeed determining, role in championing America's civil rights legislation.

Contemporary Civic Participation in the United States. A major role for civil society is a twenty-first century hallmark of the United States, as it was when Tocqueville toured. Nonprofit organizations in the United States are prohibited from endorsing political candidates or political parties, lest they lose their ability to receive tax-deductible contributions. They nonetheless exert enormous influence on American public life. Churches have been a potent force for, and against, developments in a range of sensitive political areas including racial equality, birth control and abortion, and gay rights. Most religions stress a responsibility to the poor and the afflicted, softening both the rough-and-tumble of politics and the austere dictates of the market. But civic groups can also muster champions of an obsolete status quo and prevent desirable change from happening.[35] Thus, as with most social and political phenomena, both sides are well represented.

Civic Associations and Service Delivery. US civic associations have great potential for creating public value. They coordinate the time, talents, and treasure of tens of millions of Americans. Virtually all major museums and many other cultural institutions are supported by civic associations. Charitable organizations continually search for new ways to improve society, conquer disease, and educate our citizens. Two of the three richest and most admired men in America – Bill Gates and Warren Buffett – have pledged to give the vast majority of their wealth to charity, and are now gathering other billionaires together (including in China) to make the same pledge. Gates now devotes most of his time to the Bill and Melinda Gates Foundation, using his formidable capabilities to direct its resources to conquering disease, coping with climate change, and improving education.[36] Jack Ma, whose globally renowned business acumen running Alibaba generated financial innovations that have substantially helped China's poor, recently indicated that he will step down from the helm at Alibaba, and focus his efforts on education and other philanthropic causes. Further development of China's philanthropic sector, an immense opportunity given its growing numbers of wealthy citizens, may play an important role in creating public value in the future.

---

[34] Melissa M. Mandell, November 2007, "The Public Baths Association of Philadelphia and the 'Great Unwashed'," *Pennsylvania Legacies*, 7(2), 30–31.

[35] Olson 1984.

[36] Buffett, recognizing Gates' capabilities in this regard, and also the fact that he is 25 years younger, has pledged to leave 85 percent of his wealth to the Gates Foundation.

It is important to acknowledge the time contributions that tens of millions of everyday Americans give to civic associations. Many find this an uplifting activity, undertakings that bind them to the well-being of their fellow citizens. As China gets wealthier, more and more every day, Chinese might add such community volunteer activities on behalf of "strangers" to their existing time contributions to intergenerational extended family and reciprocating social networks.[37]

Civic Associations and Policy Development. China has made tremendous progress against air pollution (Greenstone 2018) but still struggles to protect its natural environment.[38] So the experience of the United States in pursuing environmental quality may be instructive. In response to vivid evidence of air and water pollution in the early decades after World War II concerned citizens created an aggressive environmental movement. That movement in turn put pressure on the government, and much stricter environmental regulation was the result. The publication of books that sounded alarm bells, the most significant being Rachel Carson's *The Silent Spring* (1962),[39] helped create that movement and the pressure it exerted.

Civic associations in the United States have long been and remain vital in creating the pressures that led to our current environmental standards. But this pattern of nonprofit advocacy and governmental action stretches well beyond environmental policy. Whether the nation is enacting national health insurance, changing policies on overseas adventures, or revising immigration laws, civic associations get deeply involved in the political mix and push policy. There are often powerful associations on both sides. Civil society has great potential to create public value, whether through the direct provision of goods and services or through the mobilization of public opinion and the creation of pressure. This historical development of a powerful civil society in the United States bears little relationship to China's modern history. It constitutes a critical context for many of the examples of CG developed in the chapters that follow. It may portend important developments in China's future, particularly if its citizens demand more of a role in guiding its policies. Volunteering has already increased

---

[37] See discussion for example in X. Y. Dong and X. An, 2015, "Gender Patterns and Value of Unpaid Care Work: Findings from China's First Large-Scale Time Use Survey," *Review of Income and Wealth*, 61(3), 540–560; T. Brandsen, and R. Simsa, 2016, "Civil Society, Nonprofit Organizations, and Citizenship in China: An Editorial Introduction to the China Issue," *Voluntas*, 27, 2011. https://doi.org/10.1007/s11266-016-9774-4.

[38] See Greenstone, "Four Years After Declaring War on Pollution, China Is Winning," *New York Times* March 12, 2018; Y. Chen, A. Ebenstein, M. Greenstone, and H. Li, 2013, Evidence on the Impact of Sustained Exposure to Air Pollution on Life Expectancy from China's Huai River Policy. *Proceedings of the National Academy of Sciences*, 110(32), 12936–12941; and Ebenstein, Avraham, Maoyong Fan, Michael Greenstone, Guojun He, and Maigeng Zhou. "New Evidence on the Impact of Sustained Exposure to Air Pollution on Life Expectancy from China's Huai." (2017).

[39] Carson's book alerted the public to the dangers of pesticides in the environment.

significantly for specific social causes. One study estimated 58 million volunteers donated over 1.5 billion hours of service for various community services in China in 2016.[40] And in both countries, local communities displayed resilience in organizing to support those affected by the 2020 coronavirus pandemic and the associated economic recession.

ADMINISTRATIVE SUBCONTRACTS, PRIVATE ENGAGEMENT, AND SOES IN CHINA

Readers in the West will be familiar with China's dramatic economic rise and vibrant market-based economy, under the political leadership of the Chinese Communist Party (CCP). Between 1978 and 2014, the share of the state sector in the value of industrial output plummeted remarkably from 78 to 22 percent (Huang et al. 2017). Less well-known may be the continuing government control of significant shares of the economy, in parallel with development of *shehui zuzhi* (social organizations, China's generic term for nongovernment organizations (NGOs)). This section briefly describes these features of China's context for engaging private roles for public goals.

Chinese policymakers are in the process of adapting and reinventing the underlying principles of what is sometimes called the "new public management" movement in America.[41] From contracting to purchase social services to the development of collaborative arrangements across multiple sectors, China's contemporary context of private firms, corporatized SOEs, and hybrid ownership organizations reveals the power of inertia, path dependence, and serendipity.

For the United States, "private" mostly refers to domestic firms or social organizations. In China, firms wholly or partly owned by citizens of a different country – officially termed Foreign Direct Investment (FDI) and joint ventures (JVs), respectively – have greater salience. For US public managers, the menu of collaborative partners is only somewhat distorted if it is characterized as a dichotomy between for-profit or nonprofit. The Chinese menu is more complex, as illustrated in Table 2.1.

Some observers may assert that it is simply China's ideological aversion to using the term "private" that leads to a semantic jumble about ownership, where synonyms or substitutes for "private" abound, such as *fei zhengfu* (non-governmental), *shehui ziben* (social capital), or *minying*

---

[40] P.250 of Ming Wang and Shuoyan Li, "The Development of Charitable Organizations in China since Reform and Opening-Up and a New Layout for State-Society Relations," chapter 12 in Jianxing Yu and Sujian Guo, eds., *The Palgrave Handbook of Local Governance in Contemporary China*. Palgrave Macmillan, 2019: 245–266.

[41] For a classic popular book in this tradition, see Osborne and Gaebler 1993; a more recent sample is Eggers 2013. For an interesting China case, see Teets, Jessica, and Marta Jagusztyn, 2016, "The Evolution of a Collaborative Governance Model: Social Service Outsourcing to Civil Society Organizations in China," chapter 5 in Reza Hasmath and Jennifer Y. J. Hsu, eds., *NGO Governance and Management in China*, Routledge, 2016: 69–87.

TABLE 2.1 *Examples of a range of non-state organizations in China*

	Government-controlled	Domestic private	Foreign private
For-profit	SOE	Corporatized SOE, de novo private	FDI, JV
Nonprofit	Public service organization (*shiye danwei*); Government-organized nongovernment organization (GNGO)	nonprofit firm, social organization (*shehui zuzhi*)	International NGO

(people-run).[42] Categorization by the Chinese Ministry of Civil Affairs also includes *minjian zuzhi* (grassroots organizations), *minjian shehui tuanti* (grassroots social groups), *minjian jijinhui* (grassroots foundations), *minban fei qiye danwei* (grassroots non-enterprise work units). But China is not the only country with a range of ownership forms both in law and in practice.[43] And China does have a decades-long history of development of civic society and NGOs active in multiple sectors, a full treatment of which lies outside the scope of this book.[44] Government-organized non-government organizations[45] and grassroots NGOs or civil society organizations are among the many forms of NGOs operating in contemporary China.

Accordingly, as mentioned in Chapter 1, our definitions of "public" and "private" allow for a spectrum of organizational forms. State-owned enterprises are closer to the government side of the spectrum than domestic private for-profit corporations, but they are distinct from government agencies. Even between domestic private (e.g., Alibaba or Tencent) and foreign private

[42] See, for example, the official websites for China's social organizations, www.chinanpo.gov.cn /index.html, and for public-private partnerships, www.pppcenter.org.cn/. The latter, despite the domain name and embrace of the acronym PPP, avoids use of the term "private": The title is "the Government and Social Capital Cooperation (PPP) Research Center" (*Zhengfu he Shehui Ziben Hezuo Yanjiu Zhongxin*). Accessed August 31, 2019.

[43] For example, nonprofit private is not a meaningfully distinct organizational form if rules against distributing profits to owners are ineffective or unenforced.

[44] Interested readers may see Ming Wang and Shuoyan Li, "The Development of Charitable Organizations in China since Reform and Opening-Up and a New Layout for State-Society Relations," chapter 12 in Jianxing Yu and Sujian Guo, eds., *The Palgrave Handbook of Local Governance in Contemporary China*. Palgrave Macmillan, 2019: 245–266; and "Development of Chinese Grassroots NGOs" by Yan Long (https://exhibits.stanford.edu/chinese-ngos/about/ development-of-chinese-grassroots-ngos) and the extensive Chinese and English-language resources archived by the Chinese NGO web archiving project at https://exhibits.stanford.edu /chinese-ngos/feature/general-f9077f72-ce46-47ba-bcaa-90723f3eeea7.

[45] See, for example, Luo, Wenen. "From Dependence to Autonomy? Institutional Change and the Evolution of Charitable GONGOs in China." Dissertation. University of Hong Kong. 2011.

(e.g., Apple or Siemens) firms, there is an important intermediary category of overseas Chinese, Hong Kong, and Macao firms. And, of course, multiple hybrid organizational forms exist as well.

Indeed, as cases throughout the following chapters illustrate in detail, each country has a "comfort zone" for collaborating with the private sector on tasks where private discretion poses obvious risks: each tends to embrace an organizational form that is intermediary between a for-profit firm and a standard government agency. In the United States, this category is the private nonprofit (e.g., nonprofit hospitals and colleges); in China, this category is the corporatized SOE. Each form has emerged within each country's distinctive political economy as the best national answer to the puzzle of merging private efficiency with fidelity to a public mission. They have softened incentives for payoff manipulation, and manageable risks of preference discretion. US nonprofits such as hospitals can earn high net revenues, but still be more likely to offer unprofitable services than for-profits. Chinese SOEs can be strongly profit motivated, but still adhere to the spirit of government rule and regulation more faithfully than do conventional private firms. Of course, the organizational label does not automatically lead to perfect alignment with the collective good.

Some observant analysts have suggested that China's model of public–private engagement includes a learning process – sharing information, community views, professional expertise – that improves governance.[46] Nongovernment organizations work with the government not only as service providers, but also by engaging in contracting and collaborative arrangements to advocate policies and reflect the views of Chinese civil society.[47]

The incentive system for local bureaucrats strongly shapes the choice of service delivery model or project governance arrangement. Chinese local officials serve as agents for multiple principals – including the national agency in their domain as well as the provincial or municipal government. They must confront the "multiple logics" of Chinese bureaucracy, argue Xueguang Zhou et al. (2013). As mentioned earlier, they may feel themselves to be more tightrope walkers than ringmasters as they balance and adjust. In walking on the tightrope, China's local officials choose from an array of potential contracting counterparts, the choice depending on the circumstances in that province or locality, although nationally SOEs play an important role.[48]

---

[46] Teets, Jessica C., *Civil Society under Authoritarianism: The China Model.* Cambridge University Press, 2014; and Teets, Jessica C. 2013, "Let Many Civil Societies Bloom: The Rise of Consultative Authoritarianism in China," *The China Quarterly*, 213, 19–38.

[47] For an overview in the environmental area, see Teets, Jessica, 2018, "The Power of Policy Networks in Authoritarian Regimes: Changing Environmental Policy in China," *Governance*, 31(1), 125–141; and Dai, Jingyun and Anthony J. Spires, 2018, "Advocacy in an Authoritarian State: How Grassroots Environmental NGOs Influence Local Governments in China," *The China Journal*, 79(1), 62–83.

[48] SOEs accounted for approximately 23–28 percent of China's GDP in 2017, and a smaller share of employment, although assumptions have to be made in any such accounting exercise because

In Chapter 3's discussion of rail transportation, we highlight how historical context shaped China's development of regulatory structures and corporatized SOEs, starting in the 1980s phase of China's economic reforms and open-door policy. China pioneered a form of CG not between the public and private sectors, but between two different government entities to harness the benefits of competitive pressures, to harden budget constraints, and to promote the more efficient operations that the corporate form brings.[49] The relationship between administrative units of the government has been characterized as an "administrative sub-contracting system" embedded within a web of relational contracts infused with the career concerns of SOE managers (e.g., through the personnel management system within the CPC).[50]

An analysis by economist Li-An Zhou (2016) is instructive for understanding this China-specific institutional context.[51] He argues that China's "administrative subcontract" systematically differs from conventional public bureaucracy and traditional subcontracting along three dimensions: distribution of administrative rights; economic incentives; and internal assessment and control. An administrative subcontract represents "an authority relationship between a superior and a subordinate in administrative organizations, rather than contractual and equal relations between a principal and an agent in a 'pure' subcontract" (p. 40). Yet, in contrast to a standard public bureaucracy, the government "subcontractor" serves as "essentially the residual claimant and faces 'high-powered' incentives" including pressure to raise funds locally (p. 8). Moreover, in contrast with the strict rules and procedures of Weberian bureaucracy, "the internal control of the administrative subcontract features outcome-orientation and personalized accountability. ... Because the subcontractor carries out the tasks with significant discretion and controls relevant information disclosed to the

---

PRC official statistics do not report economic output in terms of public and private shares; see, Zhang, Chunlin, 2019, *How Much Do State-Owned Enterprises Contribute to China's GDP and Employment? (English)*. Washington, D.C.: World Bank Group. https://openknowledge .worldbank.org/handle/10986/32306/How-Much-Do-State-Owned-Enterprises-Contribute-to-China-s-GDP-and-Employment.

[49] For a discussion of China's policies regarding "grab the big and let go of the small" SOEs and the associated role of local governments (sometimes characterized as fiscal federalism or yard-stick competition among localities), see, Maskin, Qian, and Xu 2000; Li and Zhou 2005; Garnaut et al. 2005, Qian, Roland, and Xu 2006, Shih, Adolph, and Liu 2012, and Huang et al. 2017.

[50] See Zhou, Li-An, 2016, "The Administrative Subcontract: Significance, Relevance and Implications for Intergovernmental Relations in China," *Chinese Journal of Sociology*, 2(1), 34–74; and X. G. Zhou, 2014, "Administrative Subcontract and the Logic of Empire: Commentary on Zhou Li-An's Article,"*Chinese Journal of Sociology (Chinese version)*, 6, 39–51; Zhou, Xueguang, et al., 2003, "Embeddedness and Contractual Relationships in China's Transitional Economy," *American Sociological Review*, 68, 75–102; and Zhou, Xueguang, et al., 2013. "A Behavioral Model of 'Muddling through'. In the Chinese Bureaucracy: The Case of Environmental Protection," *The China Journal*, 70, 120–147.

[51] L. A. Zhou, 2016, "The Administrative Subcontract: Significance, Relevance and Implications for Intergovernmental Relations in China," *Chinese Journal of Sociology*, 2(1), 34–74.

superior, the superior's performance evaluation and internal controls must focus on outcomes rather than procedures" (p. 9).

Subject to these different pressures, high-powered incentives and career concerns, government officials may be risk-averse regarding the potential for contract manipulation for personal benefit (what we describe as *payoff discretion* later), or, worse, the possibility of downright corruption when working with private firms whose comparative advantages may be unfamiliar to them. In such cases, choosing a corporatized SOE as the "private" partner requires a more modest "leap of faith" for government (compared to collaborating with a for-profit private firm). The availability of corporatized SOEs as private partners makes collaborative approaches easier, because officials perceive SOEs as having their preferences better aligned with public value from the outset. (Somewhat the same argument is made about NGOs in the United States.) As many commentators on China's governance note, this alignment of interests arises in part from the ability of the CCP to select SOE managers, and from the incentives those managers' career concerns create naturally. Of course, the CCP also exerts some influence over managers of private firms, and SOEs differ in size, sector, and strategic importance. According to Milhaupt and Zheng (2015), China's government actually has less control over SOEs and more control over private firms – especially large and strategic ones – than state ownership interest in the firms suggests.[52]

Some observers view the predominance of SOEs in China's recent public–private partnerships as a weakness, arguing that it simply shifts responsibilities and debt pressures from one arm of the state to another.[53] However, the critical role of SOEs as government partners in collaborative arrangements in China also arises in part because they are often the most capable players in an industry. Efficiency considerations alone may give corporatized SOEs in some sectors an edge over de novo private firms, even apart from any presumption of better aligned incentives. Indeed, since SOEs have been retained in strategic sectors, they frequently have fewer competitors and combine considerable market power with significant symbolic power as emblems of market socialism, Chinese style.

The prominence of SOEs in the collaborative arena creates a major downside: a powerful risk of favoritism, even in the face of considerable evidence that SOEs are inefficient.[54] Many policy statements acknowledge

---

[52] Curtis J. Milhaupt and Wentong Zheng, 2015, "Beyond Ownership: State Capitalism and the Chinese Firm," *The Georgetown Law School Journal* 665(103): 665-722.

[53] "In China, Public-Private Partnerships Are Really Public-Public," February 27, 2017, www.bloomberg.com/news/articles/2017-02-27/in-china-public-private-partnerships-are-really-public-public.

[54] For example, SOEs receive preferential investment to promote innovation, but are less successful than private forms in translating investment into patents; see Shang-Jin Wei, Zhuan Xie, and Xiaobo Zhang, 2017, "From 'Made in China' to 'Innovated in China': Necessity, Prospect, and Challenges," *Journal of Economic Perspectives*, 31(1), 49-70.

favoritism, indeed corruption, as problems. For example, on September 10, 2019, top leadership called for greater support of private firms: "Both State-owned and private businesses should be guaranteed equal access to production materials, equal and open opportunities to engage in market competition and equal protection under the law."[55] President Xi's prominent anti-corruption campaign lays a foundation for better collaborative arrangements by reducing risks when either SOEs or traditional private firms engage in collaborative activities. In this way, efforts to eliminate corruption may help to make existing collaborative arrangements more effective, and to level the playing field between SOEs and other firms equally capable and motivated to contribute to public value.

THE DOWNSIDES OF COLLABORATIVE GOVERNANCE: PAYOFF DISCRETION, PREFERENCE DISCRETION, AND CORRUPTION

The magic ingredient of collaborative arrangements is simple: Discretion is granted to private parties that are better equipped than the public sector to deploy that discretion to produce public value. The great danger of collaborative arrangements, conversely, is that that discretion can be abused to promote private benefits. The hazards of CG fall into two major categories. We have alluded to these briefly in prior sections; now is the time to explore them with some care.

Payoff discretion "Payoff discretion" arises when private collaborators divert payoffs to themselves from the public at large. A private party with discretion over production often acquires some control over how value is distributed. Private players can exploit their discretion to siphon resources from the public at large, such as collecting rewards without being constrained to deliver sufficient public value, or "tuning" publicly financed production to yield mostly private payoffs.

Payoff discretion involves the distribution of value that can be expressed in relatively clear-cut economic terms.[56] A second danger arising in collaborative arrangements applies even when the augmented value from the arrangement does not take monetary form. It is what we term preference discretion.[57]

---

[55] *China Daily*, "Greater support for private firms needed, Xi says," September 10, 2019, http://en.people.cn/n3/2019/0910/c90000-9613440.html [accessed 13 September 2019].

[56] Donahue and Zeckhauser, "Sharing the Watch," in *Seeds of Disaster, Roots of Response*. Cambridge University Press, 2006, 429–456.

[57] Payoff and preference discretion bear resemblance to what social scientists sometimes call problems arising from agency theory (nonaligned incentives) and stewardship theory, respectively. See discussion and application to the case of affordable housing in China by Kerry Ratigan and Jessica C. Teets, "The Unfulfilled Promise of Collaborative Governance: The Case of Low-Income Housing in Jiangsu," chapter 16 in Jianxing Yu and Sujian Guo, eds., *The Palgrave Handbook of Local Governance in Contemporary China*. Palgrave Macmillan, 2019: 321–344.

Preference Discretion "Preference discretion" occurs when private collaborators substitute their own preferences for those of the overall community. This is a greater danger with nonprofit providers. They have limited ability to deploy their authority to increase their financial take, circumscribing the public's vulnerability to payoff discretion. But nonprofits may have strong motives to advance a narrow conception of the public good. If a collaborative arrangement is structured with insufficient attention to how the private party can redefine objectives and redirect outcomes, then public goals can be undermined. China's SOEs might engage in preference discretion, as do some nonprofits in the United States. This could take the form of tilting toward the career interests of the CEO, for example, or deferring to supervisors' desired goals even if those goals may not be aligned with the interests of the citizenry at large or even the shareholders of the SOE.

Payoff and preference discretion are always a threat. The risk becomes reality when government shares discretion inappropriately, haphazardly, or without reasonable review. Through more strategic choices among different forms of public–private interaction, and a more deliberate application of the collaborative model when it is selected, a more favorable balance between the benefits of private discretion and its costs can be achieved. The goal of this book, simply stated, is to improve the odds of this happy outcome in both China and the United States.

PART II

POLICY REALMS

3

Building the Railroads That Build the Nation

Henry David Thoreau had decidedly mixed feelings about the railroad that reshaped America during his lifetime and, quite literally, shattered the tranquility of his Walden Pond cabin several times a day. "We do not ride upon the railroad," he groused in *Walden,* "it rides upon us."[1] He relented, at least a little, elsewhere in the essay: "'What!' exclaim a million Irishmen starting up from all the shanties in the land. 'Is not this railroad which we have built a good thing?' Yes, I answer, *comparatively* good, that is, you might have done worse."[2] But his opening turn of phrase offers an apt point of departure for this chapter. A nation builds railroads and that network, from that point forward, builds the nation. This is true for both nations, but in a simpler and more dramatic way for the United States, which matured in tandem with rail transportation.

The building of America's railroads is a monumental story, stretching back to the middle of the nineteenth century. It is a history of extensive collaboration between the public and private sectors. The record is mixed, sometimes impressive and sometimes sobering. From the very beginning, the government attempted to enable, channel, and constrain private energies so as to best advance broad social goals. Three distinctive features of railroads – the costly capital investment required up front but low marginal costs of carrying freight or passengers, their need to secure rights of way, and their intricate connection to economic development – militate against simple *laissez-faire*, even in America. Given their cost structures, railroads have the potential to become either price-gouging natural monopolies setting ruthlessly high rates or victims

---

[1] Henry David Thoreau, *Walden, or Life in the Woods,* 1854, online version published by the University of Virginia Online Text Center at https://web.archive.org/web/20080918081551/ http://etext.lib.virginia.edu/toc/modeng/public/ThoWald.html, page 68. Empress Cixi in China reputedly also objected to the noise of railroads that disturbed the ancestors in their tombs.

[2] Ibid., page 42.

of regulatory exploitation forbidden to charge enough to cover their full costs. Government must promote and preserve the interests of shippers, passengers, and other stakeholders, but it must simultaneously ensure that railroads earn adequate returns to motivate continued rail investment.[3]

Some degree of cross-sectoral collaboration – in the United States as elsewhere – is all but inevitable when it comes to railroads. But American political culture discourages candor about this kind of interdependence. Since the required collaboration is too little discussed (or even honestly recognized), it has often been dealt with awkwardly, offering hard-won lessons that, despite the different circumstances, both countries might study with profit.

Those lessons apply as well whenever critical infrastructure must be built if it entails great initial expenditures and complex regulatory concerns, as it almost always does. Today that applies not just to physical assets but also to cutting-edge technologies such as 5G networks and autonomous vehicles. Things that run on tracks or on roads or, for that matter, through the ether, all involve some element of shared discretion between the government and the private sector, whether in the United States or China.

The first part of the chapter provides a highly condensed overview of the public–private relationship in the US railroad sector. It is structured around three shifting themes that also, to a substantial extent, correspond to three historical phases of that relationship: Promotion, regulation, and rescue. Most of this history happened when there was a bright line – in both technological and governance terms – between railways and urban subways, so the US story here will have less relevance to modern China's prodigious subway investments, or its unprecedented high-speed rail (HSR) network, both covered in the second half of this chapter.

The American history with railroads illustrates a recurring theme in this book. A public policy challenge arises. All parties recognize that neither the government nor the private sector can, or perhaps should, handle it on its own. Some reasonably pragmatic collaborative approach is improvised – rarely with much attention to its fundamental structure. That inattention is often promoted by parties grabbing personal value or power at the public's expense. A second common reason for inadequate structural analysis as collaborations take shape is the lack of clear conceptual guidelines for effective collaboration – a gap this book aims to help fill.

US RAILROAD DEVELOPMENT

Promotion

Centuries of improvisation with tracks to ease friction on rolling wheels, and decades of experimentation with steam power, converged around the turn of the

---

[3] This regulatory challenge applies to any industry (such as most utilities) with high fixed costs and low marginal costs. The extra challenge for rail is that vast amounts of real estate are included in the fixed costs.

nineteenth century to usher in the railroad era. In the early 1800s, the United States badly lagged rail trailblazer Great Britain. But by 1830 America's first practical steam locomotive, the *Tom Thumb*, signaled the start of a transformative period for transportation in the New World. It did not take long for entrepreneurs to recognize the vast potential for profit in a technology so dramatically superior to the boats, barges, and horse-drawn wagons that had previously been the state of the art. Nor did it take long for government to perceive the potential for public benefit from the rapid, low-cost, relatively safe conveyance of people and goods. The mid-nineteenth century featured energetic public–private collaboration for railroad expansion in which interests were substantially – though of course far from completely – aligned. Railroads enabled America to expand from a narrow East Coast strip to span the continent, at the same time building private fortunes large and small.

Abraham Lincoln, deservedly revered for preventing the separation of the nation's north and south, was a passionate advocate for a railroad to unite the nation's east and west. He signed into law the Pacific Railroad Act of 1862, which initiated the requisite construction by two private companies, financed by sales of the companies' shares, sales of land grants, and the federal government and the companies each selling bonds.[4]

Beyond mere dollars, governments at all levels aggressively promoted rail. The federal government made rights-of-way available free of charge in many or most cases for new routes, and also provided loans for rail investment. State, local, and county governments offered myriad forms of financial and in-kind support.[5] But the most ambitious tool deployed to encourage rail development in the nineteenth century – and, indeed, one of the most ambitious industrial subsidy programs ever implemented in the United States – was the federal land-grant program. The program rested on two premises. The first was that the rapid expansion of the rail network would produce immense public benefits. The second was that private investors would recoil from the risks entailed in extending costly rail lines into undeveloped regions. Big subsidies could make the risks acceptable.

In the service of this logic, as explicit quid pro quos for building designated new routes, railroads were given land amounting in the aggregate to more than 9 percent of the entire continental United States.[6] (Higher education was the other main recipient of federal land. Alternating strips of federal tracts were often allocated to railroads and colleges, respectively.) While the main justification for the land grants was the broad social benefit anticipated from rail expansion, the arrangement also featured direct advantages for

---

[4] Roger D. Billings, 2012, "The Homestead Act, Pacific Railroad Act and Morrill Act," *Northern Kentucky Law Review*, 39(4), 699–736.

[5] William S. Greever, April 1951, "A Comparison of Railroad Land-Grant Policies," *Agricultural History*, 25(2), 83–90; at 86.

[6] Greever, p. 83.

government. Railroads receiving land grants agreed to offer discounts from their regular tariffs for federal cargoes – a 20 percent discount for mail and 50 percent for other federal shipments.[7] Retrospective analyses have tried to tally this quid pro quo from the standpoint of the government, but rail moguls surely welcomed it given the combination of an immense giveaway and the low marginal costs of shipping any goods.

There has been a long-running, frequently arcane, sometimes caustic debate over where the land-grant program fell along the spectrum from the deft creation of public value to economically sterile largesse for well-connected robber barons. William Greever, writing in the mid-twentieth century, spoke for many at the time when he argued that "most of the lines ... would probably have been built without land aid, though perhaps with a little delay."[8] The economist Lloyd Mercer, in a well-reviewed retrospective analysis published thirty years later, reached a different conclusion. In his view government did a reasonably good job of structuring the deals. Not a perfect job, to be sure: For the Great Northern, Central Pacific, and Union Pacific railroads federal land grants were superfluous inducements to projects that the market would have amply repaid on its own. But for the Northern Pacific, the Canadian Pacific, the Texas and Pacific, and the Atchison, Topeka, and Santa Fe railroads, the grants were just enough (or even a little short of enough) to make the private investments viable propositions when fairly adjusted for risk.[9] Given the analytical, managerial, and political challenges inherent in targeting subsidies – challenges that can only have been greater for subsidies offered in the form of virgin real estate in undeveloped regions – this strikes us as a reasonably impressive batting average.

What of the public benefits bought for those subsidies? The lesser of the stated motives – getting bargain shipping rates for federal cargoes – was probably a bust. By one accounting the discounted rates on mail and other governmental shipments saved the government half a billion dollars by 1945. But railroads which had *not* received land grants, and thus had no obligation to offer discounts for federal shipments, generally did so anyway, suggesting that it was Washington's status as a big customer (rather than as a benefactor) that drove the discounts.[10] Yet it is important to remember that broad national development, not cut-rate shipping, was the main motive. And on this matter the land-grant program, and public promotion of rail expansion generally,

---

[7] Given that marginal costs for moving goods by rail were well below average costs, this grant-in-exchange-for-subsidized-rates structure has the qualitative features of what economists would label an efficient arrangement. Party A pays a fixed amount up front to get rates that are closer to marginal cost. This leaves aside the question as to whether the magnitude of the subsidy was appropriate, a question we take up shortly.

[8] Greever, p. 85.

[9] Lloyd J. Mercer, *Railroads and Land Grant Policy: A Study in Government Intervention*. Beard Books, 1982.

[10] Greever, p. 85.

seems like a clear-cut success. Mercer's book emphasizes that the social benefits from rail development swamped the costs of the land grants. This American episode illustrates a broader lesson: Sometimes the public and private sectors are in a position to produce such a bonanza of value through collaboration that the central challenge is to avoid undercutting the opportunity through undue squabbling over how the surplus is divided.

It may have been possible to get the same result at a little lower public cost. It may have been possible to get a similar result, some years or decades later, with less ambitious promotion policies. Had federal officials thought several moves ahead on the chess game, they may have been able to limit the concentrations of market power that would eventually prove so troublesome. But we find that the transformation of the United States over the last half of the nineteenth century, in light of the role of rail in enabling that transformation *and* government's role in promoting rail, constitutes on balance one of the more impressive episodes of collaborative governance in the dawning era of American economic power. It may thus prove instructive for our current age of China's even more rapid ascendancy.

Regulation

The late nineteenth and early twentieth centuries featured a cross-sectoral Clash of the Titans as aggressive regulatory gambits – especially the creation and strengthening of the Interstate Commerce Commission (ICC), but also the Sherman Antitrust Act and its companion measures – sought, with mixed success, to corral the market power of rail magnates such as J. P. Morgan and Cornelius Vanderbilt. Regulation was justified as essential to safeguarding precisely those broad public benefits that had motivated an earlier era's promotional stance toward rail. Private players meanwhile (by no means all of them moguls, monopolists, or malefactors of great wealth) sought to curb, evade, or control regulators – initially in search of profits, eventually in search of survival.

Regulators and railroaders, as well as the press and the public, tend to view economic regulation as a battle between powerful forces. Economists perceive a challenging intellectual puzzle beneath and beyond the political struggle. Railroads are a high fixed cost and low marginal cost industry. The usual economist's rule that price should equal marginal cost breaks down – but only in part. From one perspective that rule *does* work. If the price of rail transit is well above marginal cost, rail will be inefficiently expensive. Firms might ship their goods by truck or air, even if rail is the most technically efficient mode. Individuals might choose to drive – or even pass up worthwhile trips – instead of buying a train ticket. But from another perspective, marginal cost pricing makes no sense at all. If regulators require railroads to charge prices near marginal cost, no one will ever build a railroad. Construction is pretty much irrelevant to marginal-cost calculations – but not so irrelevant to the economics of the railroad business.

The solution in practice has been to have regulators set rates that seek to balance the need to cover investment against the desire to keep prices well below monopoly levels. Rail was perhaps the first national industry in which concerns about fundamental tensions between public and private interests spawned systematic regulatory interventions. This industry thus laid the template for the subsequent theory and practice of economic regulation more generally.[11] An early academic statement of the regulatory puzzle by transport expert Samuel O. Dunn is worth quoting at some length, not least because of its potential resonance for China a century later:

No problem more important and difficult confronts the people of the United States than that of establishing between their governments and their large business concerns relations which will promote greater equality in the distribution of the burdens and benefits of the production of wealth, without impairing the efficiency with which production is conducted. … The wisdom or folly of our regulation of railways may determine the wisdom or folly of our regulation of other classes of concerns and the success or failure of government control of business in many fields.[12]

The statute creating the ICC was enacted in the late 1880s, while the era of promotion remained in full swing, as farmers and other stakeholders began to complain that the benefits of rail expansion were tilting toward the rail companies and favored shippers at the expense of the public at large. A farmers' movement called the Grange was particularly forceful in demanding rate policies that would let the small family farm – part of the point, after all, for the original public efforts to promote rail development – survive and prosper. The legislative response broadly sought to constrain railroads' discretion to exploit the market power inherent in their capacity to offer transportation far superior to any alternative mode. Favoring big shippers over small and charging more for short hauls than longer ones (not just on a per-mile basis but for the whole trip) were among the "practices considered particularly obnoxious" that "were selected for special treatment" in the ICC's authorizing law.[13]

The next several decades were marked by a see-saw pattern of shifting public–private power over rail transportation as successive court rulings diminished ICC authority and new legislation restored and even bolstered

---

[11] The study of regulation is generally divided into two categories: economic regulation and protective regulation. The former category has a substantial focus on natural monopolies, with railroads as a salient case. Protective regulation concerns such matters as worker occupational health and safety, safety more generally, and environmental protection. It will also get attention in this book.

[12] Samuel O. Dunn, January 1916, "The Interstate Commerce Commission and the Railroads," *Annals of the American Academy of Political and Social Science*, 63, 155–172 at 155.

[13] Walter M. W. Splawn, January 1939, "Railroad Regulation by the Interstate Commerce Commission," *Annals of the American Academy of Political and Social Science*, 201, 152–164 at 152.

it.[14] Legislation enacted in 1906 was especially important in giving teeth to ICC mandates. The fortified ICC succeeded in reducing corruption and favoritism, increasing transparency, and deterring shady dealings against rail stockholders. But it also led to a steep reduction in rail profitability, in part by curbing market power over shippers and in part by mandating wage increases for rail labor.[15] In the early 1930s rail revenue was under pressure; many smaller railroads failed. This was primarily due to depression-driven declines in shipping and travel, but it also reflected tougher regulation as well as the first signs of serious competition from road transport.[16]

Worsening tensions in the business–government relationship over rail, however, were submerged during World War II (WWII). Mobilization of men and materiel massively expanded demand for both freight and passenger transport. Shortages and rationing of rubber and petroleum products imposed temporary but brutal constraints on truck transport and private autos. But with the return of peace, the tensions reasserted themselves with a vengeance.

While its founding mandate was to prevent the abuse of market power against small, isolated, or otherwise vulnerable shippers, the regulatory mission expanded to embrace other stakeholders. One of these was labor. In addition to provisions encouraging or requiring relatively high wages, rail regulations promoted work rules that were highly favorable for workers but undercut efficiency. Even though technological improvements permitted progressively smaller crews, rules required by government or by government-endorsed union agreements kept them large. A presidential commission in the Kennedy administration found that more than one in three rail workers were economically superfluous. Wages were often based on miles traveled rather than hours worked. The refrain of Steve Goodman's folk song "City of New Orleans" heralds the famous train covering "500 miles before the day is done." But pay rates based on the nineteenth-century steam locomotive speeds defined a day's work for freight crews as 100 miles. Geographic restrictions on where a crew could be required to work sometimes required swapping in a whole new crew three times over the course of a single day.[17] Costs soared; efficiency plummeted. .

Another incremental goal of regulation stemmed from the diverging fates of passenger versus freight rail. While freight faced road-based competition as well, the shift hit passenger rail sooner and harder. The private automobile came to dominate American transportation in the decades after WWII as public policy reinforced private preferences. In 1958, the ICC gained the authority to grant or deny railroad requests to discontinue money-losing passenger routes. That same year an ICC team produced a study that two leading rail scholars call a "remarkably thorough and meticulous analysis of why long-distance intercity

---

[14] Splawn, pp. 155–158.   [15] Dunn, pp. 156–158.   [16] Splawn, p. 159.
[17] John C. Spychalski, September 1997, "Rail Transport: Retreat and Resurgence," *Annals of the American Academy of Political and Social Science*, 553, 42–54 at 44.

rail passenger travel was doomed in the United States."[18] But the Commission – largely in response to pleas from rail passengers and the legislators who represented them – mostly declined requests to discontinue passenger routes. Railroads were increasingly obliged to cross-subsidize money-losing passenger operations with freight revenue.

Railroads in much of the country responded to market and regulatory pressures by merging their operations. The ICC needed to approve mergers and acquisitions, and did not always do so. But it granted consolidation requests often enough that the number of American railroads shrank dramatically as the twentieth century progressed. Growing concentration in the rail industry undercut the founding goal of regulation: supporting the interests of customers against concentrated market power. Charges of "regulatory capture" have often been leveled against the ICC.[19] Economist Marcus Alexis, writing in *Public Choice*, views the later history of the Commission as essentially a mission of suppressing competition and solidifying cartels and suggests that "[r]egulation which bestows benefits on the regulated may be endogenous in our democratic system."[20] Other economists see a more complex bottom line for rail regulation. A 1981 analysis in the *American Economic Review* finds an "interplay between ... two conflicting impulses, one toward competition and the other toward stabilizing and preserving revenue" for industry incumbents.[21]

But whatever the blend of motives, laws, institutions, technologies, and other forces behind it, the status quo of American rail was rapidly becoming untenable, and the dominant theme coloring public–private interaction was poised to shift once again.

Rescue

While the reckoning, in retrospect, was a long time coming, once it commenced the decline and fall of American rail played out with dizzying speed. Just as rail had disrupted canals and steamships with game-changing advantages in cost and convenience in the nineteenth century, now road transport (both passenger

---

[18] Robert E. Gallamore and John R. Meyer, *American Railroads: Decline and Renaissance in the Twentieth Century*. Harvard University Press, 2014, pp. 122–123.

[19] Many regulatory agencies are also accused of being captured. Prominent explanations for this phenomenon are: (1) that the regulated entities are significantly affected, and hence will devote significant resources to influence agency decisions, whereas the diffuse (albeit larger) interests of the general public do not make it worthwhile for entities to devote resources to counter these efforts, and (2) the revolving door between industry and government tilts agency officials to be more favorable to the industries they regulate.

[20] Marcus Alexis, 1982. "The Applied Theory of Regulation: Political Economy at the Interstate Commerce Commission," *Public Choice*, 39(1), 5–27 at 26.

[21] John Guandolo, May, 1981, "The Role of the Interstate Commerce Commission in the 1980's," *The American Economic Review*, 71(2), 116–121 at 116.

cars and truck freight) and air travel were disrupting rail. The inherent strengths of road and air transport were vastly magnified by favorable policy in ways both obvious and subtle. Enormous federal spending on the interstate highway system and ancillary state and local investments paved the way – literally – for an economically and culturally transformative ascendancy of the private automobile. The dispersion of housing and factories away from central cities undermined the economics of rail and reinforced the advantages of road transport. Cold War anxieties motivated Washington to maintain a huge, cutting-edge Air Force, promoting continuous technological improvement that spilled over to civilian air and ensured a steady supply of trained pilots cycling out of the military and into the civilian economy. Most of the basic infrastructure for road and air transport was paid for on the government's nickel, unlike rail. This not only drastically lowered the fixed costs for these emerging transport modes but also meant they had far less real property on which to pay taxes.[22]

Rail passenger-miles collapsed from more than 90 billion in 1944 to barely 10 billion in 1970, by which time fewer than 1 in 100 intercity trips was made by rail.[23] In 1967, the Post Office shifted most first-class mail – previously carried in special cars on passenger trains – to air and truck, at one stroke undercutting the economics of many so-far surviving routes. The situation was similar with freight. The diffusion of economic activity away from central cities was enabled by the same highway surge that helped to doom passenger rail. Trucks came to carry a soaring share of commercial cargoes, and in much of the country, the economics of rail freight became increasingly toxic. Labor complicated the problem. Work rules and lofty pay scales, won during the heyday of rail transport, made labor unions major stakeholders in rail policy while at the same time further undermining the economics of trying to ship freight at a profit. Industry-wide return on investment remained positive (though anemic) between 1960 and 1970, but dipped decisively into the red for many lines as rail lost out to air, road, and (a special threat to freight) pipelines for oil and natural gas.[24]

The trends undermining rail in general hit hardest and earliest in the northeast. The New York Central and the Pennsylvania Railroad sought to join forces in hopes of shoring up perilously thin profit margins. But it took a decade to negotiate and gain approval of the merger. Not until 1968 did Penn Central come into existence. In return for blessing the merger, the ICC obliged Penn Central to absorb the troubled New York, New Haven, and Hartford Railroad, and to continue running twenty of the thirty-four money-losing passenger lines Penn Central sought to abandon. Within two years, its stock

[22] Spychalski, p. 46, notes the importance of rail's disadvantages in terms of tax burdens.
[23] John L. Hazard, Spring 1980, "Government Railroading," *Transportation Journal*, 19(3), 38–50 at 39.
[24] Spychalski, p. 49.

fell from nearly $90 to barely $6 per share, and soon after Penn Central declared bankruptcy.[25] It was not alone: By 1973, regions served by bankrupt railroads accounted for 55 percent of American manufacturing and 40 percent of the nation's population.[26]

Penn Central's court-appointed trustees sought work-rule changes that might have given some hope of financial sustainability. But these were bitterly resisted by labor, unleashing a strike which was the trigger for stepped-up government involvement. The Nixon administration supported a Senate resolution calling for an end to the strike, a moratorium on work-rule changes, and a 45-day sprint by the Transportation Department to come up with a fix that would preserve rail service in the northeast.[27] The Nixon Transportation Department's initial bid was an "austere private-sector solution" involving only modest subsidies that "attracted the support of only Chicago School economists."[28] The ICC countered with a very different plan that gave much more weight to the interests of shippers and rail labor. A confused legislative scramble ensued to find some way to simultaneously meet the interests of customers, workers, stockholders, and managers when markets called for some significant fraction of these claims to dissolve.[29] A regulatory battle royal ensued.

Amtrak, Conrail, and the US Railway Association The outcome, perhaps predictably, was not particularly elegant. Over the course of the 1970s, the federal government created three SOEs to rescue rail and raised rail-related spending by several orders of magnitude.[30] There is little indication that this reflected a deliberate strategy rather than desperate improvisation to head off market outcomes that threatened intense political pain.

The freight rescue involved the creation of two governmental corporations with complementary functions. One was the US Railway Association, a nonprofit corporation run by a board of presidential appointees and tasked with financing and governance roles. The other, with the actual operational mandate, was Conrail – an odd organizational hybrid that was meant to be a "private, for-profit rail carrier supported by government grants and loans."[31] Penn Central along with several other bankrupt lines – not entire companies, but the dodgy parts of multiple companies – were cobbled together to constitute Conrail. (The actual list of lines to be absorbed by Conrail was reportedly drawn up not by any federal agency or by Congress, but by a private rail

---

[25] Donald Prell, *The Untold Story of the Survival of the Penn Central Company*. Strand Publishing, 2010, 6–7.

[26] Spychalski, p. 52. [27] Hazard, p. 40. [28] Ibid.

[29] According to Hazard (p. 41), the eventual solution was largely based on a proposal by an entirely separate railroad, the Union Pacific, and championed by Congressman Richard Shoup of Montana, a state with no stakes whatsoever in the issue.

[30] Hazard, p. 38.

[31] Arthur John Keefe, July, 1974, "Hear That Whistle Down the Line?," *American Bar Association Journal*, 60, 860.

trade association.) Conrail's authorizing legislation featured extensive labor protections, including lifetime wage guarantees that also extended to acquirers, if and when the industrial ward of the state were to transfer some or all of its operations back to conventional private companies. And it provided for continuing roles for both the Transportation Department and the ICC as advocates for (respectively) economic efficiency and stakeholder protection.[32]

The passenger-rail rescue was simultaneously simpler and more sweeping. Rather than taking over the unprofitable parts of private operations (as it did with freight), the government relieved the private sector of an entire unprofitable industry. While Congress, and especially the Senate, considered a plan to subsidize private rail companies to continue passenger service, the Transportation Department called instead for the wholesale governmental takeover of passenger rail.[33] The Rail Passenger Service Act of 1970 authorized the creation of "Amtrak," though one expert observes "[w]hether government was to be a distinguished undertaker for the burial of rail passenger service, the advocate for a permanent nationwide system, or the intermediate savior for private industry is unclear in the enabling legislation."[34] The Act defines Amtrak as a for-profit business, though how government was to make money on passenger rail after the private sector had despaired of doing so was by no means clear.

Amtrak's early financial performance was "disappointing but not altogether disastrous." But it would soak up $22 billion in federal spending by 1998.[35] Whether preserving passenger rail is worth the cost – and whether Amtrak should ensure *some* rail through much of the country or concentrate on a few corridors where the economics are most favorable and the social benefits greatest – continues to bedevil rail policy to this day. While the environmental, energy, and quality-of-life benefits of keeping travelers on the rails and off the roads actually did not figure in the case for Amtrak's formation,[36] these considerations later became important rationales for preserving it, even at substantial federal expense. Proponents also observe that road and air transport receive generous federal support, and they dismiss charges that if rail isn't self-supporting it is ipso facto inefficient. Many Americans (including, to varying degrees, the three coauthors) value the convenience and even the old-fashioned romance of train travel. Others, however, lament Amtrak as the creature of pork-barrel politics masked by fuzzy-minded nostalgia and exaggerated environmental claims.[37]

---

[32] Hazard, pp. 41 and 45.

[33] Hazard (p. 39) writes that the Nixon administration was following a script laid out by the private American Association of Railroads.

[34] Ibid.

[35] Ibid 43 and Federal Railroad Administration, "Privatization of Intercity Rail Passenger Service in the United States," March 1998 page 10 and Appendix A.

[36] Hazard, p. 44.

[37] David P. Baron, August, 1990, "Distributive Politics and the Persistence of Amtrak," *The Journal of Politics*, 52(3), 883–913.

There are certainly downsides, within a devoutly market-oriented culture, to assigning passenger rail to government. To maintain the broad political support on which its survival hinges, Amtrak runs operations in nearly every state. Some of these routes, such as those in the densely populated Boston-to-Washington corridor, make eminent sense by any metric one chooses to apply. Other routes, featuring sparsely peopled and elderly trains creeping along vast distances on borrowed track, are as preposterously incongruous in modern American transportation as Zeppelins. Reliance on Congress for operating funds has distinct disadvantages, particularly in these fractious times. As this chapter was first drafted, a horrific Amtrak derailment took several lives in Philadelphia. The absence of an established cause did not prevent the predictable factions from asserting with utter certainty that it was due to stingy funding, on the one hand, or elemental bureaucratic incompetence, on the other.

The situation with freight continues to be a more complicated story. Conrail, like Amtrak, was gamely described as "for-profit" in its authorizing legislation. Also like Amtrak, the label was delusional, at least at the start. Cumulative losses in its first four years of operation exceeded $1.5 billion. But new legislation in 1980 and 1981 weakened the claims of labor and shippers on rail operations, allowing Conrail (and other railroads) to streamline their operations and return to modest profitability.[38]

The abolition of the ICC in the mid-1980s, amid a broad deregulatory movement, allowed freight rail to concentrate on profitable routes and cargo. In much of the country the small family farm, whose survival had been the motive for shipping rate ceilings, had given way to factory farms capitalizing on modern methods and economies of scale. Soon the economics of the private railroad industry, now exclusively freight, were looking far more favorable. The Conrail Privatization Act of 1986 completed the round trip back to the private sector in what was then the largest initial public offering of a US industrial company in history.[39] And by 2013, the seven railroad systems that dominated the industry generated a record $73 billion in annual revenue while racking up 1.7 trillion ton-miles.[40] Both Warren Buffett and Bill Gates – neither known as a foolhardy investor – were loading up on railroad stocks.[41]

RAILWAY PROMOTION AND REGULATION IN CHINA

A central tenet of socialism is that the government controls what in 1922 Vladimir Lenin famously labeled the "commanding heights" of the economy.

---

[38] Spychalski, p. 53.   [39] Federal Railroad Administration 1998, p. 20.
[40] Office of Policy, "Freight Railroads Background," Federal Railroad Administration, April 2015, p. 1.
[41] Matthew Debord, "Why Warren Buffett and Bill Gates Are Railroad Rivals," *Business Insider* September 14, 2014.

These key sectors include not only national defense but also railways, alongside iron and steel, utilities, and telecommunications.[42] Indeed, the United States is an international outlier in not adopting a large role for government in these sectors after WWII.[43] China's leaders retain strong control of the "commanding heights," including railways. Investment in rail by the private sector only accounted for 2 percent in 2014.[44]

Given China's government control over the strategic sectors and China's pioneering work in infrastructure that has led to prominent efforts such as the Asian Infrastructure Investment Bank and the "Belt and Road Initiative" ("Silk Road Economic Belt and the 21st-century Maritime Silk Road Initiative," abbreviated BRI), one might assume that the dramatic expansion of highways and rail over the past quarter century – including the world's largest HSR network, constructed all within the first decade of the twenty-first century – were directed by a multi-year plan governing national transport development. Strictly speaking, one would be wrong; China lacked a National Transport Strategy at the time,[45] and much of the development of transport modes has evolved from local government experimentation with different ways to promote local economic growth. However, the premise of a central role for government management and fiscal investment would be correct.

Development of China's railways contrasts with that of other sectors, even transport sectors such as highways, and the differences are instructive about China's path toward contracting and collaborative governance. Railways have been more centralized, through direct government provision and then a corporatized ministry of railways, rather than through provincial-level development corporations and contracting out to private firms.[46]

The history of rail development in China illustrates many of the themes of this book. We have argued that three distinctive features of railways – their costly fixed investments coupled with low marginal costs, need to secure rights of way, and connection to economic development – require collaborative governance, or at least that government play a major role. The promotion and regulation of rail transport in China exhibit a contrasting history that converges

---

[42] According to the State Council's document guiding reorganization of SOEs, "the state should maintain absolute control over important industries that are related to national security and national economic growth" (State Council 2006, quoted p. 2462 in Z. Huang, L. Li, G. Ma, and L. C. Xu, 2017, "Hayek, Local Information, and Commanding Heights: Decentralizing State-Owned Enterprises in China," *American Economic Review*, 107(8), 2455–2478).

[43] J. Stanislaw, and D. Yergin, 1998. *The Commanding Heights: The Battle Between Government and the Marketplace That Is Remaking the Modern World*. New York: Simon & Schuster; Willoughby, Christopher. *Reforming Transport: Maximizing Synergy Between Public and Private Sectors: Background Paper for Evaluation of World Bank Assistance to the Transport Sector, 1995–2005*. Independent Evaluation Group, World Bank, 2007. http://siteresources .worldbank.org/EXTTRANSPORTATION/Resources/reforming_transport.pdf; Huang et al. 2017.

[44] National Bureau of Statistics of China, 2014.   [45] Bullock, Sondhi, and Amos, 2009.

[46] See discussion of this point in Bai and Qian 2010.

on a similar SOE structure as in the contemporary United States. The SOE approach is a rarity in the United States – an artifact of rail's peculiar history – while it is a more typical organizational form for China.

Promotion by Government: The First 100 Years

The first railway in China, constructed in 1876, was not promoted by the government in the same way as those in the United States – indeed, it was purchased by the government a year later and promptly dismantled.[47] This was not because the government disapproved of rail transport or dismissed its importance for economic development. It was because that first railway was constructed by the British, and illustrates another theme contrasting the United States with China: government interaction with the private sector often involved foreign firms and technologies; and while in the reform era these took the shape of foreign direct investment (FDI) for new technologies promoting development, there was a complicated historical legacy of imperialism.

This is hardly surprising, and does not militate against collaborative governance. Even bastions of private-sector competition, such as the United States, have sensitivities regarding foreign ownership of key sectors or landmarks. The prospect of an Arab-owned firm taking control of major East Coast ports, for example, sparked a major political brouhaha in 2006.[48] Foreign does not always mean exploitative; overseas Chinese in many cases provided constructive links between China and international technologies, resources, and expertise.[49] But what it does mean is that when public officials in China have considered collaborative arrangements, their choice set has often included a prominent SOE and a foreign firm, rather than the continuum of domestic for-profits and nonprofits available in the United States.

The People's Republic of China (PRC) inherited in 1949 a rail system ravaged by war. Although rail construction had been extensive during the late imperial period (1876–1911) and during the Republic years (1911–1949), it had not been well coordinated – serving Treaty Ports for foreign powers, lines with different gauges that did not, and could not, form an integrated network – and had been ravaged during Japan's invasion and the civil war.[50]

---

[47] X. Xue, F. Schmid, and R. A. Smith, 2002, "An Introduction to China's Rail Transport Part 1: History, Present and Future of China's Railways,"*Proceedings of the Institution of Mechanical Engineers, Part F: Journal of Rail and Rapid Transit*, 216(3), 153–163.

[48] David D. Kirkpatrick, "Pataki Joins Opposition to Takeover of Ports," *The New York Times* February 21, 2006.

[49] Chi, Cheryl S. F. and Raymond Levitt, 2011. "Multinational Teams Incorporating Freelance Expatriates in the Construction Industry: Case Studies of High-Speed Railways in China and Taiwan," *Engineering Project Organization Journal*, 1(3), 169–181.

[50] See "Impacts of Railway Construction during Late Qing and Early Republican China on the Long-term Economic Development," with Se Yan and Chong Liu, 2014. *China Journal of*

The foundation of China's truly national railway system, and the primary promotion period, began in Mao-era China in 1949. As the Mao government did with most sectors of the economy – especially those considered nationally strategic – railways were subject to centralized control and management. The government directly funded, built, and operated all rail transport through the Ministry of Railways. This rendered moot the need to cover fixed costs, hence freeing prices from any revenue requirements.

With heavily subsidized prices for passengers and freight, railways soon became the most important form of transportation in China. While careful studies of average and marginal costs for Mao-era railways are unavailable, prices certainly were well below average costs and in some cases may not have covered even marginal cost. For example, in the 1950s the uniform national price for passengers was 0.0149 yuan per person-kilometer, and for freight 0.0165 yuan per ton-kilometer (declining to 0.01438 in the 1960s).[51] Plans focused on development and improvement of the trunk lines, and catered to political exigencies as well, such as investments in the western mountainous regions during the 1960s to prepare for a feared invasion.[52]

Government promotion through direct delivery of the technology and operations continued throughout the first 30 years of the PRC, with various breakthroughs in domestic production technology for steam, diesel, and electric locomotives, as befitted the input-intensive economic development model.[53] The system operated under rigid planning and low prices, managed by fourteen geographically based railway administrations.

To understand the significance of contemporary China's transformation after this central planning phase, one has to appreciate that the Ministry of Railways, like other work units, provided cradle-to-grave "iron rice bowl" employment and social support to their employees and dependents. Thus, beyond rail-related activities, the Ministry of Railways also owned and managed many ancillary facilities and services, such as postal and telecommunication systems, public security, and health service providers for their employees, even high schools and colleges.

Promotion and Regulation since the 1980s

China came to recognize that its fully centralized provision of railroad services created rigidities, sacrificed valuable price signals, and more generally was

Economics, 1(3), 1–20; and X. Xue, F. Schmid, and R. A. Smith, 2002, "An Introduction to China's Rail Transport Part 2: Urban Rail Transit Systems, Highway Transport and the Reform of China's Railways," *Proceedings of the Institution of Mechanical Engineers, Part F: Journal of Rail and Rapid Transit*, 216(3), 165–174.

51 Bai and Qian 2010, p. 300.
52 During the Third Front Construction program, many SOEs were relocated inland to be far away from external threats (Huang et al. 2017).
53 Xue, Schmid, and Smith, 2002.

inefficient. During the early phases of reform in the 1980s, promotion continued but with a little more flexibility and some cautious explorations of engaging the private sector, primarily in the form of welcoming partial funding by foreign capital for several rail lines in the 1980s.[54] The later 1980s and early 1990s brought more autonomy, with the Ministry of Railways given a little more control of prices. Tax and profit payments that had previously been paid to the State Treasury were now retained by the Ministry to invest in the railway system.[55] Technological improvements proceeded apace.[56]

This phase arguably also saw the birth of China's modern regulatory state, in an interesting parallel with the United States. A major difference for China was that the promotion and regulatory phases all proceeded within a strictly government-provided rail service; the government was regulating its own Ministry. During this early phase of China's economic reforms and open-door policy, a regulatory system gradually took form across a wide variety of industries as they were separated from direct government operations, and separate agencies were tasked with regulation and monitoring. Thus for China, regulation and promotion in support of economic development coincided, albeit with a severely limited private role. The propelling factor was a growing recognition of the benefits of competitive pressures, hard budget constraints, and the more efficient operations that corporatization might harness.

In 1993, it was announced that the state railway monopoly would end. The Guangdong railway bureau was the first to be restructured into a corporate group in February 1993. Others followed over the 1990s until the whole system was corporatized in 1999.

Prices were allowed to depend on the route, season, and quality of service, and finally by 2002, railway prices were put under government "guidance" rather than determination. Regional authorities acted as profit centers responsible for their own net revenue, each paying a dividend to the Ministry for capital deployed and rent on wagons in use. The Ministry also encouraged regional authorities to build and operate their own railways, constructed usually with a mixture of central and local funding.

Corporatization marked the Chinese route toward remedying the fiscal drag from inefficient directly provided services and paved the way for private sector

---

[54] The first joint-venture railway was the Sanshui–Maoming Route, co-funded by the Ministry of Railways, Guangdong Province and the Asian Development Bank (J. Wang, F. Jin, H. Mo, and F. Wang, 2009. "Spatiotemporal Evolution of China's Railway Network in the 20th Century: An Accessibility Approach," *Transportation Research Part A: Policy and Practice*, 43(8), 765–778).

[55] C. E. Bai, and Y. Qian, 2010, "Infrastructure Development in China: The Cases of Electricity, Highways, and Railways," *Journal of Comparative Economics*, 38(1), 34–51.

[56] X. Xue, F. Schmid, and R. A. Smith, 2002. "An Introduction to China's Rail Transport Part 1: History, Present and Future of China's Railways," *Proceedings of the Institution of Mechanical Engineers, Part F: Journal of Rail and Rapid Transit*, 216(3), 153–163.

engagement within many economically strategic sectors. The railway system became more strongly exposed to market competition from other forms of transport. It also started to divest its many ancillary social service functions to focus on its core railway operations. Non-core businesses including engineering, construction, equipment, materials, and communications were separated from the Ministry of Railways and became independent enterprises in 2000.[57] Moreover, the Ministry removed itself from running the ten Ministry-owned railway universities and over 400 secondary schools.

China's new corporate structure for the railways – bearing many similarities to Amtrak in the United States, but never requiring a rescue – proceeded to raise efficiency and modernize rail infrastructure. For example, the core rail network shed 100,000 staff positions in 2001 in pursuit of enhanced labor productivity.

In the first decades of the twenty-first century, China's corporatized rail firms built over 1,500 kilometers of new lines each year, focusing on 'corridor-building,' reducing regional disparity, and supporting national growth. As the next section discusses, HSR also developed quickly.

Thus, government control in rail transport continued, without ever having to rescue private enterprises as the United States had done. The principal explanation of more robust passenger revenues, of course, is that a goodly fraction of Chinese travel by rail each month, but only a tiny percentage of Americans do. But even in China, the railroads now face profit pressures from the *relative* decline of rail compared to other transport modes such as roads and aviation.[58] The technical efficiency of railways improved in the 2000s, but growth rates in terms of passenger-kilometer and ton-kilometer hardly matched that of GDP.[59]

Investment has evolved from traditional direct spending by central government into greater partnership with provincial investment corporations.[60] The railway system has been profitable since 1998. However, the rate of return to investment in railways is low, below what is required to attract private investors. Whereas the average rate of return on equity for highways has been estimated at 10.5 percent, for rails it has been in the low single digits,[61] and considerably below the average for the whole transport sector.

Certainly this strong government role has its rationale, and a cautious approach toward sharing discretion with private for-profit companies to

---

[57] Bai and Qian, 2010.
[58] F. Jin, T. Dai, and J. Wang, 2005, "Modeling of Economic Effect of Transport Investment in China," *Journal of the China Railway Society*, 27(3): 9–14 (in Chinese); J. Wang, F. Jin, H. Mo, and F. Wang, 2009, "Spatiotemporal Evolution of China's Railway Network in the 20th Century: An Accessibility Approach," *Transportation Research Part A: Policy and Practice*, 43(8), 765–778.
[59] Bai and Qian, 2010.
[60] J. Scales, and J. Sondhi, 2009. China's Railway Development Program and the Vision for the Future. In *Indian Railways Strategy Workshop New Delhi*; Wang, et al., 2009.
[61] Bai and Qian, 2010.

avoid payoff discretion could be warranted in pursuit of broader public value. The government role is critical for many reasons, especially regarding access to land concessions and nationwide coordination of rail development. Economic promotion required substantial investments to bridge regional disparities, efforts that pure private investment would have been reluctant to support, including expansion in the inland mountainous regions of the country. Lhasa was the latest provincial capital city connected to the railway network with the opening of the Qinghai–Tibet route in 2006.

Nevertheless, China has relied on some private engagement even within this strategic sector. In 2002, the Ministry of Railways declared that China would allow foreign companies to enter its cargo market through joint ventures. Moreover, corporatization entailed divesting government ownership from the vertically integrated, sprawling organization, to instead focus on the core functions of building and operating the railways. Spinning off all the complementary products and services required contracting out many parts of the supply chain. Authorities managing the railways are under pressure to become efficient or else face further restructuring. This path toward China's world-class railway system surely has delivered substantial public value, despite numerous disturbing cases of corruption and inefficiencies, and steady erosion of market shares by other forms of transport. Recently, HSR helped to revive the high-tech 'glamor' of rail transport, which we turn to next.

High-Speed Rail

During the first decade of this century, China constructed the longest HSR network on the globe. How? Not with collaborative governance, but by continuing the Chinese tradition of a strong government role in rail transport promotion and development. Officially announced in the early 1990s, China's HSR system began operations in the early 2000s. Chinese authorities quickly signed a series of technology transfer agreements with leading international firms to import and absorb HSR technologies, albeit with a series of relatively standard contracts that involved little shared discretion.[62] China's current HSR system – already two-thirds of global HSR and planned to reach 30,000 kilometers of lines in 2020 – operates over 4,000 bullet trains carrying about 4 million daily passengers. It has transported more than 7 billion passengers since 2008, and started express cargo delivery in 2016.[63] Much of the HSR network has been constructed and operated under collaborative

---

[62] This is not to deny that disputes arose regarding the intellectual property rights; see Lin, Yatang, Yu Qin, and Zhuan Xie. *International Technology Transfer and Domestic Innovation: Evidence from the High-Speed Rail Sector in China*. London School of Economics and Political Science, LSE Library, 2015.

[63] "All Aboard: A Look at China's Highspeed Rail, 10 Years on," *China Daily* Hong Kong Edition, August 2, 2018.

arrangements between central and local governments, with the latter's contribution often coming in the form of land[64] – echoing the land-grant financing saga of the US rail development.

Construction of the Beijing–Shanghai High-Speed Railway provides an illustration. It was a government-led mega project following in the footsteps of the Three Gorges Dam and the Qinghai–Tibet Railway, with a total investment of 220.9 billion Renminbi (RMB, about US $32 billion).[65] China's State Council established the Leading Group of Beijing–Shanghai High Speed Rail Construction, chaired by a vice premier and with the director of the National Development and Reform Commission and the Minister of Railways serving as vice chairs, and prominent officials from all the affiliated government agencies, from the Ministry of Finance and Ministry of Science and Technology, to the governors and mayors of Beijing, Shanghai, and Shandong Province.[66]

Financing came primarily from central government fiscal investments and local government provision of land access rights procured from farmers. The managing entity, the Beijing–Shanghai High Speed Railway Co. Ltd, was founded by controlling shareholder China Railway Investment Corporation (a corporate entity funded by the Ministry of Railways, with 56.267 percent of shares); Ping'an Asset Management Co. Ltd (an SOE, leading a group of four similar companies, with 13.913 percent); the National Council for the Social Security Fund (a government agency, with 8.896 percent), and local governments (21.124 percent).[67] Only the approximately 14 percent of shares owned by Ping'an and other Asset Management firms under various insurance company holding companies could be construed as private investments.

During the process of construction and operations, these private partners did not substantially share in the oversight and management.[68] Though a modest amount of private ownership in a massive infrastructure project may be insufficient to promote efficient production, it may provide some assurance that the project is economically sound. We employ the term *sliver solution*

[64] Martha Lawrence, Richard Bullock, and Ziming Liu. 2019. *China's High-Speed Rail Development*. The World Bank, p. 9.

[65] Ouyang, B. (July 1, 2011). "The Total Investment of Beijing-Shanghai High-Speed Rail Reached 220.9 Billion Yuan" (JingHu Gaotie Zongtouzi Da 2209 YiYuan). Retrieved January 24, 2019, from www.chinanews.com/cj/2011/07–01/3149637.shtml.

[66] "Notice on the establishment of the construction leading group of Beijing-Shanghai high-speed railway" (Guowuyuan Bangongting Guanyu Cheng Li Jinghu Gaosu Tielu Jianshe Lingdao Xiaozu de Tongzhi). Retrieved January 24, 2019, from www.gov.cn/zwgk/2007–10/30/content_789767.htm.

[67] http://news.xinhuanet.com/fortune/2007–12/27/content_7323235.htm.

[68] Reportedly some of the private parties wanted to sell back their shares in 2012 because of complaints of lack of transparency, although these news reports have subsequently been suppressed. "Some investors in Beijing-Shanghai high-speed rail proposed to withdraw" (Jinghu Gaotie Bufen Touzizhe Tiyi Tuichu). Retrieved January 24, 2019 from http://companies.caixin.com/2013–02-03/100489062.html.

when the public sector wishes to secure a modest amount of participation from private parties in a project to test and demonstrate that the project is economically sound.[69] Such testing is particularly important, whether in China or the United States, if there may be substantial political pressures for the government to undertake such a project.

Some aspects of the Beijing–Shanghai line construction, such as technological development of the high-speed trains, involved contracting relationships among SOEs, prominent public universities and research organizations. Although this was hailed as "collaborative innovation"[70] and no doubt contributed substantially to the ability to deliver the ambitious project in record time through domestic resources, the project overall could not be considered as a pioneering effort in collaborative governance. And the comfortable working relationships with SOEs for HSR projects did not prevent corruption and questions about quality and safety, as we shall see.

Demand has been robust, and the Beijing–Shanghai High Speed Railway Co. apparently started making a profit in 2014.[71] Its experience can be contrasted with that of the California High-Speed Rail Project (linking Northern and Southern California) to highlight differences in the governance mechanisms used for rail promotion in China and the United States. Project management for China involved a strict internal power hierarchy within the Chinese leading group, with members having unequal status and vertical working relationships. By contrast, the California High-Speed Rail Project featured a coalition-building group with closer to equal-status membership and relatively horizontal working relationships. This stark difference clearly reflected divergent institutions in the two countries.[72] So too did the schedules for construction. China's lasted three years.[73] The California project, which must contend with many objecting parties, began construction in the same year (2008) but is scheduled for completion in 2033.

Even as construction progresses – and investment costs mount – the California project remains controversial. There are at least three kinds of objections to the

---

[69] Author Zeckhauser, advising Treasury Secretary Lawrence Summers, recommended a sliver approach when in 1999 a group of legislators from disaster-prone states asked to have the federal government offer a catastrophic insurance program for natural disasters. Thus, private insurers might offer 5 percent of the coverage, and the government would use their price as a benchmark. The legislators hoped for a much heavier subsidy.

[70] Cao Jianlin, Vice Minister of Science and Technology, used this term in a speech in May 2012. www.qstheory.cn/kj/kjcx/201205/t20120530_161181.htm.

[71] It is not clear if depreciation and other costs were accounted for in standard ways in some of the announced net revenue figures.

[72] X. Chen, and M. Zhang, 2010, "High-Speed Rail Project Development Processes in the United States and China," *Transportation Research Record*, 2159(1), 9–17; California High Speed Rail Authority. www.hsr.ca.gov/.2016 Business Plan, available at www.hsr.ca.gov/docs/about/business_plans/2016_BusinessPlan.pdf [accessed 4 August 2017].

[73] Construction work on the Beijing-Shanghai high-speed railway project started in April 2008; the track laying was completed by 2010, and the line opened in June 2011.

enterprise. Some critics simply think that California's version of HSR is a bungled version of a good idea. Others charge that California – a state that grew up with the auto and air industries – is just the wrong place for HSR. And still others decry what they see as massive investments in the last gasp of a dying, dated transport mode, calling instead for truly new transport technologies such as the "hyper-loop" that rockets magnetically levitated pods through near-vacuum intercity tubes.[74]

In China, HSR projects and the railways, in general, have not been immune from controversy. The fatal crash of two high-speed trains in July 2011 near Wenzhou, Zhejiang province stirred considerable controversy about the pros and cons of China's approach toward rail infrastructure and, indeed, the breakneck speed of infrastructure investment in general. Corruption led to the dismissal of the Minister of Railways and many other officials.[75]

Since then, China's rail system has continued robust government-led development with a gradually increasing private role, as HSR reaches most major cities.[76] Critics contend overdependence on government subsidies and unsustainable debt that might trigger a rail debt crisis.[77] Others estimate that despite the originally rigid fare structure that discouraged private investment, "the economic rate of return of the network as it was in 2015 is estimated at 8 percent, well above the opportunity cost of capital adopted in China and most other countries for such major long-term infrastructure investments."[78] The Hangzhou–Shaoxing–Taizhou line south of Shanghai is the country's first privately managed one, with the private firm Fosun holding a 51 percent stake.[79]

---

[74] James Fallows, "California High-Speed Rail: The Critics' Case," *The Atlantic Monthly* July 2014 summarizes the critiques. A talented friend of two of the authors recently became CEO of the leading hyper-loop company; they wouldn't bet against this technology. *Atlantic*: Web Edition Articles (USA), July 11, 2014 News, 6pp.

[75] In 2013 (the same year Xi Jinping formally launched the anti-corruption crackdown in China), Minister of Railways Liu Zhijun was convicted of taking over 60 million yuan in bribes and abuse of power; he was given a suspended death sentence commuted to life in 2015. See "The contract that brought down China's rail minister Liu Zhijun," *South China Morning Post* July 21, 2015; and the 'genesis of the tiger hunt' of Xi's anti-corruption campaign, discussed by Andrew Wedeman in his chapter "Anti-corruption Forever?" in Thomas Fingar and Jean C. Oi, eds., *Fateful Decisions: Choices That Will Shape China's Future*, Stanford University Press, 2020.

[76] After the 2011 accident in Wenzhou in which forty people died, HRS trains slowed down from 400 kilometers per hour, with 350 kilometers per hour restored as the highest speed. Babones, S. (February 14, 2018). China's High-Speed Trains Are Taking On More Passengers in Chinese New Year Massive Migration. McHugh, F. (September 27, 2018). China's high-speed railways have finally reached Hong Kong. Retrieved November 10, 2018, from www.telegraph.co.uk /travel/rail-journeys/china-high-speed-railways-new-hong-kong-train/.

[77] T. Mitchell and X. Liu, "China's high-speed rail and fears of fast track to debt." Retrieved November 10, 2018, www.ft.com/content/ca28f58a-955d-11e8-b747-fb1e803ee64e.

[78] Martha Lawrence, Richard Bullock, and Ziming Liu, 2019, *China's High-Speed Rail Development*. The World Bank. Quote on p. 4.

[79] Dong, Z. (June 19, 2018). High-speed rail on public–private partnership track. Retrieved November 11, 2018, www.chinadaily.com.cn/a/201806/19/WS5b28abcda310010f8f59da52.html.

China's rail firms have also actively worked abroad, constructing high-speed railways or contracting to do so in Turkey, Russia, and Indonesia, among other nations.[80]

Municipal Subway Systems

Public transport systems developed wholly within a region or municipality present greater opportunity (and necessity) of variation in governance and style. It is hardly surprising that among rail transport projects, municipal subway systems represent a broad spectrum of modes of private sector engagement, with a few becoming the most active in embracing aspects of collaborative governance. In the United States, subway construction is mostly a history lesson, since cost and politics have made new or dramatically expanded systems prohibitive to build. Washington, DC, completed the last major system in 2001.

As in other sectors discussed in the next four chapters in this book, in China it has often been the local governments with strong regulatory and procurement backgrounds – generally those in higher income provinces like Zhejiang (home to the Hangzhou–Shaoxing–Taizhou HSR line), and megacities, like Beijing and Shanghai – which first embrace the collaborative governance approach. Orchestrating effective collaborative arrangements calls upon a broad range of skills, from the ability to run a professional tendering process, to commitment to creating and enforcing accountability mechanisms, and generally guiding the discretion shared with private contractors and partnering organizations in the direction of public value.

The cooperation between the Beijing Government and Hong Kong's Mass Transit Railway (MTR) Corporation [81] – for Beijing subway Line 4, and then two more lines – well illustrates the increasing private engagement for construction and operation of infrastructure in China, and a stepping stone toward collaborative governance, Chinese style.

In 2005, MTR, Beijing Infrastructure Investment Co. Ltd (BII), and Beijing Capital Group Co. Ltd (BCG), signed an agreement with the Beijing Government on investment, construction, and operation of Beijing Subway Line 4. BII is a state-owned company solely held by the State-owned Assets Supervision and Administration Commission of Beijing Municipal Government (Beijing SASAC). It is responsible for investment, financing, planning, and capital operation for infrastructure-related projects. BCG, founded in 1995, is

---

[80] "All Aboard," *China Daily* Hong Kong Edition, August 2, 2018.
[81] Hong Kong's MTR, with controlling shares held by the Hong Kong Special Administrative Region Government and listed on the Hong Kong exchange, has cooperated with several other municipal governments in China, including Shanghai, Shenzhen, Hangzhou, and Shenyang, for subway metro investment, construction, and operation.

also a large state-owned company affiliated with Beijing SASAC, engaged in infrastructure, real estate, and financial services.[82]

Beijing Subway Line 4 crosses western Beijing from the north to the south, linking a residential area with the 'Beijing Silicon Valley' high-tech area of *Zhong Guan Cun*, major universities, and historical sites. The investment for construction followed the 70–30 public–private split dictated by Beijing policy for rail infrastructure. The entity that holds the operating rights of subway line 4 for thirty years, Beijing MTR, is held primarily by MTR and BCG (each with a 49 percent share; BII holds 2 percent of shares).[83] Beijing MTR makes profits through ticket revenue, rentals to commercial businesses inside subway stations, and some specified fiscal subsidies. The Beijing Government sets subway prices and subsidizes Beijing MTR based on the difference between the actual set price and the calculated expected price. Beijing MTR appears to have started making a reasonable return within a few years, and residents and visitors to Beijing have benefited from smooth operations of the new line.[84]

This relatively successful example of private engagement has been emulated for related projects, such as the Daxing Line (an extension of Line 4 from its southern end) and Line 14 (crossing southern and eastern Beijing). Development toward sharing of discretion is evident from Beijing MTR being involved in Line 14 at an earlier stage than for Line 4, providing input on key issues such as route selection and design.[85]

Another case of collaboration held up as a potential model for China's national PPP projects is that of Beijing subway Line 16, a 50-kilometer-long subway line in southwestern Beijing. Constructed between 2013 and 2018, the Line 16 project utilized collaboration for resources, with authorized franchising and equity investment attracting private investments.[86] According to participants, the Line 16 governance and accountability mechanisms drew from the experiences of Line 4 and improved upon them both in terms of project design – dividing the investments according to the actual amounts of

---

[82] *Beijing Morning Post.* "700 million Hong Kong capital injected into Beijing Metro Line 4 The first PPP model" (Qiyi Gangzi Zhuru Beijing Ditie Sihaoxian: Shouchuang Gongsiheying Moshi). News. Retrieved January 24, 2019, from www.bii.com.cn/p669.aspx; http://finance .sina.com.cn/g/20050208/08281356844.shtml; www.capitalgroup.com.cn/html/alhxs.html.

[83] "Beijing-Hong Kong Subway" (Jinggang Ditie). Retrieved January 24, 2019, from www .mtr.bj.cn/xljj/shx.html; www.bjpc.gov.cn/zhjh/jjshfz/2005/2005_1_5_1_1_1/200511/t100266 .htm.

[84] MTR (Xianggang Tielu Youxian Gongsi). Retrieved January 24, 2019, from www.bjpc.gov.cn /zt/wzz/al/201307/t6486611.htm.

[85] Caixin, "Beijing-Hong Kong subway is deeply involved in the construction and operation of Beijing Metro Line 14" (Jinggang Ditie Shendu Jieru Beijing Ditie Shidihaoxian Yunying). Retrieved January 24, 2019, from http://companies.caixin.com/2013-01-06/100479907.html.

[86] *Beijing No. 16 Subway Line PPP Model Case Analysis*, The Government And Social Capital Cooperation (PPP) Research Center, August 2015, http://pppcenter.cn/alfx/swal/jcss/201508/ 091951YKD.html.

capital they entailed, working with professional auditing firms for budget estimation – as well as in terms of sharing more operational discretion with the private counterpart. Engaging private investors earlier in the project process aims to smooth the transition from construction to operation, while enabling the private partners' information and expertise to be incorporated into the design.[87]

Even if later experience shows that these specific projects yielded fewer public benefits than had been expected, or that corruption marred their implementation, they nevertheless illustrate the active experimentation with private sector engagement and sharing of discretion in China.

RECAPPING THE JOURNEY

Lincoln and Mao were both railroad visionaries as well as nation-builders. They understood how railroads could unite their countries. Lincoln preceded Mao by almost a century, just as the nation-uniting rail efforts in the United States preceded those in China. The approaches in the two countries differed drastically. America worked hand-in-glove with bold entrepreneurs, quite a number of whom made vast fortunes. These railroad tycoons regularly drew on public resources. This represented collaboration to be sure, but it also entailed payoff discretion on a vast scale. The PRC first developed its conventional railway network through state-led construction and operation under the Ministry of Railways, frequently called "the last fortress of China's planned economy"; and then developed the world's largest system of HSR through strong central government leadership, partnering with local governments, SOEs and a supply chain of multiple ownership forms, a process lauded as a model for other countries in a recent World Bank report.[88]

The history of railways revealed fundamental tensions between public and private interests and therefore spurred development of economic regulation – in the United States, through the land-grant program, public promotion of rail expansion, and later a template for rate regulation; and in China, in separating corporatized SOEs from government ministries and cultivating a supply chain with public and private participants. Development of rail transport infrastructure – from low-speed rails to subways to HSR – also illustrates how *path dependence* (how the ease, or even the possibility, of reaching a given destination depends on the journey's earlier steps) strongly shapes contracting and delegation.

The United States built its railroads on a collaborative basis up through the early twentieth century, with positive results. Yet, the record suggests that the government was too generous to the bold men who built it. The failure of

---

[87] *Beijing No. 16 Subway Line PPP Model Case Analysis.*
[88] Lawrence, Martha, Richard Bullock, and Ziming Liu, 2019, *China's High-Speed Rail Development.* The World Bank.

the United States to keep pace with passenger rail developments in the twenty-first century appears more due to the distinctive political system of the United States and priorities given to other transport modes, rather than to the failure to find the right formula for collaboration or non-collaboration.[89]

China's government-led approach built more HSR in a decade than the rest of the world combined has yet constructed. To be sure, some other rail infrastructure development (such as municipal subway systems) drew increasingly on public–private collaboration, especially when commissioned by local governments with strong regulatory backgrounds and skills – illustrating the local heterogeneity in "collaborative governance, Chinese style." The story of rail transport thus previews many of the similarities and contrasts between the two countries' histories of public–private collaboration that we explore in the next several chapters, starting with the extraordinarily active and consequential arena of real estate.

[89] Democracies, particularly democracies with elaborate checks and balances, have their advantages. One of them is not the ability to lay straight track over land that is owned by a great variety of parties.

4

Real Estate's Intricate Tangle of Public and Private

One stormy night in our species' long prehistory, somebody got tired of sleeping in the rain and couldn't find a cave. She leaned a well-leafed broken branch against a big rock, or maybe bent a low-hanging bough to the ground, weighted it with a stone so it would stay put and crawled in out of the worst of the weather. This unnamed innovator slept a little drier that night, and in the process invented real estate. Fossil evidence makes it clear that this happened 30,000 years ago at the very latest, though humans may well have been building shelters as early as they started wearing clothes 140,000 years before that.[1]

Real estate is a fertile domain for public–private collaboration in all its rich, unruly diversity. In most times and places, the private sector is better than the public sector at erecting and managing buildings. But always and everywhere there are crucial collective interests tied up with real estate. The interaction of the sectors around land, dwellings, and other structures is sometimes simple and straightforward. Frequently, though, it evolves into the kinds of complex relationships, featuring shared discretion, that we term collaborative governance. This chapter begins with a high-level overview of real estate in the United States, organized by three broad sub-categories: owner-occupied housing; rental housing (especially subsidized low-income rentals); and commercial (office, retail, hotels, and industrial) real estate.[2] It then segues to cover the parallel story – radically different in some ways, strikingly similar in others – in China.

---

[1] "History of Architecture" on History World website, www.historyworld.net/wrldhis/PlainTextHistories.asp?historyid=ab27, and *Science Daily*, "Lice DNA Shows Humans First Wore Clothes 170,000 Years Ago," January 27, 2011 at www.sciencedaily.com/releases/2011/01/110106164616.htm, both accessed August 2015.

[2] As noted later, for some purposes rental housing is counted within commercial real estate, but here it makes sense to separate the categories.

UNITED STATES

Owner-Occupied Housing

In 2014, there were about 117 million occupied housing units in the United States, roughly two-thirds inhabited by owners and one-third by renters. American homeownership rates have been trending down in recent years but are still relatively high by international standards; about 80 percent of families above the median income own their own home, as do about half of below-median-income families.[3] While not the only reason for high levels of ownership in the United States, one major factor is massive, multifaceted governmental support for owner-occupied housing. Americans and their political leaders, across most of the ideological spectrum, consider homeownership to be desirable on political and social as well as economic grounds. Owners are thought to be more committed and engaged citizens than renters, and home equity can provide economic and even cultural ballast.

A network of institutions supports homeownership by subsidizing long-term mortgages, making them cheaper and more readily available than would the untrammeled market. Government-sponsored enterprises (GSEs) are relatively rare in the United States, but the housing sector is an exception. During the Great Depression's widespread concern over locked-up residential lending and swooning home-buying and home-building – housing starts had dropped by 95 percent between 1929 and 1931 – the federal government created the Federal National Mortgage Association (better known as "Fannie Mae," for its acronym FNMA) to establish an orderly secondary market for long-term mortgages.[4] A sibling organization with much the same mission, the Federal Home Loan Mortgage Association (also called by a variant of its acronym, though a rather strained one: Freddie Mac) joined Fannie Mae during the Nixon administration.

It worked. Private banks naturally hesitated to make thirty-year housing loans on the strength of deposits that (as the run-up to the Depression vividly demonstrated) can be withdrawn in an instant. Likewise, they found it uncomfortable to offer stable interest rates to borrowers when the rates depositors can demand zig and zag dramatically. But, the confidence that a network of government-sponsored intermediaries stands ready to orchestrate the sale of mortgages into the secondary market encourages banks to issue them. Concerted, cooperative action by a range of institutions – purely public, purely private, and a multitude of hybrid forms – powered a decades-long surge in homeownership and transformed American culture. (This has mostly been a matter of middle-class homeownership; not until 2014 were

---

[3] Robert Callis and Melissa Kresin, Social, Economic, and Housing Statistics Division, Census Bureau, US Department of Commerce, Press Release CB15-08, January 29, 2015.
[4] David M. Kennedy, Summer 2009, "What the New Deal Did," *Political Science Quarterly*, 124 (2), 251–268, at 257.

Fanny and Freddie required by law to emphasize lending for low-income homeowners or the builders of affordable rental housing.[5])

Lending by Fannie, Freddie, and the other, smaller GSE intermediaries was not actually supported by government guarantees. But markets long believed that Washington would step in, if necessary, to protect the system that had served American homeowners so long and so well. Early in the twenty-first century, as investors worldwide know to their sorrow, this system went haywire, degenerating into one of the more costly perversions of public–private collaboration in modern times. A mix of moral hazard due to the implicit governmental guarantee, confusion due to ever-more-exotic derivative securities that hid risk rather than reducing it, and what in retrospect seems like a vast epidemic of garden-variety foolishness led to the gradual inflation and abrupt collapse of a housing bubble. It would take over a decade for the world to recover, and some of the damage – including a whole generation's hobbled entry into the workforce – will never be fixed. This debacle is not the topic of this book, but it is a useful object lesson in how disastrous collaborative governance can be when it is carelessly managed.

Other governmental undertakings, beyond fervent support for long-term mortgages, promote homeownership in America. One is the dense skein of highways built in the twentieth century, which gave urban workers access to the vast expanses of less-developed areas where homes were more affordable. Probably more important and more expensive is a vast array of special tax rules for housing. Such targeted incentives in the tax code are often termed "tax expenditures," to the irritation of those who insist that declining to collect taxes that would otherwise be owed, in order to support some function or activity, is nothing at all like direct public spending to support the same function or activity. However one feels about the term, it is indeed true that tax expenditures are harder to measure with precision than are conventional budgetary outlays. The magnitudes involved are sufficiently prodigious, however, that even rough estimates are enough to signal strenuous governmental effort to encourage housing through the tax code. Official estimates by the Office of Management and Budget point to tax expenditures to support homeownership totaling over $3 trillion for the decade from 2015 through 2024.[6] Table 4.1 gives some of the major categories.

Tax expenditures for homeownership are by no means classic collaborative governance. Government has little or no discretion with respect to any particular

[5] Dionne Searcey, "Low-Income Housing Goals Set for Fannie Mae and Freddie Mac," *The New York Times*, August 19, 2014; Denise DiPasquale, 2011, "Rental Housing: Current Market Conditions and the Role of Federal Policy," *Cityscape*, 13(2), Rental Housing Policy in the United States, 57–70.

[6] US Office of Management and Budget, Fiscal Year 2016, Budget of the United States Government, Analytical Perspectives Volume, Chapter 14, "Tax Expenditures". Table 14.1, "Estimates of Total Income Tax Expenditures for Fiscal Years 2014–24" (The title is a little misleading, since the aggregate figures are for the 10 years from 2015–24.)

TABLE 4.1 *US tax expenditures to support home ownership*

Tax preference for homeownership	Total 2015–2024 cost
Deduction for mortgage interest	$1.1 trillion
"Imputed rent" not counted as income for owner-occupied housing (as it would be for rental housing)	$1 trillion
Capital gains on home sales mostly untaxed	$500 billion
Deduction for state and local property taxes (this one benefits rental as well as owner-occupied housing)	$450 billion

housing decision. It set the special tax rules for mortgage interest long ago. Individuals can decide whether, when, and how to respond to the incentives those rules establish. Nor is the policy entirely coherent. A Congressional Budget Office study of *all* housing-related tax policies found that the net effect is, as intended, to make owning cheaper than renting; in many circumstances, that is, not in all. And especially for the well-off. Poorer people can be better off renting, though they often don't realize this. There is no reason to believe that this tangle of divergent effects is intentional.[7] Inelegant though it may be, however, tax policy clearly has powerful impacts on housing. More resources go into real estate than they would in the absence of tax preferences, and greater generosity toward owner-occupied housing tilts private decisions toward owning rather than renting.

Low-Income Rental Housing

Unlike owner-occupied housing, subsidized rental housing for low-income Americans represents a textbook case of collaborative governance. For a large share of the 3 million families housed, in part, at public expense, the private sector actually delivers the housing. Private collaborators, moreover, enjoy substantial discretion, deciding whether and to what degree to participate in subsidized housing programs. Government, meanwhile, deploys a flotilla of rules, regulations, and incentives that endeavor (with uneven success) to require private collaborators to deliver public value in exchange for governmental monies.

It was not always so. Low-income housing long operated at the two extremes of public or private discretion – direct governmental action or pure private philanthropy. From colonial times local authorities maintained "poor houses," institutions that were generally preferable to homelessness but not by much. Religious organizations and other private charities also provided housing for the poor – often better than the public variety, sometimes not – as part of their

---

[7] Larry Ozanne, "Taxation of Owner-Occupied and Rental Housing," Congressional Budget Office, November 5, 2012.

broader ministries to orphans, widows, and paupers. Not until the Great Depression did the balance shift decisively toward government, driven by powerful forces on both the supply and demand sides. The economic calamity left many once-solvent American families unable to afford market-rate housing. And the Public Works Administration at the heart of the New Deal seized on residential construction as an ideal way to reduce mass unemployment. John Maynard Keynes personally urged President Roosevelt to fight the depression by pouring public money into residential construction.[8] (Interestingly, the Hoover administration that preceded Franklin Delano Roosevelt (FDR) had employed a delegated approach to anti-depression housing efforts, offering low-interest construction loans to corporations, but found too few takers to put a dent in either joblessness or homelessness.[9])

Title II of the National Industrial Recovery Act of 1933 authorized subsidized housing construction. But it was not until 1937, when the Wagner-Steagall Act established institutions and financial flows specifically dedicated to public housing, that construction began to explode.[10] Within three decades, there was public housing in every state. More than 2.1 million Americans – well over one percent of the population – lived in subsidized public rental housing by 1966.[11] There were more than half a million public-housing tenants in New York City alone.

But dissatisfaction with the direct governmental approach to housing the poor had already begun to deepen and spread. Conservatives hated the idea of millions of families so abjectly dependent on benefits funneled through governmental bureaucracies. Liberals hated seeing the poor warehoused into separate residential developments that were often squalid and dangerous. Social scientists documented the pathologies that flowed from packing disadvantaged people together with nobody but other disadvantaged people. And just about everybody found "the projects" aesthetically repellent and culturally repugnant.

The Nixon administration (and especially Nixon's Secretary of the Department of Housing and Urban Development (HUD), George Romney) began developing market-based housing reforms during their first term, though they didn't come to fruition until after the president resigned. The kernel of the reform effort was to shift away from take-it-or-leave-it public housing projects and toward housing vouchers that boosted poor families' ability to pay for rental housing, but let them decide on their own what and where to rent. While the

---

[8] David M. Kennedy, Summer 2009, "What the New Deal Did," *Political Science Quarterly*, 124 (2), 251–268 at 257.

[9] Robert G. Barrows, June 2007, "The Local Origins of a New Deal Housing Project: The Case of Lockefield Gardens in Indianapolis," *Indiana Museum of History*, 103(2), 125–151 at 127.

[10] Ira S. Robbins, "A Brief Summary of the Wagner-Steagall Housing Bill," The Compass, 18(7), 4–5, April 1937.

[11] Lawrence M. Friedman, "Public Housing and the Poor: An Overview," *California Law Review* May, 1966, 642–669 at pp. 643–644.

details have changed over time, the basics of the voucher program – called Section 8, after the legislative provision authorizing it – have been fairly stable: HUD sends funds to state and local housing authorities for rent-subsidy programs. Low-income families (and in some cases individuals) apply to participate. If selected, participants shop for their own rental units, give their voucher to the landlord (who is paid part of the rent by the government) and pay the remainder of the (regulated) rent themselves.[12] Participants' own housing payments are pegged to a percentage of their income.

By the mid-1990s, more than 700 thousand dwellings were occupied by Section 8 beneficiaries as the Clinton administration embraced the program. Early in the twenty-first century, the Bush administration doubled down on the voucher approach, accelerating the demolition of public-housing projects to general acclaim. To somewhat *less* general acclaim, the Bush team curbed the budget for Section 8. Much of the downward pressure on Section 8 in the Bush years came from budget concerns; growth trends in spending for low-income housing had alarmed budget hawks. But opposition on other grounds was brewing as well.

Howard Husock of the conservative Manhattan Institute and Hanna Rosin, a prolific and often provocative freelance writer, separately raised a common alarm. Lowlifes and criminals brandishing housing vouchers, they charged, were breaking free of the central cities that had previously contained them and scattering into vulnerable suburbs.[13] Rosin, in particular, made much of maps showing the overlap between high-crime areas and neighborhoods where Section 8 families chose to cash in their rental vouchers. Section 8 participants surely include bad actors, as does any large group. But, the notion of a HUD-subsidized spread of predators is far-fetched. Indeed, Greg Anrig and Harold Pollock showed that the causal arrow probably pointed the other way. Even after the vouchers boost their purchasing power, Section 8 families remain pretty poor; if they're not poor they're not eligible. Poor people tend to seek cheap housing. And housing tends to be cheap in dicey neighborhoods.[14]

It may well be that Section 8 benefits low-income participants without, to any great degree, harming the public at large, but that does not imply that this collaborative model is good housing policy. The voucher approach could be unduly expensive – either because expected private-sector efficiency advantages fail to materialize, or because private landlords charge excessive rents and thereby claim for themselves all those advantages (and more). There *does* appear to be some over-charging in the smaller, non-voucher component of

---

[12] Housing Vouchers Fact Sheet, US Department of HUD website at http://portal.hud.gov/hud-portal/HUD?src=/topics/housing_choice_voucher_program_section_8, accessed August 2015.

[13] Hanna Rosin, "American Murder Mystery," *The Atlantic Monthly* July/August 2008; Howard Husock, "The Housing Reform That Backfired," *City Journal*, The Manhattan Institute, Summer 2004.

[14] Greg Anrig and Harold Pollack, "False Accusation," *The American Prospect*, July 30, 2008.

Section 8. In this "project" component, the government does the shopping itself, paying private landlords for whole housing complexes to which low-income families are assigned. Over time, as landlords learned what they could get away with from government, costs crept up for this part of the program. But when families did the shopping themselves – as they did for most Section 8 rentals – they tended to get better deals, leading the Clinton administration to call for phasing out direct payments to landlords and moving entirely to the voucher model.[15]

Careful economic studies by both academics and the Government Accountability Office, spanning the range from five years after the program's launch to three decades later, have found Section 8 vouchers to be a generally effective model for housing America's poor.[16] By 2015, over 2000 state and local housing authorities administered Section 8 vouchers, and 2.1 million families comprising over 5 million people benefited from them – more than twice the number residing in the big housing developments that had previously dominated low-income housing.[17]

Even if *generally* effective, Section 8 is of course far from flawless. In most locales, landlords aren't obliged to accept Section 8 tenants. Even augmented by the vouchers, eligible families still have limited means, and the rentals they can afford are far from luxurious – indeed, often not even particularly safe. Whether because of overt discrimination or simple economics – and in a disappointing departure from one of the program's founding goals – Section 8 families tend to be concentrated in relatively segregated neighborhoods.[18] But while improvements are certainly possible, imperfection is the way of social programs, and on balance, the collaborative approach to low-income housing represents definite progress from "the projects." We could do a lot worse on housing for the poor. Indeed, we have.

It is worth noting briefly that there are policies apart from Section 8 for low-income housing in America. Some of them feature the collaborative approach to an even greater degree. Housing policy has incubated some exotic institutional and transactional hybrids, such as specialized intermediaries that link nonprofits that build low-income housing with for-profits able to benefit

---

[15] James R. Barth and Robert E. Litan, "Uncle Sam in the Housing Market: The Section 8 Rental Subsidy Disaster," *The Brookings Review* Fall 1996, 14(4), 22–25 at 22–23.

[16] Edgar O. Olsen and William J. Reeder, "Does HUD Pay Too Much for Section 8 Existing Housing?" *Land Economics* May 1981; Positive net benefits found in Deven Carlson, et al., "The Benefits and Costs of the Section 8 Housing Subsidy Program," *Journal of Policy Analysis and Management*, Spring 2011; US Government Accountability Office, "Housing Choice Vouchers: Options Exist to Increase Program Efficiencies," GAO-12-300, March 2012.

[17] Center on Budget and Policy Priorities, "Policy Basics: The Housing Choice Voucher Program," Center website updated July 2015 at www.cbpp.org/research/housing/policy-basics-the-housing -choice-voucher-program, accessed August 2015; "The Sequester and the Homeless" *The New York Times* March 23, 2014, p. 12.

[18] John Eligon, "A Year After Ferguson, Housing Segregation Defies Tools To Erase It," *The New York Times* August 8, 2015, p. 1.

financially (unlike the nonprofit builders) from tax incentives.[19] And not all public–private interaction on rental housing is focused on the poor. The nearly half-trillion in estimated tax expenditures (for the decade starting in 2015) related to deductions for state and local property taxes mentioned in Table 4.1 earlier includes rental as well as owner-occupied housing. There are also special tax preferences for rental housing with an estimated ten-year cost summing to about a quarter trillion – a good deal less than tax preferences focused on homeownership, but by no means trivial.[20] We also note that, while the focus here has been on the federal government, states and localities also seek to promote housing. But sub-national housing policy, however important in absolute terms, is limited in scale relative to federal direct spending and (especially) tax expenditure. Total state and local spending on housing and community development – a category that includes housing and a range of other functions – was about $50 billion in 2012, less than 2 percent of state and local spending overall and an order of magnitude lower than education budgets.[21]

Commercial Real Estate

Loath to dwell upon the squalor and gore of World War I trench warfare in letters to his children, Englishman Hugh Lofting instead crafted elaborate fantasies about a physician who could converse with animals. Lofting's wartime inventions evolved into his enormously popular series of "Dr. Dolittle" books. Among the most memorable denizens of Dr. Dolittle's fabulous menagerie was the Pushmi-Pullyu, a beast with a head at either end. (In the movie version, the Pushmi-Pullyu was a rather pedestrian two-headed llama, but in the books it was a gazelle-unicorn hybrid.) Long past the peak of Dr. Dolittle's popularity with British and American children, the Pushmi-Pullyu remains a favored metaphor for situations featuring forces that are both linked and in opposition. The Pushmi-Pullyu would be a wonderfully apt mascot for the public–private relationship over commercial real estate.

Commercial real estate is an umbrella term that covers most nonresidential structures, though some definitions also incorporate rental housing. Its major categories include office buildings, retail space, industrial buildings, and hotels. Public actors (including federal, state, and local agencies as well as special authorities) and private actors (ranging from big national and international

[19] Ellen W. Lazar and Michael S. Levine, "Community-Based Housing Development: The Emergence of Nonprofits, Enterprise, and LISC," *American Bar Association Journal of Affordable Housing and Community Development Law*, 1993 2(2), 6–9.

[20] US Office of Management and Budget, Fiscal Year 2016, Budget of the United States Government, Analytical Perspectives Volume, Chapter 14, "Tax Expenditures". Table 14.1, "Estimates of Total Income Tax Expenditures for Fiscal Years 2014-24."

[21] Jeffrey L. Barnett et al., "2012 Census of Governments: Finance—State and Local Government Summary Report," U.S. Department of Commerce, December 2014.

corporations to tiny mom-and-pop operations, and including some nonprofit players within a predominantly for-profit game) interact in complex and frequently contradictory ways to generate America's vast endowment of commercial buildings. When the Pullyu end is in charge, government promotes commercial real estate through direct subsidies, tax incentives, and other special deals, motivated by hopes of job creation, economic development overall, and broader cultural vibrancy. With the Pushmi end ascendant, government restrains or simply pushes away commercial real estate to ward off congestion, overdevelopment, or undesirable patterns of growth. Sometimes (from the perspective of a particular developer) some public actors are pushing and others pulling at the same time; sometimes the same actors push one year and pull the other; sometimes the pushing and pulling happens simultaneously from the same units of government seeking to balance the upsides and downsides of commercial real estate.

One obvious and consequential domain of public–private interaction around commercial real estate – though an exceedingly complex one that features more unintended than intended consequences – concerns the intimate linkage between real estate and the macroeconomy. Booms (often but not always related to fiscal and monetary policy) inspire private actors to develop more space to accommodate offices, stores, and assembly lines. Busts make developers push away, curtailing new projects and sometimes canceling developments in the works or even mothballing completed buildings. Commercial real estate can be excruciatingly sensitive to economic cycles. In one admittedly extreme case, the same office tower in Lowell, Massachusetts, sold for half a million dollars in a mid-1990s slump and changed hands again for over $100 million just four years later when good times returned.[22] Valuations are so volatile in part because projects can take a decade or more to come to fruition. A development launched in a boom can land in a bust (or vice versa). Not just overall economic conditions but also regulations and tax rules can shift in the meantime.[23] The cross-sectoral pushing and pulling goes in the other direction as well. Decisions by developers to plunge ahead or pull back powerfully shape (for good and for ill) the economic vitality and cultural complexions of cities, metropolitan areas, even entire states. And in the aggregate, such decisions can trigger turning points between recession and recovery and back again in the broad macroeconomy.

Beyond this general interconnection (and interdependence) lies a range of specific policy arenas and instruments of public–private collaboration over real-estate development.

---

[22] Karl E. Case, Edward L. Glaeser and Jonathan A. Parker, 2000, "Real Estate and the Macroeconomy," *Brookings Papers on Economic Activity*, 2000(2), 119–162 at 121.

[23] Ibid 137; see also Edward Glaeser, 2013, "A Nation of Gamblers: Real Estate Speculation and American History," *American Economic Review*, 103(3), 1–42.

Firm-targeted inducements States, cities, and other jurisdictions use direct financial lures to attract commercial real estate (as well as other development considered desirable).[24] Occasionally subsidies come as cash, though in-kind benefits are more common, such as free or cut-rate transit or utility connections. Subsidies ostensibly from states and localities can actually originate with the national government. Among the many purposes for which federal Community Development Block Grants can be used is "financial assistance to for-profit businesses" in the name of economic development.[25]

Even more common than direct subsidies, and almost certainly far larger in financial terms, are targeted tax subsidies. A city or state government will agree to forgo the collection of taxes that would otherwise be owed – typically property taxes, though sometimes also other types of taxes – in exchange for developers investing in (or simply remaining in) the jurisdiction. Research from 2010 found that two-thirds of the states and over half of all municipalities offered targeted tax abatements to lure development. There is no reason to expect such tax preferences to have become less popular since then.[26] The economic scale of targeted tax subsidies is hard to estimate, in part because of conceptual issues but more importantly because full transparency is in the interest of neither the public actors who offer them (who might worry about demands from other firms for equal treatment, or tough questions from constituents) nor of the private actors who receive them (who would prefer not to have to face journalists or citizens demanding detailed accounts of the public benefits delivered in exchange for the subsidies.)

Place-targeted inducements "Place-based" policies offer benefits to *any* developer who invests within a particular area—usually but not only urban areas suffering from high levels of poverty and unemployment. Geographically circumscribed incentive systems have a long history. In some countries (including Mexico, China, and even North Korea), special economic zones (SEZs) are carved out where the normal rules don't apply, in order to promote exports without making wholesale changes in economic laws and regulations. In the United States, such zones usually represent an awkward compromise between conservatives (whose first choice would be to reduce taxes and regulations everywhere) and liberals (who doubt the public benefits of such policies, in general, but concede they might be useful in nudging development from one side to the other of a zone's boundary.) Two-thirds of states had "enterprise zones" by the early 1990s. The details of what this entails

[24] The frenzy to attract Amazon's second US headquarters in 2016–2017 featured remarkably promiscuous subsidy offers by a long list of cities and states.
[25] Government Accountability Office, "Community Development Block Grants: Program Offers Recipients Flexibility but Oversight Can Be Improved," GAO-06-732 released August 28, 2006, Table 1, page 9.
[26] Mark K. Cassell and Robert C. Turner, December 2010, "Racing to the Bottom? The Impact of Intrastate Competition on Tax Abatement Generosity in Ohio," *State & Local Government Review*, 42(3), 195–209.

vary from one state to another and even from one zone to another, but there is usually a range of tax preferences for building and operating within the designated boundaries.[27] Researchers have found little evidence to suggest that state enterprise zones make a major difference in reversing the fortunes of targeted locales, but the policy interventions are of moderate scale and the market dynamics they are meant to deflect tend to be potent. Later the Federal government created its own "empowerment zones" that featured direct spending and regulatory waivers as well as tax incentives to steer investment to eight economically troubled locales. Evaluations point to mixed results. There has been some decline in poverty and joblessness within the targeted zones, relative to comparable locales that aren't included in the program. But there has been little discernible increase in residents' earnings. The gains, while far from trivial and for some zone residents perhaps transformative, have probably been below the costs of the empowerment zone movement.[28]

Business Improvement Districts Business Improvement Districts (BIDs) are a hybrid form of public–private interaction around commercial real estate as exotic as anything in Dr. Dolittle's menagerie. Government (sometimes state legislatures, sometimes city councils, sometimes other kinds of authorities) sets up the laws by which a BID can be formed and delineate their rights and responsibilities. Property owners and other businesses come together to form a BID and define its mission, which may include stepped-up investments in infrastructure and amenities within the district, marketing and promotion efforts, parking and transportation improvements, even private policing. These activities are funded by special taxes on businesses operating within the district. Closing the loop back to the public sector, these taxes are collected by government – usually from all businesses within the district, even those who did not advocate for or feel they benefit from the BID – and turned over to the BID. The Bryant Park Restoration Corporation, on which two of us have written elsewhere, is among the most famous BIDs, but there are hundreds in operation in the United States alone and many more BIDs or comparable organizations elsewhere.[29]

These are the major categories of public–private collaboration around commercial real estate, but many other formats exist. A city government might build and operate a money-losing convention center to pump up the market for hotels and restaurants. Or it might waive costly regulations in one domain (such as building height or minimum setbacks) in exchange for concessions in another area (legal ones such as affordable housing or

[27] Edward L. Glaeser and Joshua D. Gottlieb, 2008, "The Economics of Place-Making Policies," *Brookings Papers on Economic Activity*, 155–239, at 201.

[28] Ibid.

[29] Robin Reenstra-Bryant, March 2010, "Evaluations of Business Improvement Districts: Ensuring Relevance for Individual Communities," *Public Performance & Management Review*, 33(3), 509–523.

sustainable construction, or illegal ones such as donations to a reelection fund.) Governments can even invoke eminent domain to force one private property owner to yield to the interests of another, if those interests can be persuasively described as instrumental to those of the public at large.[30]

Yet the distinguished urban economist Edward Glaeser, among other scholars, believes that, on balance regulations pushing away commercial real estate (as well as housing) tend to be stronger than subsidies and other policies meant to pull it in. The right approach – from the perspective of environmental sustainability and cultural vibrancy as well as economic efficiency – would be to pull people and capital into high-productivity urban areas until density's downsides start to swamp its advantages. But most of the time political preferences of people and businesses who have already found their place in the urban sun – and whose political clout dwarfs that of those outside looking in – lead to policies that repel new development far before the sweet spot of optimal density is reached.[31] As is often the case, the key question concerns not how much public–private collaboration there should be, but rather details of structure and purpose.

CHINA

In real estate, China presents a vastly different picture from the United States. The government or collective owns all the land. Population movement from rural areas to cities is a contemporary tsunami, not a century-long phenomenon. Yet the key question for China also involves the details of structure and purpose of public–private cooperation. China's real estate policies have shifted dramatically in recent decades. Its system, once dominated by direct provision, today prominently features private engagement and aspects of collaborative governance. Private firms partner with local governments not only to develop real estate but also to solicit investment, provide logistical support, and manage a full range of business development services. These collaborations can bring great public value, or fail as the "ghost cities" discussed later.

The municipal government owns the land in urban areas; in rural areas, the owner is the village collective. Private parties have land use rights only, although leases can extend to fifty or seventy years. This feature gives rise to distinctive aspects of China's real estate development, notably including the government promotion of housing construction and use of land financing – selling land use

[30] Wendell E. Pritchett, Winter, 2003, "The 'Public Menace' of Blight: Urban Renewal and the Private Uses of Eminent Domain," *Yale Law & Policy Review*, 21(1), 1–52.

[31] Edward L. Glaeser, *Triumph of the City: How Our Greatest Invention Makes Us Richer, Smarter, Greener, Healthier, and Happier*. New York: Penguin Press, 2011. For a dissenting study, see Albert Saiz, August 2010, "The Geographic Determinants of Housing Supply," *The Quarterly Journal of Economics*, 125(3), 1253–1296.

rights to commercial developers – as a primary means to fund local governments.

Real estate development is highly consequential in China, given its rapid economic development enabled by the movement of hundreds of millions of people from village agriculture to urban life. Just within the few years of the New National Urbanization Plan (2014–2020), ambitious targets called for increasing urban residents from slightly over half to more than 60 percent of the population and granting urban *hukou* to 100 million rural migrants.[32] The unprecedented scope of the housing boom in China has global implications. As Glaeser and colleagues (2017) phrase it, compared to this Chinese real estate boom, US housing gyrations look "stable and dull."[33] Residential property investment in GDP tripled from 2 percent in 2000 to 6 percent in 2011 (Du and Zhang 2015); real land prices in thirty-five Chinese cities increased five-fold between 2005 and 2015.[34] As in the United States, and ominously, investors believe that the government will step in to stabilize housing markets. Their expectations have been reinforced by the numerous and frequent interventions in the market, including policies that helped soften the economic hardships associated with control of COVID-19 in 2020.

Accordingly, households and other stakeholders perceive a government commitment that housing markets are "too important to fail."[35] Could comparable missteps trigger a crisis in China in the way US real estate went off the rails early in the twenty-first century, ultimately shaking the world financial system? Liu and Xiong (2018) note that nationally, the dramatic increase in housing prices – 4.5-fold between 2003 and 2017 – was accompanied by similar growth in per capita income, alleviating some concerns. However, middle- and low-income households have purchased homes at large multiples of annual income (averaging eight to ten times) in expectation of future income growth, and firms, banks, and local governments are all substantially exposed to real-estate investments.[36] The health of the

[32] Urbanization spurs China's dramatic growth and promises to continue as an engine of development even as the country faces headwinds from nearing the technological frontier and the Lewisian turning point after reallocating labor from lower productivity agriculture to higher productivity industrial and service sectors, as well as population aging. Karen Eggleston, Jean Oi, and Yiming Wang, 2017. "The Political Economy of Urbanization in China," chapter 1 in Karen Eggleston, Jean Oi, and Yiming Wang, eds., *Challenges in the Process of China's Urbanization*, Stanford University Walter H. Shorenstein Asia-Pacific Research Center series with Brookings Institution Press.

[33] E. Glaeser, W. Huang, Y. Ma, and A. Shleifer, 2017. "A Real Estate Boom with Chinese Characteristics," *The Journal of Economic Perspectives*, 31(1), 93–116.

[34] Glaeser et al. 2017, p. 108.

[35] Fang, Hanming, Quanlin Gu, Wei Xiong, and Li-An Zhou, 2016. "Demystifying the Chinese Housing Boom," *NBER Macroeconomics Annual*, 30(1), 105–166.

[36] C. Liu, and W. Xiong, 2018, *China's Real Estate Market* (No. w25297). National Bureau of Economic Research.

global economy could well hinge on sound public–private interactions in China's real-estate sector.

Owner-Occupied Housing

Political leaders in China, like their US peers, strongly support homeownership, on political, social, and economic grounds. Homeownership in China is extraordinarily high: 85 percent according to the 2010 census, higher in rural (95 percent) than urban areas (75 percent),[37] and more than 90 percent currently.[38] However, the quality of housing is highly heterogeneous. More than one-third of all houses – especially in rural or peri-urban areas – lack piped water and more than one-quarter lack in-home toilets.[39] On average, Chinese homes are fairly large – comparing favorably with many high-income countries – but the average masks considerable disparities, with about one in ten citizens – and a much higher share in crowded mega-cities – residing in homes offering fewer than 13 square meters per person.[40]

Historical stages of policy development. Although China was the most urban society in the world 1,000 years ago, during the Song Dynasty, it started the modern era as a predominantly agricultural society. Some scholars argue that Chinese cultural traditions and historical legacies that emanate from agricultural roots foster especially high rates of homeownership.

In Mao era China (i.e., after the PRC was founded in 1949 through the 1970s), housing was the sole responsibility of the government, through an urban work unit (*dan wei*) like a SOE or a rural collective, with most rural homes originally self-constructed. Work units provided employees with heavily subsidized housing as part of a comprehensive package of welfare support. Larger work units negotiated with farmers for the acquisition of rural land and then contracted the development work to construction teams. The central government paid the bill. Municipalities allocated their housing budgets to municipal housing bureaus to develop public housing for employees of smaller enterprises or public employees, like teachers. Rents were extremely low.

While this system guaranteed housing to all, it encountered multiple problems: funding constraints meant that supply fell behind demand; maintenance lagged; and complaints of unfair housing allocation proliferated. Work units objected to the great financial burden of providing housing. Residents expressed discontent with low quality housing. And the government knew that success of its macroeconomic reforms depended on delinking

---

[37] Data from the 2010 census and more recent statistical updates and news; see Niny Khor and Jean Oi, "Institutional Challenges in Providing Affordable Housing in the People's Republic of China," chapter 11 in Karen Eggleston, Jean Oi, and Yiming Wang, eds., *Challenges in the Process of China's Urbanization*, Stanford University Walter H. Shorenstein Asia-Pacific Research Center series with Brookings Institution Press, 2017.

[38] Glaeser et al. 2017, p. 105.   [39] Khor and Oi 2017, p. 221.   [40] Khor and Oi 2017, p. 227.

employing work units from mini social welfare states. Thus, housing reforms began.

Several experiments in the 1980s tested the feasibility of rent adjustment and privatization[41] before the central government issued "The Decision on Deepening the Urban Housing Reform" in 1994. Its vision was that middle- and lower-income households would purchase subsidized affordable housing units produced through a program (discussed in more detail later) called economical and comfortable housing (ECH), while higher-income families would purchase housing at market prices.[42]

On the financing side, potential homebuyers would get subsidized mortgage loans through a compulsory housing saving program called the Housing Provident Fund (HPF) as well as by applying for commercial mortgage loans. Modeled after Singapore's Central Provident Fund, China's HPF is a compulsory housing-saving program in which both employers and employees contribute a certain percentage of the employees' salaries, initially set at 5 percent, to HPF accounts. In return, employees get low-interest mortgage loans for their home purchase. Since 2005, the program has required that both public and private employers participate. Actual participation varied widely across cities. Local governments manage the HPF fund and have used it to keep local real estate markets vibrant.

Starting in the early 1990s, mortgage loans became available to homebuyers nationwide (Di et al. 2008), but banks were not comfortable providing loans to individual households and usually imposed strict restrictions on loan originations.[43] Later the standards were relaxed somewhat. In 1998, the Chinese central bank, the People's Bank of China (PBoC), published the Residential Mortgage Lending Regulations, which established a maximum loan-to-value ratio of 70 percent, mandatory income verification, maximum mortgage term of twenty years, and a mortgage rate for all borrowers set at ten basis points below commercial loans with the same terms.[44] (Standard terms in the United States are much laxer.)

As one component of these housing reforms, public housing units throughout the country were sold to their sitting tenants at heavily discounted prices.[45] Enjoying the new fiscal freedom that economic reform allowed, many

---

[41] Wang, Ya Ping, and Alan Murie, 2000, "Social and Spatial Implications of Housing Reform in China" International Journal of Urban and Regional Research, 24(2), 397–417.

[42] State Council of PRC, 1998.

[43] For example, loans were available only to those who had bank savings equal to 30 percent of the home's value. Moreover, the loans had to be paid back in five years, and the first payment had to be no less than 30 percent (Zhang 2000). Most urban households could not meet these criteria.

[44] Deng, Yongheng, and Peng Fei, 2008, "The Emerging Mortgage Markets in China," in D. Ben-Shaher, C. K. Y. Leung and S. E. Ong, eds. Mortgage Market Worldwide. Blackwell Publishing, 2008: 1–33.

[45] Households living in state-owned housing were given the opportunity to buy either full or partial property rights to their current homes at prices far below market values; the vast majority

work units significantly expanded housing production for their employees. Thus, reforms included both privatizing the existing housing stock and expanding new construction, with many of the newly constructed housing units initially purchased by work units and then resold at deeply discounted prices to their employees.[46] Housing privatization appears to have been a success, and this collaborative approach to housing policy made Chinese households better off, on balance, than they had been with the prior arrangement of direct government provision and its associated misallocations.[47] Sociologists have noted that despite greater access to better housing for elite occupations in China, "housing privatization distributed home equity widely across those who were resident in public housing immediately prior to privatization," with less inequality than in many established market economies, like the United States.[48]

In the wake of the late-1990s financial crisis, China's government required work units to shift from direct provision of housing to subsidies to help employees buy homes. This change in policy reflected China's broader effort to restructure its economy toward domestic consumption rather than reliance on export-led growth. Housing represented a promising new growth engine.[49] Reforms varied significantly by region, reflecting the prominent role played by local governments, which control both the land supply and zoning regulations. Moreover, the central government committed only limited resources; local governments bore most of the burden of paying for housing reforms.[50]

Still, national housing patterns were radically transformed within a decade, with the homeownership rate increasing from around 55 percent in the early 1990s to over 80 percent by 2004.[51] China became the largest residential mortgage market in Asia by 2005.[52]

Jing Ji Shi Yong Fang ("Economic and Comfortable Housing," ECH). Established in 1994, the ECH program aimed to serve lower- and middle-income urban families who could not afford housing purchases at market

purchased full property rights, with no restrictions on the sale of their homes and the right to retain all profits earned from any such sales (Wang 2011).

[46] Wang, Ya Ping and Alan Murie, 1996, "The Process of Commercialization of Urban Housing in China," *Urban Studies*, 33(6), 971–990.

[47] Wang, Shing-Yi, 2011, "State Misallocation and Housing Prices: Theory and Evidence from China," *The American Economic Review*, 101(5), 2081–2107.

[48] Walder, Andrew G. and Xiaobin He, 2014, "Public Housing into Private Assets: Wealth Creation in Urban China," *Social Science Research*, 46, 85–99.

[49] Lee, James and Ya-peng Zhu. 2006, "Urban Governance, Neoliberalism and Housing Reform in China," *The Pacific Review*, 19, 39–61.

[50] Wang 2005.

[51] S. Y. Wang, 2011, "State Misallocation and Housing Prices: Theory and Evidence from China," *American Economic Review*, 101(5), 2081–2107.

[52] Deng, Yongheng, and Peng Liu, 2009, "Mortgage Prepayment and Default Behavior with Embedded Forward Contract Risks in China's Housing Market," *Journal of Real Estate Finance Economics*, 38(3), 214–240; L. Deng, Q. Shen, and L. Wang, 2009, Housing Policy and Finance in China: A Literature Review. *US Department of Housing and Urban Development*; Zhu 2006.

prices. The contrast with affordable housing in the United States was stark: All the ECH units were developed for sale, not for rent. Indeed, purchased rather than rented housing accounts for 3/5ths of affordable housing (*baozhang fang*) in China.[53]

To get this housing built, the government adopted a two-step collaborative approach. Construction was contracted out to for-profit real estate developers (sometimes SOEs), and then sold to eligible families through market transactions. Some ECH projects were cooperative housing developments sponsored by work units, a phenomenon distinctive to China in its transition.[54] Discount housing helped work units attract and retain talented workers, and to get their feet wet in the profitable real estate industry. This intricate collaborative arrangement served multiple public and private purposes, and with much sharing and shifting of discretion. One longer term consequence – probably not anticipated – was that many such spin-off development companies later grew into large commercial housing developers serving regional housing markets.[55]

Economic and comfortable housing relied heavily on local governments, who were expected to provide subsidies through free or low-cost land to ECH developers, as well as through reductions or even waivers of various development fees and real estate taxes. In exchange, local governments regulated the sales price of ECH units; the profit margin could not exceed 3 percent. Nationwide, the prices of ECH units were usually 15 to 20 percent lower than market prices.[56]

Construction supported by the government might be justified if supply was constrained and subsidizing households to purchase on the private market would have been difficult. Increasing supply can reduce the price for all consumers, something that cash transfers, like America's section 8 vouchers, cannot. Relying on such logic, many European governments built social housing after the destruction of World War II. Whether or not this was an explicit objective of China's ECH program, research suggests that the program only moderately crowded out market supply.[57]

Critics questioned the rationale for providing subsidized housing to a majority of the population, and local governments objected to the fiscal

[53] Khor and Oi 2017, p. 216.

[54] Wang, Ya Ping, Yanglin Wang, and Glen Bramley. 2005. "Chinese Housing Reform in State-Owned Enterprises and Its Impacts on Differential Social Groups," *Urban Studies*, 42(10), 1859–1878.

[55] Wang et al. 2005.

[56] Rosen, Kenneth T and Madelyn C Ross, 2000, "Increasing Home Ownership in Urban China: Notes on the Problem of Affordability," *Housing Studies*, 15, 77–88; Liu, Zhi-Feng, and Jia-Jing Xie. 2000. The Speeches at the Meeting about the Progress of Housing Monetary Allocation in 35 Large and Middle Size Cities.

[57] J. Chen, and H. Nong, 2016, "The Heterogeneity of Market Supply Effects of Public Housing Provision: Empirical Evidence from China," *Journal of Housing Economics*, 33, 115–127.

burdens of unfunded mandates for affordable housing. But following on from the Asian Financial Crisis, policymakers apparently believed that below-market prices for ECH units were necessary to push most urban households into the market. Arguably, the primary goal of ECH was to stimulate housing consumption, not necessarily to help the neediest families. Given this background, it is perhaps not surprising that the program often missed the target of target efficiency. Wealthy households often purchased the ECH units, pushing both development standards and housing prices beyond the reach of middle- and lower-income families.[58] Officials' response to this slippage in policy intent, and the criticism it aroused, took the form of stricter regulation. The program continued as part of the 2008 stimulus package to combat the near-global recession induced by the housing market debacle of the United States.

Links to the macroeconomy. As in the United States, homeownership in China plays a major role in the macroeconomy. First and most prominently, Chinese households view homeownership as the best way to invest their savings, given that other options are few: average real interest rates on bank deposits tend to be extremely low, domestic stock markets are notoriously volatile, and tight capital controls restrict investment beyond the nation's borders.[59] Investment in housing is also strongly linked to local government financing and to demographic changes. The tradition of providing housing for sons and the large gender imbalance increases current demand;[60] but in the longer run, China's shrinking working-age population and overall aging population suggest that demographics may "put great pressure on the demand for housing ... because houses currently owned by the older generation will be eventually transferred to the current younger generations, which are smaller."[61]

Thus demographics, direct housing policy, and the indirect effects of a range of macroeconomic policies all work together to create large potential fluctuations in housing markets that threaten macroeconomic stability. Over the past decade, these forces have pushed housing demand exceptionally high – so much so that housing policy swiveled sharply toward constraining rather

[58] Cai, Jiming. 2009, "Stop Building the Economic and Comfortable Housing, Let Cheap Rental Housing Benefit People (Ting Jian Jing Ji Shi Yong Fang, Rang Lian Zu Fang Qie Shi Hui Min)," *China Construction Newsletter (Zhong Guo Jian She Xiao Xi)*, 2009(7), 48–51; Zhang, Chunxiang. 2007, "The Discussion on the Reform of Economic and Comfortable Housing (Jing Ji Shi Yong Fang De Gai Ge Tan Tao)," *China Price (Zhong Guo Wu Jia)*, 2007(4), 57–59; Duda, Mark, Xiulan Zhang, and Mingzhu Dong. 2005. China's Homeownership-Oriented Housing Policy: An Examination of Two Programs Using Survey Data from Beijing. W05(7). Retrieved from http://citeseerx.ist.psu.edu/viewdoc/download?doi=10.1.1.110.575&rep=rep1&type=pdf.

[59] Glaeser et al. 2017, p.105.

[60] Wei, Shang-Jin, and Xiaobo Zhang, 2011, "The Competitive Saving Motive: Evidence from Rising Sex Ratios and Savings Rates in China," *Journal of Political Economy*, 119(3), 511–564.

[61] Liu and Xiong 2018, p. 31.

than promoting demand, then swiveled again toward local government stimulus during the COVID-19 outbreak in the first quarter of 2020, moderating as the market surged.

As early as 2002, China's central bank issued a report warning state-owned commercial banks to be cautious about potential housing bubbles. Local governments were pushed to tighten the supply of land. But prices still climbed in response to market forces. As many citizens acquired dwellings for investment purposes, vacancy rates across Chinese cities surged to more than 20 percent[62] – levels unheard of in other countries. Unsurprisingly, the ownership of vacant housing increases with household income.[63]

After the financial crisis in 2008, policy once again shifted toward promotion, as evidenced by the large share of fiscal stimulus devoted to low-income housing.[64] Experts argue about the eventual fate of China's housing boom, but a preponderance of opinion seems to favor the view that a housing crash is not inevitable. The future largely depends on government policy choices.

> With sufficiently controlled housing supply, current prices can be maintained, but if housing supply continues to aggressively deliver new space, prices will fall. ... If the government buys up excess housing inventory—perhaps to convert it to social housing as it started to do in 2015—it can further bolster softening prices. There does appear to be a feasible public path towards housing price stability.[65]

Time will tell if the government has the ability, the resources, and the desire to make purchases on the scale that would be required.

While both China and the United States promote homeownership, their policy instruments differ sharply. One major difference, as we have noted, is China's heavy emphasis on ownership rather than rentals to promote affordable housing. Another is that conventional tax policy plays far less of a role in China than the United States – though, one could argue that China's "tax expenditures" are also quite formidable. For example, residential properties are exempt from property tax.

A third is that US land use regulations often restrict construction of new housing, whereas in China, local governments have strong incentives to promote new construction for both residential and commercial properties. The central government has imposed several policies to restrain localities, such as strictly limiting local government requisition of land to the residential land of rural households (*zhaijidi*), rather than agricultural land. Policies also restrict private developers from procuring the rural residential land directly, so local governments mediate the process and reap the revenue benefits: they

---

[62] K. Chen, and Y. Wen, 2017, The Great Housing Boom of China. *American Economic Journal: Macroeconomics*, 9(2), 73–114.

[63] About 40 percent of households in the top decile of income own vacant houses, which is about 22 percentage points higher than among households in the lowest income quartile (Chen and Wen 2017).

[64] Deng, Shen, Wang, 2009.   [65] Glaeser et al. 2017, pp. 113–114.

purchase land at its (low) value in agricultural use, and sell it at its (high) value in urban use, leading to large revenues from "land financing," as described in greater detail in the section on commercial real estate later.

Many other policies indirectly support urban homeownership in China as well as the desirability of living in cities. These range from extensive investments in urban public transportation (buses, subways, highways) and high-speed railways, to the concentration of the best arts, entertainment, health-care providers, and educational opportunities in urban centers. These factors conspire to push up the value of urban housing, fueling concerns about the future affordability of housing as China attempts to urbanize hundreds of millions more Chinese.

Within the span of little over a decade, construction of floor space shifted sharply toward the private sector. Between 2000 and 2013, the share of China's floor space built by SOEs and housing collectives plummeted from almost three-quarters to only 13 percent.[66] This public–private relationship encompasses collaborate governance in policies that grant private developers considerable discretion, and government-controlled banks are pressured to provide favorable credit policies with developers bearing very little risk.[67]

The government's fairly visible hand powerfully shapes the housing market and overall economy. Vastly more resources go into real estate than they would in the absence of land financing and exemption from property tax. Policies favoring owner-occupied housing feed back onto rental markets. Freed from property taxes and other carrying costs, owners often need not rent out properties, even if they are second or third residences. Ballooning numbers of vacant homes have resulted. Owners' buy-and-hold strategies limit the potential for Section8-like collaborative approaches to affordable housing, our next topic.

Low-Income Rental Housing

Lian Zu Fang (literally, low-price or cheap rental housing, CRH), as a component of China's affordable housing (*baozhang fang*), holds enormous untapped potential for collaborative approaches. Cheap rental housing in fact is a more accurate name than low-income rental housing, because all China's affordable housing programs have been plagued from the outset with poor target efficiency. Certainly, any government finds monitoring and enforcement of income eligibility to be a challenge. China has employed two factors – not always intentionally – to encourage self-targeting of CRH units to those urban residents whose incomes are lowest. First, as noted, the high demand for homeownership naturally promotes self-selection. Second, CRH developments are often relegated to the least desirable locations, with few amenities, long commute times, and poor public transport connections.

---

[66] Glaeser et al. 2017, p. 103.   [67] Glaeser et al. 2017, p. 104.

Local governments resist CRH projects not merely to avoid subsidies, but also because they are concerned that such projects would diminish property values in the surrounding areas. In addition, deploying land for affordable housing brings high opportunity costs. Their alternative is to reap the net revenue from selling land use rights to commercial developers (discussed later). The central government's focus on ownership and the modest enthusiasm of local governments for CRH – combined with citizens' preferences – keep subsidized rental housing far scarcer in China than in the United States. Nationally, only 1 percent of residential homes are *lian zu fang*.[68]

Public rental housing (*Gong zu fang*, PRH) is intended to serve the same population. Here too policies differ significantly by locality.[69] Whereas in Beijing, PRH constitutes only a small share of affordable housing and has strict eligibility criteria, Chongqing widely promoted PRH under its now imprisoned former leader, Bo Xilai, with relatively lenient eligibility thresholds. Cities also differ in their private engagement in the construction of PRH, with some working exclusively with large SOEs, while others contract out to a variety of private real estate developers.

Sometimes collaborative activities with the private sector help local governments convert central government mandates into policies tailored to economic development. For example, in southern coastal China, such as in Guangdong province, factories have long been staffed by migrant workers, who require affordable housing. Originally, the central authorities had requested estimates of the scale of these requirements from local governments. But the localities, anticipating prorate subsidies, inflated their estimates – a tactic that backfired when it turned out that local government would have to pay for what was often surplus housing. Meanwhile, many local firms had already built housing for their employees, responding in part to large tax preferences for housing benefits.

In other cases, efforts to harness collaborative governance fall short of their full potential. Ratigan and Teets (2019), for example, argue that affordable housing policies in Jiangsu Province fell prey to a kind of self-fulfilling spiral of underdevelopment: when government could not find private partners with enough capacity, they abandoned the spirit of collaboration if not the rhetoric, and without investment and contracts to bolster development of capable private partners, collaborative approaches to affordable housing floundered. They recommend central government investment in developing nonprofit organization capacity, as well as attention to the fundamental contradictory incentives for local officials, who gain more from cultivating commercial development (see discussion of land finance later).[70]

---

[68] Khor and Oi, p. 217.

[69] Jing Zhou and Richard Ronald, 2017, "Housing and Welfare Regimes: Examining the Changing Role of Public Housing in China," *Housing, Theory and Society*, 34(3), 253–276.

[70] Kerry Ratigan and Jessica C. Teets, "The Unfulfilled Promise of Collaborative Governance: The Case of Low-Income Housing in Jiangsu," chapter 16 in Jianxing Yu and Sujian Guo, eds., *The*

China's policies on affordable housing remain in flux. No final grade for collaborative approaches should be given. And when it is, it will vary by grader. Policies to date have been reasonably effective but far from perfect. Further evolution should be expected. Textbook approaches to improve target efficiency, such as vouchers, may get a trial. Moreover, the market for rental housing in general is sure to rapidly change as China's economy develops further into a knowledge-based service economy and labor is pulled to new activities.

Commercial Real Estate

The Pushmi-Pullyu metaphor invoked for American commercial real estate policy is an equally apt mascot for the public–private relationship in China. On the one hand, world-class rates of industrial and service-sector growth epitomize China's great economic success. On the other hand, the intimate linkage between real estate and the macroeconomy, along with China's unprecedented pace and scope of urbanization, dictate a strong and continuing role for government at all levels. With local government leaders' careers closely linked to success in stimulating economic growth during their tenure in office, strong incentives push real estate development and the collaboration with the private sector it requires. Indeed, the central government Pushmi struggles to direct and constrain the local government Pullyu, motivating multiple directives to protect collective interests (such as restriction on requisitioning agricultural land from peasants), to constrain overbuilding and housing bubbles, to target affordable housing, and to root out corruption in property development. In China, as in the United States, great fortunes have been built in real estate. Unfortunately, those fortunes have sometimes relied on political favors, and not infrequently on shady practices and direct corruption.

Firm-targeted inducements are officially rare in China (or perhaps common but illicit, as some argue[71]), but *place-targeted inducements* have been pervasive in China's development. For example, anti-poverty policies usually feature place-based targeting. Officially designated poverty counties and poor villages receive earmarked transfers.[72]

More generally, national strategy for economic development utilized policy experiments in different localities, dating back to the famed SEZs. While

Palgrave Handbook of Local Governance in Contemporary China. Palgrave Macmillan, 2019: 321–344.

[71] Bai, Chong-En, Chang-Tai Hsieh, and Zheng Michael Song. 2019. "Special Deals with Chinese Characteristics." NBER Working Paper 25839, National Bureau of Economic Research, Cambridge, MA.

[72] Park, Albert, and Sangui Wang, 2010, "Community-Based Development and Poverty Alleviation: An Evaluation of China's Poor Village Investment Program," *Journal of Public Economics*, 94(9), 790–799.

ostensibly set up to spur exports, China's SEZs embraced policy experimentation and institutional innovation. Shenzhen is the premier example, having blossomed from rice fields into one of China's four tier-1 cities. Indeed, Shenzhen was a pioneer city in China's reform and opening process, with a highly collaborative process involving the municipal government, developers, and SOEs. They collaborated in its real estate development as in virtually all facets of its development.[73]

Special industrial parks across China compete fiercely to attract investment. One of the earliest and ultimately among the most successful, the China–Singapore Suzhou Industrial Park (SIP), well illustrates several lessons of collaborative governance. Established in 1994 with strong support from the two countries' governments, SIP at first lost money but later attained considerable success by adhering to several key steps of the AADA cycle. Flexibility in redefining the participants' stakes (transferring in 2001 majority ownership from the Singapore consortium to the China consortium of central and local government representatives and SOEs), and flexibility adjusting the incentive structure to better align goals, contributed to attracting over $17 billion in FDI and over 500,000 jobs.[74] Both sides also committed to strong knowledge transfer about urban planning, making SIP an exemplar of collaboration for information as well as productivity.

Real estate development gets its major spur from local governments' reliance on land financing. This practice powerfully shapes all forms of property development in China. It is the centerpiece of commercial real estate development. Land-lease revenue as a share of local government fiscal revenue ballooned from a trivial fraction to very high shares in the most recent decade.[75]

Of course, countries around the world have the power to requisition land for public infrastructure through eminent domain, but the process may be tortuous, the payments significant, and takings for commercial development politically toxic and thus rare, as it is in the United States.

However, what is rare elsewhere is common in China. Its approach to land taking is pervasive and distinctive. First, a bit of background: One might think that since all land belongs to the state or collective, authorities find it easy to

---

[73] J. Zhu, 1999a, "The Formation of a Market-oriented Local Property Development Industry in Transitional China: a Shenzhen Case Study," *Environment and Planning A*, 31(10), 1839–1856; and J. Zhu, 1999b, "Local Growth Coalition: The Context and Implications of China's Gradualist Urban Land Reforms," *International Journal of Urban and Regional Research*, 23 (3), 534–548.

[74] Min Zhao and Thomas Farole, "Partnership Arrangements in the China-Singapore (Suzhou) Industrial Park: Lessons for Joint Economic Zone Development," in Farole, Thomas, and Gokhan Akinci, eds., *Special Economic Zones: Progress, Emerging Challenges, and Future Directions*. The World Bank, 2011. Also see Inkpen, Andrew C., and Wang Pien, 2006, "An Examination of Collaboration and Knowledge Transfer: China–Singapore Suzhou Industrial Park," *Journal of Management Studies*, 43(4), 779–811.

[75] Liu and Xiong (2018).

allocate land toward commercial development. It is true that government ownership of land avoids the endless wrangling over land rights that befuddles real estate development in many developed countries. But "easy" it is not. Fierce controversies and perverse incentives plague the process. The government does not in fact directly control all the land. Local governments in China requisition land from rural collective ownership, and must compensate peasants and their village collectives for their loss of land use rights. Since private developers cannot directly procure rural land from villagers, government steps into the frequently profitable role of middleman. Gains from acquiring land on the cheap and reselling it covers an increasingly large share of local government expenditures in China, and lurks behind the troubling issue of large local government debt. Local governments have direct control over urban land, and monopsonistic power in acquiring rural land for urban use. They use that power to earn revenue from the real estate development process, and thereby support themselves.

Commercial real estate has been a fertile arena for experimentation with government–private coalitions and collaboration. The early years of commercial real estate development built on the fiscal foundation of local state corporatism initiated by rapid rural industrialization,[76] which then morphed into rapid urbanization.

Current real estate development in China more closely resembles standard collaborative approaches drawing on the private sector, albeit manifesting several characteristics of China's distinctive approaches to public–private engagement. Thus, most efforts are government-led, and involve international private firms and SOEs as much as de novo private (i.e., not corporatized public) domestic firms, and at times with creative hybrid organizational forms. Unsurprisingly, approaches differ significantly across regions.

One could argue that real estate development projects exhibit collaboration for resources, information, and productivity. Collaboration for legitimacy also plays a role, but with a strong Chinese twist. Local government leaders gain legitimacy through promotion of local economic development; private firms gain legitimacy and access to coveted resources such as land[77] and contracting revenues from being chosen for development projects.

As for rental housing, substantial regional variation in real estate development approaches fosters experimentation with collaborative models. For example, prominent property development projects in Chongqing featured

---

[76] Jean C. Oi, 1992, "Fiscal Reform and the Economic Foundations of Local State Corporatism in China," *World Politics*, 45(1), 99–126.

[77] Chen and Kung (2018) show how politically connected firms had obtained "sweet deals" in local land markets and how Xi Jinping's anti-corruption campaign reduced inside dealing; see T. Chen, and J. K. S. Kung, 2018, "Busting the 'Princelings': The Campaign Against Corruption in China's Primary Land Market," *The Quarterly Journal of Economics*, 134(1), 185–226.

stronger government direction than those in Shanghai, such as the Lujiazui and Xintiandi developments discussed later.[78]

Diverse motivations drive property-led development at different levels of the government. They include transforming urban land use functions, showing off the entrepreneurial capability of local government, and maximizing negotiated land benefits and profit.[79] The dual objectives of stimulating economic growth and enhancing political legitimacy call for a collaborative approach. Municipal leaders seek to enhance their profile to the national leaders, since promotions follow spotlighted accomplishments. They also seek to bring in tax revenues. Developers seek land resources and a smooth regulatory pathway for development projects.

Of course, there have also been far less successful cases of urban development, including "ghost towns" such as northern China's Kangbashi,[80] Inner Mongolia's Ordos, and Henan Province's Zhengdong.[81] Such cases often arise because fundamentals of commercial real estate development were ignored, highlighting the importance of geographic location and the need for urban planning beyond simple construction of physical infrastructure. Migrants may not be attracted to affordable dwellings if they are in locations without jobs, schools, or hospitals.

More successful cases illustrate the multiple motivations and enabling factors – notably, shrewd and creative government leadership. As a prime example, the Shanghai Municipal Government desired Lujiazui Central Finance District, a sub-zone in the Pudong New Area, to become the symbol of twenty-first century Shanghai – the Chinese equivalent of creating a new Manhattan for New York. Lujiazui's development drew liberally upon private partners granted discretion. Foreign and Hong Kong architects were heavily involved, and at least two-thirds of its high-rise buildings secured investment from outside mainland PRC, notably Hong Kong and Taiwan; several were wholly foreign-invested.[82]

The transition from government-led redevelopment – fueled by China's administrative decentralization and intense competition among cities – to

---

[78] See discussion in Eggleston, Oi and Wang 2017; T. Zhang, 2002, "Urban Development and a Socialist Pro-growth Coalition in Shanghai," *Urban Affairs Review*, 37(4), 475–499; and S. S. Han, and Y. Wang, 2003, "The Institutional Structure of a Property Market in Inland China: Chongqing," *Urban Studies*, 40(1), 91–112.

[79] S. He, and F. Wu, 2005, "Property-led Redevelopment in Post-reform China: A Case Study of Xintiandi Redevelopment Project in Shanghai," *Journal of Urban Affairs*, 27(1), 1–23.

[80] "CFLD's Gu'an New Industry City: A New Kind of Public-Private Partnership," Knowledge@Wharton in collaboration with E-House China, March 2, 2018 http://knowledge.wharton.upenn.edu/article/cflds-guan-new-industry-city-new-kind-public-private-partnership/ [accessed December 28, 2018].

[81] Liu and Xiong 2018.

[82] Z. Fu, "The State, Capital, and Urban Restructuring in Post-Reform Shanghai," Logan, J. ed., *The New Chinese City: Globalization and Market Reform*, Blackwell Publishers Ltd, 2002: 106–120.

privately funded property redevelopment with larger private discretion can be illustrated with many cases. Xintiandi, part of the Taipingqiao redevelopment area in Shanghai, is a spectacular exemplar.[83] A cooperative agreement dating back to 1996 between the Luwan district government and the Hong Kong Shui On Group planned that every year two to three blocks would be leased out and redeveloped based on negotiated land prices, with a leasehold of 50 years.[84] Now it thrives as a pedestrian area famed for arts, shopping, and entertainment. Xintiandi, with lofty home prices rivaling Tokyo and Manhattan, represents a relatively early and highly successful case of public–private partnership in urban renewal.[85]

Suburban and rural areas face additional challenges. Local governments need expertise in attracting and retaining investment, not merely erecting and managing buildings. New kinds of collaborative arrangements have emerged to fill this need. For example, the government of Gu'An near the Beijing–Tianjin urban corridor entered into a collaborative governance arrangement with the China Fortune Land Development Co. (CFLD) with incentives similar to revenue sharing.[86] In such collaborative arrangements, local governments share considerable discretion with private development firms to access the information and expertise to attract and retain high-growth firms in their localities.

COMING HOME

The inherent publicness of the built environment, combined with the private sector's characteristic advantages in many of the tasks required for building, has made real estate a fertile area for collaborative arrangements throughout the world. The move of populations and economic activities into cities, and the steep escalation in land values this entailed, priced housing beyond the budgets of vast swaths of the population. Governments have responded with housing policies that predominantly call on the private sector. Both the United States and China have employed an array of collaborative policies to promote and steer real estate development.

Given its monumental process of urbanization, its unprecedented economic success, and its government's ability to impose policies without tussle, China has experimented much more aggressively. Its cities brim with innovation, and

---

[83] He and Wu (2005).

[84] M. Xu, 2004. Study on the Renewal and Development Patterns of the Old Settlements in the Inner City of Shanghai. *Unpublished doctoral thesis*, Tongji University, Shanghai. (In Chinese).

[85] Y. R. Yang, and C. H. Chang, 2007, "An Urban Regeneration Regime in China: A Case Study of Urban Redevelopment in Shanghai's Taipingqiao Area," *Urban Studies*, 44(9), 1809–1826.

[86] This case draws primarily from "CFLD's Gu'an New Industry City: A New Kind of Public-Private Partnership," Knowledge@Wharton in collaboration with E-House China, March 2, 2018 http://knowledge.wharton.upenn.edu/article/cflds-guan-new-industry-city-new-kind-public-private-partnership/ [accessed 28 December 2018].

with the evidence those innovations generate. There is much success to celebrate. But the empty empires of vacant apartments in both established and new cities, and the overstretched financial institutions that supported their construction, reveal a fundamental failing: imprudent, and even corrupt, approaches to public–private collaboration. Past a certain point, land that is too cheap and regulation that is too lax unleashes investments that are foolhardy and not infrequently crooked.[87] It is no surprise that real estate firms and real estate tycoons have been a major focus of President Xi's anti-corruption campaign.

America's most prosperous cities also glisten, though their growth has been slower and, for the most part, has a subtler connection to governmental policy than in China. Their blemishes, which like skin blemishes tend to be confined to certain areas, relate more to social policy than to real estate policy. Homelessness, poor schools, and urban crime are the most salient examples. And in a stark contrast to China, America's secondary cities have suffered economically. That they have lost population in recent decades is both cause and effect. Tolstoy famously wrote that: "Happy families are all alike; every unhappy family is unhappy in its own way." So too, successful cities have marked similarities. Their flaws are what make them distinctive. But well-crafted collaborative arrangements have the potential to help ease those flaws by bringing innovative approaches to urbanization in China, and to the rejuvenation of downtrodden cities in the United States.

---

[87] See Chen and Kung (2018) *Quarterly Journal of Economics* article "Busting the 'Princelings'" and sources cited therein.

5

A Game like No Other

Delivering the Olympics

For roughly a millennium in ancient Greece, pan-Hellenic athletic competitions were held in Olympia every four years. With an eye to resurrecting the Games, the International Olympic Committee (IOC) was formed in the late nineteenth century and the first modern Olympics were held in Athens in 1896. Since then the Olympics have taken place at regular four-year intervals, with time out for a couple of world wars. In the mid-twentieth century, winter competitions for cold-weather sports were added, first as an adjunct to the long-standing warm-weather competition and then as a separate event held in a different city and on a different quadrennial cycle from the Summer Games. Beijing will be the first city in modern times to host both the Summer (2008) and Winter (2022) Games.

Certain aspects of the Olympics are classically governmental, such as their exploitation as tools of statecraft by the Hitler regime in 1936 and by both the United States and the Soviet Union during the Cold War. And a few aspects mostly involve the private sector's interests and authority, especially the big-bucks bets connected with broadcasting rights. But for the most part, the Games are collaborative by their very nature, with vital roles for both public and private players. No country's private sector – no matter how flush or enthusiastic – could host the Olympics without the support and involvement of its government. While in principle, the public sector could go it alone in hosting the Games – and as we will see, China came closer than most to doing so in 2008 – in practice it would be close to impossible and, at best, grossly inefficient to run the Games without the significant involvement of business, nonprofits, and civil society.

A complex, years-long, and highly visible process determines where on the globe each iteration of the Olympics will be held. Cities (with the concurrence of their national governments) submit bids roughly a decade in advance for the right to host the Games. The IOC weighs a range of factors – including each locale's climate and ease of access, the quality and suitability of sports venues, athlete housing, and other facilities (whether new or existing), and other inducements offered by aspiring hosts in choosing among competing bids. There are multiple motives for a city to seek the Games. A higher global profile is one perennial and important goal. In an age when media lovingly transmit every ceremony, competition, and interview to screens across the planet, a host city can count on an intense burst of attention. Success in hosting the Olympics has often been a coming-of-age ceremony, as it was for Tokyo (1964), Seoul (1988), Barcelona (1992), and Beijing (2008). Another frequent motive is the hope that the Games will be a spur to long-term economic development. The expectation here is that the athletic facilities, housing, transportation assets, and other infrastructure built for the Olympics will provide a permanent boost to prosperity. A related but distinguishable goal is a short-term stimulus, the expectation that the years of construction that precede the Games and the intense months of running the events and catering to the flood of athletes and spectators will reduce unemployment and lift wages.

These objectives are all sound. But, they do not justify hosting an Olympics unless they will be met. The actual realization of the benefits a host city might anticipate depends on specific circumstances that can be hard to pin down with precision. A high-profile turn on the global stage can be a boon to a city – spurring visitors, luring investment, promoting local businesses – but only if two conditions hold: First, the city is to some extent a mystery to the rest of the world, ready to be unveiled by the Games. Second, the surprises revealed by the Olympic spotlight are likely to be *good* news, previously unrecognized economic or cultural or natural delights. To the extent a city is already well-known, or the news to be unveiled is a mixed bag, the benefits of Olympic attention are attenuated. Likewise, Olympic investments will only be a long-term boon to the extent that the stadiums, pools, housing, roads, and subways aren't only useful for the Olympics but will have broader and enduring value – and despite this would not have been built without the Olympic spur. And only if a city would otherwise be plagued by unemployment or underemployment can the Games provide a fiscal stimulus.

Of course a city that is already world-famous, is already well-endowed with infrastructure and housing and stadiums (or is perfectly capable of investing in what it needs without an Olympic pretext), and has little joblessness or underemployment might still bid for the Games if particular groups – hoteliers or construction workers or the owners of the land where the stadiums would be built – stand to reap private benefits and have political leverage over bidding decisions. And even if cynicism or self-dealing on the part of narrow constituencies doesn't drive an economically ill-considered bid, a community might seek the Olympics for the simple fun of it; its residents would like to attend or have foreigners in their midst. Nothing wrong with that, if it is an eyes-open choice. But, it can be a tricky business to judge how rich a bid to offer and still have hopes of reaping net benefits from the Games, and more than a few cities have lived to regret winning the Olympics.

Without exception, every modern iteration of the Games has cost more than anticipated. It is inherently hard to predict the costs and benefits of big, novel undertakings, and the Olympics can be a special occasion for rose-tinted self-deception.[1] Calibrating costs fairly and closely can be especially difficult, since host city officials tend to have both the means and the motive to obscure them; the host committee of the 1998 Nagano Games went so far as to incinerate its financial records.[2] But there is enough available evidence to reveal that cost overruns – exceeding 150 percent on average – have been even worse for the Olympics than for other "mega-projects."[3] For some Games, however – including those in Beijing – the overruns have been minuscule. And there is at least some evidence that hoped-for benefits do indeed materialize. Two economists have found that hosting the Olympics is associated with a major increase in exports, and hypothesize that a bid to host signals economic openness. Indeed, even a *losing* bid seems to spur exports.[4] There is some evidence that hosting the Olympics leads to a big increase in philanthropy and civic engagement on the part of the local private sector.[5] (A natural disaster, not welcomed for other reasons, seems to have the same effect so long as it isn't *too* disastrous.) On balance, however, payoffs to host cities are usually disappointing, according to a careful 2016 study, and a winning Olympic bid will "result in positive net benefits only under very specific and unusual circumstances."[6]

RECENT AMERICAN GAMES

Los Angeles Summer Games 1984

Los Angeles (LA) was emphatically *not* a regretful winner when it hosted the Summer Games a generation or so ago, which helps to explain why it will be hosting again in 2028. In pure financial terms, LA netted $250 million from the 1984 Games, and almost surely harvested other benefits as well.[7] But it had

[1] Andrew Zimbalist. *Circus Maximus: The Economic Gamble Behind Hosting the Olympics and the World Cup.* Brookings Institution Press, 2016.
[2] Robert A. Baade and Victor A. Matheson, Spring 2016, "Going for the Gold: The Economics of the Olympics," *The Journal of Economic Perspectives*, 30(2), 201–218 at 205.
[3] Bent Flyvbjerg, Allison Stewart, and Alexander Budzier, *Oxford Olympic Study 2016: Cost and Cost Overrun at the Games*, Said Business School Research Paper 2016–2020, page 2.
[4] Andrew K. Rose and Mark M. Spiegel, 2011, "The Olympic Effect," *The Economic Journal*, 121 (553), 652–677.
[5] András Tilcsik and Christopher Marquis, 2013, "Punctuated Generosity: How Mega-events and Natural Disasters Affect Corporate Philanthropy in U.S. Communities," *Administrative Science Quarterly*, 58(1), 111–148.
[6] Baade and Matheson, p. 202. See Zimbalist 2016 as well as Baade and Matheson's Table 4, p. 208 for a summary of scholarly studies.
[7] Jeré Longman, "Olympic Officials Move Closer to Giving Bids to Paris and Los Angeles," *The New York Times* July 11, 2017.

some special advantages. After the ghastly terrorism that marred the 1972 Munich Games, the financial debacle of the 1976 Montreal Games, and the US-led boycott of the 1980 Moscow Games (to protest the USSR's invasion of Afghanistan), there was limited worldwide appetite to bid for 1984. As the IOC neared a decision, LA shared the short list. There was just one other contender, Tehran. When an Islamist revolution overthrew Iran's government, Tehran dropped out and rival-free LA was suddenly in a position to dictate terms to the IOC. Usually a host city agrees to build a vast array of brand-new sports facilities and other assets customized to the needs of the Games. But the LA organizing committee got the IOC to settle for stadiums and pools and dormitories that in most cases were already in place. Where incremental spending *was* required, LA was able to negotiate cost-sharing terms with the IOC that host cities facing real competition could only envy. Even though most Soviet bloc countries stayed away – in a tit-for-tat response to the 1980 boycott – a record 140 countries participated. The 1984 Summer Games were a rousing success.[8] Los Angeles will be hosting the Summer Olympic Games again in 2028.

Atlanta Summer Games 1996

Hosting rights for the 1996 Summer Olympics were announced in 1990, and Atlanta's prospects were considered dim since another American city had so recently hosted. But Andrew Young, Atlanta's energetic and well-connected mayor, led a concerted and ultimately successful campaign to sway the IOC. Young and the rest of Atlanta's leadership believed that the city's global reputation – as a backwater still plagued by racism – was damagingly outdated in a way the Olympics could fix. So, Atlanta bid aggressively, promising a portfolio of sports-related facilities that eventually cost over $4 billion.

Despite some complaints of crowding and price-gouging and a fatal terror bombing by an anti-abortion extremist, the Atlanta Games were generally graded as a success on both the athletic and financial fronts. Cost overruns for the Atlanta Games, at 150 percent, roughly accord with the modern average.[9] Employment in Atlanta and surrounding communities directly involved in the Games was somewhat higher than in otherwise-similar Georgia cities, both during and immediately after the Olympics. However, wage levels barely budged, suggesting that Atlanta reaped a limited economic payoff on its investment.[10] But on a narrow financial basis, the 1996 Games were reasonably

---

[8] China also enjoyed rousing success. The first gold medal at the games, and China's first medal ever, went to Xu Haifeng for the 50-meter pistol.

[9] Flyvbjerg, Stewart and Budzier 2016, Table 1 p. 8 and Table 3 p. 12.

[10] Julie L. Hotchkiss, Robert E. Moore, and Stephanie M. Zobay, January 2003, "Impact of the 1996 Summer Olympic Games on Employment and Wages in Georgia," *Southern Economic Journal*, 69(3), 691–704.

successful as generous corporate sponsorship and lucrative broadcasting arrangements offset the cost overruns, and presumably the corporate sponsors thought that they received their moneys' worth.

A detail of the Atlanta Summer Games illustrates an interesting example of collaborative governance. One way a host city can offset at least a little of its costs is by charging high fees to vendors of food, drink, apparel, and assorted Olympic paraphernalia while restricting competition to let licensed vendors recoup those fees from customers. In principle, Atlanta could have set up its own vendor-licensing operation. But, the city opted instead to enlist the private sector, perhaps motivated by what two academics characterize as the suspicion that a "bureaucracy would have no incentive to maximize [financial gains] but would instead maximize a utility function that would include non-pecuniary goals."[11] A marketing company with close ties to Atlanta's mayor proved willing and (mostly) able to strike deals that siphoned resources from visitors to the city's coffers (while taking a healthy cut for itself), though vendors subsequently complained of insufficient vigilance against non-licensed competitors.[12]

Salt Lake City Winter Games 2002

Dismay over America's meager medal count in the 1988 Calgary Winter Olympics inspired a Congressional investigation and a shift in the criteria for choosing which US cities could bid for the right to host. Only communities that were ready to invest in assets and institutions that promised to advance American athletics beyond the Games themselves would get the nation's nod to submit a bid. Salt Lake City, already a winter-sports powerhouse, assembled a plan for new sports venues and other facilities, winning it the right to bid and eventually the IOC's designation as the host for the 2002 Winter Games.[13]

Salt Lake City turned out to be a generally successful iteration of the lower-profile Winter Games, but it had to overcome a rough start. The co-chairs of the Salt Lake City Olympic Committee, officially the Salt Lake Organizing Committee (SLOC), were accused of bribing IOC decision-makers to improve the odds of bringing the Games to Utah and were forced to resign. A number of

---

[11] Ralph C. Allen and Jack H. Stone, 2001, "Rent Extraction, Principal-Agent Relationships, and Pricing Strategies: Vendor Licensing during the 1996 Olympic Games in Atlanta," *Managerial and Decision Economics*, 22(8), 431–438 at 435P.

[12] If attendees could know in advance about vendor prices, it would not make sense to have above-market prices for items such as food, paraphernalia, and souvenirs. If such items were sold at competitive prices, the tickets themselves could have been priced higher; efficiency losses would be less. Gabaix, Xavier and David Laibson, 2006, "Shrouded Attributes, Consumer Myopia, And Information Suppression in Competitive Markets," *Quarterly Journal of Economics*, 121 (2, May), 505–540.

[13] Salt Lake City Olympic Committee, "Salt Lake 2002: Official Report of the XIX Olympic Winter Games," 2002, p. 5.

IOC members were expelled for accepting unseemly gifts, but no charges of criminal bribery were ever proven.[14] Nevertheless, the leadership vacuum threatened to undermine the Games before they even began. Into the breach leapt Mitt Romney, a remarkably able businessman and public servant – virtually the only failure of his career was his 2012 Presidential run – with deep ties to Utah. Romney operated deftly on both the private front (rallying corporate sponsors and soliciting massive donations from prominent local Mormon families) and on the public front (lining up an unprecedented level of funding from the Federal government, for highways and rail projects). From the opening ceremony featuring the Mormon Tabernacle Choir singing the Star-Spangled Banner to the closing ceremonies, the 2002 Winter Games were broadly successful. The one major exception was the revelation that the figure-skating competition had been rigged by corrupt judges, prompting changes in the structure and process of awarding medals for subsequent Olympics.[15]

In distinctly American fashion, the Olympics were conducted by a nonprofit corporation. This facilitated fundraising, in part, because it made private donations tax deductible and assured donors that no one would profit from their generosity. Romney donated his total salary as chief executive officer to charity, and an additional $1 million to the Olympics. The legitimacy benefits of collaboration played a significant role in assuring the Olympics' success.

In terms of broad and enduring benefits, the 2002 Games – like most Olympics – were a mixed bag. Romney and his team sought to minimize Olympics-only investments and most of the assets built for Winter 2002 – including the housing units for athletes, which were deliberately constructed to serve subsequently as student housing – have seen significant post-Games use. A light-rail system built for the Games has proven useful in later years. Even though the vast majority of Salt Lake City area commuters travel by car, between a quarter and a third of those traveling to areas where the 2002 events had been held (the university area and downtown) take the transit system.[16] So this may be an example of the Games prompting a host city to make a valuable investment that it otherwise would have foregone. Or it may not, depending on a more comprehensive tally of costs and benefits. During the Games people from around the world flocked to Salt Lake City, and the hotels and restaurants were packed. So were the few highly regulated bars that operated in heavily Mormon Utah. But, Salt Lake City tourist facilities are pretty much always packed in the winter, and there is evidence that visitors

[14] Lex Hemphill, "Acquittals End Bid Scandal That Dogged Winter Games," *The New York Times* December 6, 2003.
[15] J. Atsu Amegashie, 2006, "The 2002 Winter Olympics Scandal: Rent-Seeking and Committees," *Social Choice and Welfare*, 26(1), 183–189.
[16] Lee Davidson, "The Utah Effect: 25% of downtown Salt Lake travelers use mass transit, just 3.4% for metro area," *The Salt Lake Tribune*, June 15, 2015.

who came to Salt Lake City for the 2002 Winter Games displaced as much as they supplemented the regular flow of ski-season tourists.[17]

Salt Lake City seeks to build on this success, and the facilities now available, with its official bid for the 2030 Winter Olympic Games. It has but two competitors.

Overall, the Salt Lake and Atlanta Olympics were relatively benign from the cities' perspectives. The Los Angeles Olympics were a moderate plus, since LA did not have to build many new facilities.[18] In all cases, the approach was broadly collaborative.

BEIJING TAKES ITS TURN – TWICE

China had been a planetary pacesetter until its trouble-plagued nineteenth and twentieth centuries. In the summer of 2008, the entire world got the word that China was back in a big way. The Beijing Olympics featured eye-popping architecture, a transformation of the city's infrastructure, thrilling displays of athletic prowess,[19] and intricately choreographed ceremonies produced at a staggering scale. Even by the over-the-top standards of many recent Olympics, the Beijing Summer Games represented audacious ambition, realized more completely than many would have dared to predict.

Accomplishing such a feat required the contributions of a vast number of people from a diverse array of organizations. The work of winning, planning, and delivering the Games was by no means a monolithic governmental effort. The Beijing Organizing Committee for the Olympic Games (henceforth BOCOG) – the summit organization – was technically not part of China's formal, permanent governmental structure. There were individuals and institutions outside of China's conventional public sector – indeed, individuals and institutions outside of China altogether – that played key roles in the triumphant project. The Olympic Games, as noted, is the sort of undertaking that is particularly well-suited to collaborative governance. Yet, the Beijing Olympics contrasts with most other recent Games – in the United States, Europe, even other Asian countries – which featured a vast and diverse menu of public–private interaction. It does not diminish in the slightest the success of the 2008 Olympics to observe that they featured very little that can be considered collaborative governance. To the contrary, it magnifies China's remarkable feat of accomplishing so much with a relatively restricted repertoire of delivery models, and suggests that there remains a great deal of

---

[17] Bruce L. Jaffee, 2002, "Should Budapest Bid for the Olympics? Measuring the Economic Impacts of Larger Sporting Events," *Society and Economy*, 24(3), 403–408 at 405.
[18] Andrew Zimbalist, personal communication 9–15-19.
[19] In less than a quarter century, China had gone from no medals to the most gold medals at an Olympics.

room for China to develop its own ways to create public value through the effective engagement of the private sector.

The highlights of the Games are familiar to just about anyone on the planet who had access to a working television in 2008: the globe-spanning torch relay (including a run up Mount Everest); the cutting-edge architecture of the Beijing National Stadium that will always and everywhere be known as the "Bird's Nest"; the astonishing spectacles of the opening and closing ceremonies. We will thus not recap those visible elements here, but briefly tour a bit of the prodigious behind-the-curtains work that enabled them. And, we will consider some of the organizational details of the components and precursors of the Games – not because they exemplify collaborative governance as we know it in the United States but because, compared to their western analogs, they generally do not.

The summit organization responsible for the Games was the BOCOG. It has sometimes been described as a nongovernmental organization, and if pushed we might classify it that way. But essentially all of its authoritative members were either Beijing municipal officials or representatives of major national ministries. Even so, the "Action Plan" that BOCOG issued soon after it formed clearly envisioned an Olympics with significant private involvement – or at least a significant role for market principles and institutions. It called for assembling resources from the market sector, aligning Olympics-related infrastructure with broader economic imperatives, and recruiting nongovernmental organizations into the enterprise.[20] But as deadlines approached, with the whole world watching and China's reputation riding on a successful outcome, hopeful calls for innovation in cross-sectoral interaction generally gave way to comfortable habits of command and control. We offer a few specifics from the Beijing Games, contrast them briefly with western practice, and suggest what this episode shows for the current limits and future potential of collaborative governance in China in 2022 and beyond.

Building the Bird's Nest

In principle, the watchword for the construction of the National Stadium and other Olympics facilities was "government leads, market operates."[21] In practice – while the private role was undeniably extensive, especially by comparison to past norms in China – government was heavily involved in the operational side of building the Bird's Nest. An entity blandly named the National Stadium Co. Ltd was established late in 2003 as a joint venture of

---

[20] Beijing Organizing Committee for the Olympic Games (BOCOG). (2002) Action Plan for the Beijing Olympic Games. (In Chinese) Retrieved from www.china.com.cn/chinese/PI-c/124760 .htm.

[21] Sohu News. 2002–2003 Big Event: Bird Nest Design Won. Retrieved from http://2008.sohu.com /20071212/n254238827.shtml.

the Beijing State-Owned Assets Management Company (the majority owner, controlled by the Beijing municipal authorities) and a consortium led by China International Trust and Investment Company (CITIC).[22] CITIC is a state-owned company whose 1979 launch was supported by Deng Xiaoping. The consortium it led consisted of multiple organizations, most or all of them difficult to classify cleanly as either "public" or "private" by standard western definitions, but generally leaning toward the governmental mold. One of the consortium members, the Beijing Urban Construction Group, in turn had forty subsidiaries, and the notionally "American" member of the consortium (apparently recruited because of tax advantages for projects involving foreign capital) was headquartered in Beijing.[23] A separate consortium – this one consisting of a Swiss firm, a firm with British roots, and a Chinese organization – was responsible for the design work.[24]

The deal struck between the CITIC consortium and Beijing's city government called for the consortium to raise about 40 percent of the capital required for the project. In exchange, the consortium rather than the city would hold rights to the post-Olympics use of the stadium for 30 years, at which point control would revert to Beijing. A key player – if not entirely private by western standards, at least external to the core public entity responsible for the Games – would thus be compensated by expected future commercial return, and engaged on terms of risk and discretion that echo collaborative governance. To sweeten the deal, the municipal government also provided on very favorable terms the land on which the Bird's Nest would sit, and built a dense web of complementary infrastructure to the stadium. In China, where all of the land is owned by the government – represented by local governments for urban land and collectives for rural land – granting of such land use rights is usually key for real estate projects (see Chapter 4). The municipal government also embraced policies to promote the stadium's future profitability, including blocking the construction of competing facilities for the thirty-year post-Olympics period. The intricate coordination of design and construction for the Bird's Nest itself, and many iterative rounds of adjustments such as plans for the stadium and the ceremonies it would house, evolved together as the games approached; most and were unambiguously reserved as governmental responsibilities.[25] Even by

[22] S. Wang and Y. Ke, *Fund Raising for Franchised Projects: BOT, PFI & PPP.* Tsinghua Press, 2008.

[23] W. Yi, 2008. Investment Path of CITIC on Bird Nest. *Manager.* 7, p. 44; Bloomberg/Business Week Website http://investing.businessweek.com /research/stocks/private/snapshot.asp?privcapId=36219135 accessed July 30, 2014.

[24] Sohu News 2002–2003 Big Event: Bird Nest Design Won. Retrieved from http://2008.sohu.com /20071212/n254238827.shtml.

[25] Y. Liu, Research on the Government Responsibility in the City Infrastructure PPP Project. *Master's Thesis, Southwest Jiaotong University,* 2010.

the original intent of the deal, the private sector's discretion was tightly circumscribed.

Unsurprisingly, perhaps, a complex and novel undertaking involving many different organizations, whose histories, cultures, and interests differed, generated a fair degree of friction. In addition, stakeholders within entities sparred over the sharing of risk, return, and control. The design consortium and the construction consortium wrangled repeatedly over arrangements that were both operationally and economically consequential. Where there were tensions between the goal of delivering a high-quality facility in time for the Olympics and the interests of the players outside city government – and such tensions were frequent and intense – the general tendency was for municipal government's strong commitment to delivering a successful Olympics to trump other goals and subordinate other stakeholders.

Parking capacity steadily evaporated, the moveable roof that meant to make the Bird's Nest an all-weather stadium was canceled, plans for concessions and other commercial space in the stadium were drastically reduced, and the consortium's ability to sell "naming rights" to the stadium was revoked. These are only four of many changes that undercut the expected post-Games profitability of the project. An independent post-Games analysis predicted that while the stadium might break even on its current operations, it would never earn enough for CITIC to recoup its investment costs.[26] Rounds of renegotiation ended up with Beijing's city government, rather than the CITIC group, in control of the Bird's Nest amid much-diminished commercial ambitions.[27] The Bird's Nest was a glittering focal point for the Games themselves, and a valuable long-term municipal asset for Beijing – no shabby outcome by any reckoning, but not quite what was intended or advertised up front. It now serves as a tourist attraction and occasional venue for sports or entertainment events, including for the 2022 Winter Olympics. A truly collaborative model for creating the iconic physical asset for China's showpiece Olympics proved too much of a stretch.

Behind the Curtain of the Opening Ceremonies

At 08:08:08 PM on the 8th day of the 8th month of 2008 – making the most of the country's favored good-luck numeral – a capacity crowd in the Bird's Nest, and countless millions tuning in all over the planet, heard the thunder of 2008 traditional drummers that marked the start of an unforgettable opening ceremony. A trail of footprints forged in fire leading into the stadium;

[26] Wang Zipu, Liang Jinhui, Lu Weiping, and Huo Jianxin, 2010, "Investment and Financial Models of National Stadium and Financial Analysis of Its Operation after Olympic Games," *China Sport Science*, 30(1), 16–29.

[27] Xiao, T. and Zhu, H. *Annual Report on Development of Sports Industry in China: 2013.* Social Sciences Academic Press (China).

Buddhist deities spookily floating in mid-air near massive Olympic rings; dazzling homages to Chinese culture and inventions; 2008 tai chi masters followed by 2008 dancers, with astronauts, acrobats, and musicians interspersed. A spectacle before the speeches got underway and the torch was formally ignited by a seemingly levitating gymnast, Li Ning. The opening ceremony lasted over four hours and ended after midnight, but few attendees flew from the Bird's Nest. To western sensibilities it seems strikingly odd, and indeed almost inconceivable, that so flamboyant a show could have been the product of top-down governmental planning. But this would be only the slightest of exaggerations for the process by which the opening ceremonies, and the equally magnificent closing ceremonies, were developed and delivered.

In the spring of 2005, BOCOG issued what was essentially a request for proposals for the opening and closing ceremonies, and about a year later announced the winners. This was not, on its face, at odds with standard international practice. Almost any Olympics host would have put out such a request. The timing was somewhat unusual; two years' lead time for a high-stakes ceremony would be considered cutting it very close in most other settings, and indeed the relatively late request for proposals reportedly unnerved some foreign consultants unaccustomed to the speed with which official China could operate when it was focused on a goal.[28] Eleven designers or design teams were specifically invited to submit proposals; all eleven were selected for further stages of the competition. (Another 398 submissions came in without targeted invitations; only two survived the first phase).

The organizational apparatus for the opening and closing ceremonies was an intricately structured matrix. There were three levels: a decision-making "leading group" consisting of BOCOG Chair, Liu Qi (whose day job was as Party Secretary of the Beijing Committee of the CCP) and Chen Zhili, the State Councilor who served as BOCOG Deputy Chair, along with three slightly-less-senior deputies including Zhang Heping, Vice Chair of the Beijing Committee of the Chinese People's Political Consultative Conference.[29] Zhang Heping, in turn, headed the second tier, the "working department," responsible for oversight and coordination. The actual work was done by the ground-level "Operation Center." This Center, in turn, was divided into three main components, a "creative and idea" team, a "technology and production" team, and a management team.

The creative and idea team was led by Zhang Yimou – the internationally acclaimed director of some of China's most celebrated films of the past several decades. Somewhat rare among accomplished elites of his generation, Zhang

[28] Sohu News. (2008a) The birth story of Opening Ceremony for Beijing Olympic Games: Chinese civilization soaked with wisdom and sweat. Retrieved from http://2008.sohu.com/20080809/n258700832.shtml.

[29] BOCOG, Official Report of the Beijing 2008 Olympic Games. Volume 3 Preparation for the Games: New Beijing, Great Olympics (English version), 2010.

had had no major roles in formal government, and his engagement with the Olympics was essentially as an independent artist analogous to (for example) his admirer Stephen Spielberg.[30] The vice directors of the creative and idea team – eminent artists as well, but by no means independent of government – were Zhang Zigang, with links to the People's Liberation Army Core Group of Creative Planning, and Chen Weiya, whose affiliations included China Central Television. The rest of the Operation Center was even more firmly anchored in China's governmental structure, with lead roles for the head of the People's Liberation Army's Armaments Department and Chief Engineer of the space program. This was hardly unexpected. In China, government is simply where much of the top talent is to be found, even in the creative arts. This contrasts starkly with most western countries, where fewer than 1 percent of their most creative arts people would work for the government. In the United States, it would be less than one-tenth of 1 percent.

The Beijing Organizing Committee for the Olympic Games explicitly rejected outsourcing the production of the ceremonies to nongovernmental entertainment companies, in part on the grounds that engaging for-profits would boost costs, and in part due to the desire to maintain close control over the complex and high-stakes undertaking.[31]

The same pattern appears recurrently throughout the elements of the Beijing Olympics. Private organizations were indisputably involved. In the historic torch relay, for example, important roles were played by both Chinese (Lenovo, China Mobile, China International Airlines) and foreign corporations (Volkswagen, UPS, Samsung).[32] The recruitment of volunteers involved universities and other organizations outside the core agencies represented by the BOCOG and, by some conceptions, outside formal government. Greenpeace, the United National Environmental Program, and other environmental groups were involved in efforts to make the Olympics as environmentally benign as so massive an undertaking could aspire to be.[33] But in virtually every case, the private role was more limited than it had been in comparable undertakings in recent Olympics in the west. And even to the extent private entities *were* involved, it was rarely if ever on terms of truly shared discretion. While, as we have noted, there is seldom a bright line between the public and the private in China, in virtually every important example from the Beijing Games the guiding hand was governmental, and it was far from invisible.

---

[30] Our extraordinary research assistant, Wang Yuzhou, who searched long and diligently for examples of classic collaborative governance in the Beijing Olympics, nominates the role of the "creative and idea team" for the ceremonies as the closest approximation.

[31] Sohu News, 2008a.

[32] BOCOG Official Report of the Beijing 2008 Olympic Games. Volume 3 Preparation for the Games: New Beijing, Great Olympics (English version).

[33] UNEP *Beijing 2008 Olympic Games: Independent Environmental Assessment.* United Nations Environment Programme, 2009.

The 2002 Salt Lake City Winter Games offered a useful and stark contrast; many elements exemplified the collaborative governance model. The Olympic Village housing complex was essentially a joint venture between the University of Utah and the SLOC – the analog of BOCOG but, unlike its Chinese counterpart, more the orchestrator of a network of collaborators than the master of a hierarchy. The university put up 80 percent of the construction cost and had the lead in designing the buildings, tuned primarily to their long-term role as student housing. The SLOC contributed a fifth of the investment, in exchange for the right to make minor and sometimes temporary modifications to suit the short-term Olympics role, and then essentially rented the complex from the University for the period of the Olympics.[34] Anheuser-Busch, Coca-Cola, and other firms made major contributions to emissions-reduction and other environmental efforts for the Olympics in exchange for favorable publicity opportunities.[35] In perhaps the greatest contrast with Beijing – though not with at least five other Olympics that used the same company – the Salt Lake City torch relay was handled by a Colorado-based for-profit events-management firm, Alem International Management.[36]

Let us be clear about what we intend – and, perhaps as importantly, do *not* intend – to suggest by this overview of the organizational structure of the 2008 Beijing Games. Most fundamentally, we are not shocked to discover that the People's Republic of China (PRC) tilts more toward government when hosting the Olympics than does, say, the United States, Canada, Britain, or even Russia. While skyrocketing growth, institutional complexity, and a vibrant and highly profitable private sector sometimes obscure the fact, China *is*, at the core, a country where the Communist Party and the government call the shots. Hard as it may be to unambiguously apply international metrics to Chinese institutions, most of the organizations that matter most are more "public" than "private," and in all but a few domains – the cinematic career of Zhang Yimou may be one of few exceptions – the path to accomplishment and advancement for talented people still tends to pass through government.

These observations do not diminish in the least China's accomplishment in delivering a magnificent round of the Olympic Games. Neither are we suggesting that China should have, or reasonably *could* have, embraced an approach that relied on a less dominant role for government in producing the 2008 Beijing Games. Top-down government is China's strong suit, and in a high-visibility, high-stakes, limited-time setting, it makes sense to play to your strengths.

---

[34] Mike Gorrell "U. Backs Going for Olympics Again, Wants Rest of Fort Douglas," Salt Lake Tribune, June 1, 2012 at www.sltrib.com/sltrib/news/54218687-78/games-olympic-report-olympics.html.csp; Robert J. Martinson, "A Real Options Analysis of Olympics Village Development: How Design Flexibility Adds Values," http://dspace.mit.edu/bitstream/handle/1721.1/54860/609677156.pdf; Scott Taylor, "Olympic Village a Class Act," Deseret News, January 27, 2001.

[35] Salt Lake City Olympic Committee, *"Official Report of the XIX Olympic Winter Games,"* http://library.la84.org/6oic/OfficialReports/2002/2002v1.pdf.

[36] Ibid.

Preparation for the 2022 Winter Olympics

But China's strengths have diversified. Beijing's hosting of the 2022 Winter Olympics Games may well illustrate the evolution of China's approach toward collaborative arrangements, although it remains unclear to what extent the firms involved will have autonomy in the final decision-making or reap long-term benefits.

Compared to the extravagant spending on the 2008 Olympics, the 2022 Winter Olympics "economical budget"[37] embraces collaborative approaches for some aspects of the preparations – collaboration for productivity and resources. In part, this approach stems from differences between the Summer and Winter Olympics, as well as China's differing economic position compared to 2008: Rather than decades of double-digit growth, China confronts a declining growth rate, local government debt, environmental concerns, and other challenges that commend a more collaborative approach.

The Beijing Organizing Committee for the 2022 Olympic and Paralympic Winter Games (BOCWOG) draws from the experience of the BOCOG, with government officials from different municipalities and ministries,[38] as well as drawing on experience from other Winter Olympics. The BOCWOG sent 254 staff members to the 2018 PyeongChang Winter Olympics as interns or observers, together compiling a list of more than 2,000 critical issues related to facility planning, games coordination, service provision, and city administration in preparation for 2022.[39]

The 2022 Games will actually be held in Beijing, Yanqing, and Zhangjiakou, since Beijing lacks the Alpine landscape. Collaborative approaches have been discussed for creating the transportation infrastructure connecting the host locations as well as other aspects of regional development. The budget for venues is 1.51 billion, with 65 percent planned to come from private investments. Plans call for the Olympic Villages at Beijing and Chongli, Zhangjiakou, to be sold after the Games as commercial housing, and the Olympic Village at Yanqing is slated to become a vacation resort.[40] Among

---

[37] Xi Jinping, http://103.42.78.227/Discipline_Inspection/content/2018-03/20/content_7500820.htm?node=84346.

[38] Cai Qi, the Chairman of BOCWOG, is also the Beijing Municipal Party Committee Secretary. Other executive chairmen in the committee include the Director of General Administration of Sport, the Provincial Governor of Hebei where Zhangjiakou city is located, the Mayor of Beijing, and the Chairman of China Disabled Persons' Federation which is a quasi-governmental organization founded by the son of China's former leader Deng Xiaoping. www.beijing2022.cn/en/about_us/leadership.htm.

[39] Wang, Y., and Ji, Y. (April 20, 2018). www.xinhuanet.com/politics/2018-04/20/c_1122715829.htm.

[40] See news report July 31, 2015 at www.xinhuanet.com/world/2015-07/31/c_128078040.htm.

the eighteen sports facilities in Beijing, eight will be newly built, two will be temporary, and the remaining eight will be renovated 2008 facilities.[41]

Although government clearly continues to orchestrate and dominate the host preparations, the potential for an enhanced embrace of collaboration is illustrated by several aspects of the preparations for 2022 such as the National Speed Skating Oval. Private partners were invited to build and operate the new speed skating venue for the 2022 Winter Olympics. The public–private partnership is overseen by the Beijing Major Projects Construction Headquarters Office, the regulator of the city's major building projects. The eventual bid winner is authorized to transform and operate the venue for commercial purposes for 25 years after the Games, together with Beijing State-owned Assets Management Co., the governmental stakeholder in the joint venture. According to Wang Gang, Party Chief of the office, "It will be an effective model for sharing construction costs and encouraging the private sector to offer innovative and commercially practical solutions for the sustainable use of the venue."[42] In January 2018, four companies won the bid and signed the contract.[43]

The development of Zhangjiakou as co-host also embraces a collaborative approach, using in part a "rebuild-operate-transfer (ROT)" model (with the private companies in charge of reconstruction and operation after the Olympics until transfer back to the municipal government) and in part a "build-own-operate (BOO)" model thirty-year contract, with private capital owning 60 percent of the equity.[44]

In addition to private participation in the construction process, BOCWOG has also recruited corporations such as Hylink and International Data Group to enhance marketing and post-game development.[45] While BOCWOG also signed two official private collaborators (Yili Group and Anta Sports) and various private sponsors such as Snickers and EF Education First, whether these partners share any discretion in key decisions remains unclear.[46] Moreover, International Data Group's extensive effort in bringing foreign brands such as Rossignol into the Chinese market, some through the construction of complementary long-term winter sport infrastructure, also hints at the increased role of international organizations in post-game development.[47] Despite the coronavirus outbreak in early 2020, most projects

---

[41] See August 10, 2018. http://zhengwu.beijing.gov.cn/zwzt/dah/bxyw/t1556296.htm.

[42] Sun, X. (July 15, 2018). Private sector to help build skating oval. *China Daily*. www.chinadaily.com.cn/china/2017-07/15/content_30122069.htm.

[43] Previously available at www.bjzdb.gov.cn/bjzdb/tzgg/2018-01/05/content_1050648.shtml.

[44] See www.ccgp.gov.cn/cggg/dfgg/zgysgg/201804/t20180403_9743019.htm (April 3, 2018).

[45] Yi, Yuan. (December 9, 2019). www.beijing2022.cn/a/20191209/005352.htm and October 10, 2019, at www.xinhuanet.com/english/2019-10/10/c_138461425.htm.

[46] Yi, Yuan. (December 26, 2019).www.beijing2022.cn/a/20191226/022601.htm.

[47] World Winter Sport Beijing Expo Official Site. (January 18, 2019). www.wwse2022.com/xiang-qing_en.aspx?id=193.

have continued construction, with intensive health monitoring onsite and reduced teamwork, to meet the year-end goal for completion.[48] The coronavirus crisis did, however, delay several testing events for completed competition sites in Yanqing.[49]

THE CLOSING CEREMONY

Both China and the United States have conducted highly successful Olympics recently, a task where many other nations have stumbled. Both did so on a collaborative basis, with significant contributions from both the government and for-profit sectors. The official organizing arrangements reflected the differing strengths and inclinations of the two nations. The United States relied on a nonprofit entity in the lead, which is the normal arrangement there for most cultural events. In China the government led, though it expects to cede more authority elsewhere in 2022.

Unlike the other policy realms we address, the Olympics is far from a year-in-year-out responsibility. That poses some special challenges for delivering the Games. Its organization has to be recreated on each occasion, and a single city rarely hosts two Olympics even many decades apart, though Beijing and LA will do so, and Salt Lake City may do so as well. That one-time-through element creates a challenging problem where vastly expensive sports, housing, and transportation facilities have to be built for events lasting less than three weeks, and then have to be repurposed. Such repurposing almost always entails a lesser value in use, and often the need to provide benefits, such as swifter transport, whose value is not easily recouped. This makes the requirement of significant government support, which almost always entails a nontrivial degree of governmental discretion, inevitable.[50]

Compensating for the steep challenges faced by the hosts, a hometown Olympics enjoys significant advantages. Despite many scandals in Olympics past, and not so past,[51] they bring great prestige. They help to put cities and countries on the map. That prestige rubs off on those associated with an Olympics. It can induce participation from many parties, including the athletes, and direct donations from others. Some of the most talented people in the nation will work tirelessly to assure their success, as did Mitt Romney in Salt Lake City and Zhang Yimou in Beijing.

"We're going to put on an Olympics. Let's all work together." That is a rallying cry that has been heard in both the United States and China. It has

---

[48] See news report on Feburary 18, 2020, at www.beijing2022.cn/a/20200218/003884.htm.

[49] Hang, Chen. (January 29, 2020). https://m.chinanews.com/wap/detail/zw/ty/2020/01-29/9072912.shtml.

[50] For example, a for-profit sports operation, a staple on the American scene though still in a developmental stage in China, would be impossible to employ for a brief set of Olympic events.

[51] Andrew Zimbalist. *Circus Maximus: The Economic Gamble behind Hosting the Olympics and the World Cup*. Brookings Institution Press, 2016.

worked well in these two highly pragmatic nations. While many nations do not even try to compete – cowed by witnessing the difficulties the quadrennial show has entailed for others – both China and the United States will do it all again in coming years.

Hosting the Olympics also illustrates another aspect of our conceptual framework articulated in Chapter 2, regarding "collaborative governance, Chinese-style." China's economic accomplishments, the evolution of new institutional forms, and some of the experiments in public–private cooperation and even true collaborative governance that we describe elsewhere in this book demonstrate that, as it moves into the future, China is developing a broader and more nuanced repertoire of ways to create value. It is increasingly employing the collaborative approach when it believes it to be beneficial. When it presented its first Olympics in 2008, China almost entirely eschewed collaboration. Somewhat paradoxically, its reluctance to embrace the collaborative model in prior Olympics highlights the potential for this approach as China becomes more comfortable with its challenging but promising features – not only in hosting the 2022 Olympics but also in many other realms.

6

The Truest Wealth of Nations

Creating Human Capital

Any culture's human potential for work and wisdom accounts for a significant share of its resources. Developing that potential – a process termed education, training, or human capital development – is a major responsibility of government. Spending for human capital development, using a conservative definition, averaged 5 percent of gross domestic product (GDP) for all Organization for Economic Co-operation and Development (OECD) countries in 2015.[1] In most rich countries, education comes second only to health care as a claim on public spending, as it does in the United States, at 6.1 percent of GDP.[2] China, as a middle-income country, not surprisingly spends a somewhat lower share: 4.14 percent of GDP in 2017 for primary, secondary, vocational high school, and higher education.[3]

Lofty public spending on human capital development can make eminent sense. Education allows greater access to life's possibilities, in part by increasing citizens' earnings, but more broadly it widens the scope for the pursuit of happiness. Human capital policy is classically framed as benefiting individuals, such as enabling more-skilled workers to earn higher wages. But the benefits of education also ripple through the larger society, helping employers, increasing tax revenues,[4] and enriching culture. Government support for human capital development can also work to reduce economic inequality, which increasingly plagues both China and the United States. If all human capital spending were private, rich families would vastly outspend poor ones; disparities would be magnified.

---

[1] Definitions, even when standardized across countries, usually omit (among other things) all forms of on-the-job training and the opportunity cost of students' time. OECD *Education at a Glance 2018: OECD Indicators*, OECD Publishing, Paris, 2018. https://doi.org/10.1787/eag-2018-en.

[2] OECD (2018) OECD Indicators (ibid).

[3] *Ministry of Education of PRC*. (2018, October 8). www.moe.gov.cn/srcsite/A05/s3040/201810/t20181012_351301.html.

[4] An additional $1,000 expenditure by government may generate significantly less than $1,000 in additional discounted taxes. Posit that it generates $600. A benefit-cost analysis should then weigh the human capital benefits against the $400 net cost.

In both theory and practice, human capital development presents a rich array of possibilities for cross-sectoral collaboration. The intricate mixture of costs, benefits, incentives, and information in this domain enhances the potential for public–private interaction. But those complexities also make it difficult to identify and implement desirable arrangements. Results often disappoint. This chapter offers a high-level overview of the public, private, and mixed models that have been employed in the United States; it then segues to China. For neither country is the material selected to give an up-to-the-minute picture of the current scene; rather, it illustrates broad developments, such as the US' extensive, hard-earned menu of public–private options. The discussion for both countries is organized into three broad segments: Elementary and secondary schooling for children and youth, education in colleges and universities, and postsecondary worker training.

Before diving into this discussion, we should note a major source of productivity gains in both China and the United States, related to but distinguishable from education and training: In both countries, massive numbers of individuals migrated from rural to urban areas, from farm to factory, and from areas where productivity was low to areas where those relatively unskilled workers could earn significantly more. In the United States, the farm population fell by half from 1970 to 1990. In China, a third of the population moved from village to city in the thirty years following 1980. Both the Chinese migrants and their American counterparts, on average, experienced enormous gains in income and living standards.

PUBLIC–PRIVATE ROLES IN EDUCATION IN THE UNITED STATES

Ethnicity and Human Capital

Throughout this book, we have noted that China and the United States are more similar, in many meaningful ways, than surface impressions might suggest. In the human capital realm, however, there is one fundamental difference with enormous implications: America is racially and ethnically diverse; China is not. Han Chinese represent 92 percent of the population, a share that has changed little since the People's Republic's founding in 1949. Although the fifty-six officially recognized ethnic minorities[5] total about 112 million Chinese, more than one-third of the US population, they constitute only 8.4 percent of the overall population.[6] Of course there are many deep disparities in China that affect human capital, including controversy about what China characterizes as "vocational education and

---

[5] See Thomas S. Mullaney 2010, "Seeing for the State: The Role of Social Scientists in China's Ethnic Classification Project," *Asian Ethnicity*, 11(3), 325–342; and Thomas Mullaney, James Leibold, Stéphane Gros, and Eric Armand Vanden Bussche, eds., *Critical Han Studies: The History, Representation, and Identity of China's Majority.* Berkeley, California: University of California Press, 2012.

[6] National Bureau of Statistics, *Tabulation on the 2010 Population Census of the People's Republic of China*, 2012, cited at www.unicef.cn/en/atlas/population/774.html.

TABLE 6.1 *US population by ethnicity, all ages*[7]

	White (%)	Black (%)	Hispanic (%)	Asian (%)	Other[8] (%)
All ages, 1980	79.7	11.5	6.5	1.6	0.6
All ages, 2017	60.8	12.5	18.0	5.6	3
Ages 5 through 17 only					
Age 5–17, 1980	74.6	14.5	8.5	1.7	0.8
Age 5–17, 2017	51.2	13.7	24.9	5.0	5.2

training centers"[9] for Uyghurs and other Muslims in western Xinjiang province, recently decried by twenty-two countries in a United Nations statement.[10] Arguably the most consequential of China's human capital disparities, affecting hundreds of millions, is the urban–rural divide in school resources and educational attainment (discussed in more detail in the China section later).

While we will not explore race or ethnicity in either country at any length, it is important to note its salience for practically the full gamut of issues surrounding education and training in the United States. Once overwhelmingly white, today's United States is multiethnic; tomorrow's will be more so. On the eve of World War II, America's population was 90 percent white, with African–American descendants of enslaved peoples accounting for the vast majority of the nonwhite population.[11] Whites were still nearly 80 percent as recently as 1980. But by 2017, they were not quite 61 percent (see Table 6.1), with the Black share edging up only modestly from 11.5 percent to 12.5 percent. Soaring rates of immigration – both documented and undocumented – have overlaid a multihued mosaic onto the simpler black-and-white pattern that prevailed from colonial times. The Hispanic share of the US population surged nearly threefold after 1980 to 18 percent, and the Asian share rose even more sharply to 5.6 percent.

---

[7] From the US Department of Education, *Digest of Education Statistics,* Table 101.20: Estimates of resident population, by race/ethnicity and age group, selected years 1980 through 2017, at https://nces.ed.gov/programs/digest/d17/tables/dt17_101.20.asp?current=yes, accessed August 28, 2018.

[8] "Other" includes two or more races (the largest category) as well as Pacific Islanders and Native Americans or Alaskans.

[9] See, for example, the *People's Daily* coverage (e.g., http://en.people.cn/n3/2019/0904/c90000-9611994.html), compared to that of others such as Al Jazeera (e.g., www.aljazeera.com/news/2019/06/concerns-official-trip-china-xinjiang-190615060808708.html).

[10] See www.hrw.org/sites/default/files/supporting_resources/190708_joint_statement_xinjiang.pdf.

[11] Calculated from the US Department of Commerce, *Historical Statistics of the United States, Colonial Times to 1957,* Series A 23–33, Estimated Population by Sex, Age, and Color 1900–1957, Page 8, online version at www.census.gov/library/publications/1960/compendia/hist_stats_colonial-1957.html, accessed August 28, 2018.

Of special significance for the theme of this section is the fact that divergent rates of immigration and fertility have made the shift even more striking for school-age children. The white share of children age 5 to 17 years has fallen from three-quarters of the total to barely half as other groups – especially Hispanics – have grown dramatically.

Ethnic and racial diversity affects how the US experience with human capital policy is, and is not, relevant to China. For one thing, American educational attainment differs meaningfully – even though somewhat diminishingly – by race and ethnicity, making any statements about general tendencies misleading. By 1980, more than seven in ten white adults were high school graduates, compared to just over half of Blacks and fewer than half of Hispanics (see Table 6.2). The gaps had narrowed by 2017, though with a white-Black differential of six percentage points and a white-Hispanic differential of nearly fourteen percentage points they were still significant. Both the gaps and their narrowing are starker in higher education. In 1980, white Americans were much more likely than their nonwhite counterparts to have a bachelor's degree or better. In 2017, whites still graduated from college at twice the rate of Hispanics. But the Black-white gap had narrowed markedly – and Asian Americans were considerably *more* likely than whites to have earned at least a bachelor's degree.

But beyond the numerical importance of these disparities in educational attainment for getting a sense of America's stocks and flows of human capital, race and ethnicity permeate debates over education and training policy in ways

TABLE 6.2 *Educational attainment percentages of Americans twenty-five and older, 1980 and 2017*[12]

	White (%)	Black (%)	Hispanic (%)	Asian (%)
Primary and secondary education				
High-school diploma, 1980	71.9	51.4	44.5	unavailable
High-school diploma, 2017	94.1	88.1	70.5	90.9
Higher education				
Bachelor's degree or higher, 1980	18.4	7.9	7.6	unavailable
Bachelor's degree or higher, 2017	38.1	24.3	17.2	55.4

[12] *Digest of Education Statistics,* Table 203.50, Enrollment and percentage distribution of enrollment in public elementary and secondary schools, by race/ethnicity and region: Selected years, fall 1995 through fall 2027 at https://nces.ed.gov/programs/digest/d17/tables/dt17_203.50.asp?current=yes, accessed August 29, 2018.

that they do not in China. This holds, albeit in somewhat different ways, for both K-12 and higher education.

Immigration, differential fertility, and "white flight" have combined to end what was once white dominance of public elementary and secondary schools. As recently as 1995, white students constituted about 65 percent of public K-12 enrollment. The non-Hispanic white share slid below half in 2014, and is projected to continue dropping.[13] In the largest urban school districts, white students are already a decided minority. For districts enrolling more than 15,000 students, Hispanics are (by just a bit) the plurality, with 34.3 percent versus 34.1 percent for whites, 20.4 percent for Blacks, and 6.6 percent for Asians. In the very biggest districts, the ethnic tilt is even more dramatic. In Los Angeles, with more than 600,000 students or Chicago, with more than 400,000, white students comprise less than a tenth of the total; and whites are just 15 percent of New York City's population of nearly a million K-12 students.[14] Whites are overrepresented among the roughly one-tenth of all students in private schools – but significantly *less* likely than Blacks or Hispanics to be among the 4.6 percent of students attending charter schools (which we will discuss shortly), most of which are part of large urban districts.[15]

The preponderance of Black and Hispanic students in troubled urban schools can make for toxic politics. White families are tempted to wash their hands of responsibility for schools that mostly enroll students of other races, and that often underperform despite relatively high levels of funding. Nonwhite families complain that their children are abandoned to institutions with inadequate facilities and underqualified teachers, schools that can't possibly overcome the damage done by poverty, family dysfunction, and racism.

The same story of diminishing white dominance applies to higher education. The white share of enrollment in American colleges and universities overall fell from about 84 percent to about 57 percent in the 40 years after 1976 (see Table 6.3).[16]

---

[13] *Digest of Education Statistics*, Table 104.10, Rates of high school completion and bachelor's degree attainment among persons age 25 years and over, by race/ethnicity and sex: selected years, 1910 through 2017, at https://nces.ed.gov/programs/digest/d17/tables/dt17_104.10.asp?current=yes, accessed August 29, 2018.

[14] *Digest of Education Statistics*, Table 215.10, Selected statistics on enrollment, teachers, drop-outs, and graduates in public school districts enrolling more than 15,000 students: Selected years, 1990 through 2014 at https://nces.ed.gov/programs/digest/d16/tables/dt16_215.10.asp?current=yes, accessed August 28, 2018.

[15] As of 2016 private schools accounted for 9.5 percent of K-12 students, with whites disproportionately likely to attend private schools (11.5 percent of whites versus 8 percent of Blacks and 6 percent of Hispanics). But the ethnic breakdown is quite different for charter schools: 2.7 percent of whites versus 8.5 percent of Blacks and 6.7 percent of Hispanics attend public charter schools. *Digest of Education Statistics*, Table 206.30, percentage of students enrolled in grades 1 through 12, by public school type and charter status, private school type, and selected child and household characteristics: 2016, at https://nces.ed.gov/programs/digest/d17/tables/dt17_206.30.asp?current=yes, accessed August 28, 2018.

[16] All figures in the table and in this paragraph are from *Digest of Education Statistics*, Table 306.20, Total fall enrollment in degree-granting postsecondary institutions, by level and control

TABLE 6.3 *White share of enrollment in postsecondary institutions (percent)*

	1976	2016
All	84.3	56.9
Public four-year institutions	86.1	59.5
Private four-year institutions	86.7	61.0
Public two-year institutions	80.2	50.6
Private two-year institutions	80.3	38.0

But the change has been uneven across categories of institutions. Whites still account for around 60 percent of students at colleges and universities granting four-year degrees. But the nonwhite share has soared at community colleges and other two-year institutions – some of which are heroically efficient engines of opportunity, others of which are expensive dead ends.[17] At private two-year schools, nonwhites now comprise over 60 percent of the total. (Asian-American students haven't been tallied separately for all kinds of schools, but for the largest category – public four-year institutions – their share has ballooned from around two percent to around eight percent.) Whites and Asian Americans are overrepresented, and Blacks and Hispanics are underrepresented, at the most highly selective public and private postsecondary schools.

The ethnic politics of higher education in America are, if anything, even more contentious than for K-12 education. Blacks and Hispanics (and their liberal allies) deploy political pressure and legal gambits to reduce racial and ethnic disparities in higher education, especially at the top schools that have long been anterooms to privileged positions in American society. Some whites and Asian Americans – aided by traditionalists, advocates of color-blind meritocracy, and foes of "political correctness" – wield similar weapons to opposite ends. Students, faculty, alumni, and politicians all participate in the battles. Bad data, bad logic, and bad faith abound on both sides.

Ethnicity is thus a first-order feature of human capital policy in the United States – and a rather dispiriting one. If we were writing a book about American education and training policy, we would have no choice but to address race and ethnicity at length. Since our topic is collaborative governance with a special focus on lessons relevant to China, we sidestep this complex, and for the most part idiosyncratically American, set of issues.

of institution and race/ethnicity of student: Selected years, 1976 through 2016 at https://nces.ed.gov/programs/digest/d17/tables/dt17_306.20.asp?current=yes, accessed August 29, 2018.

[17] Clive R. Belfield, 2013, "Student Loans and Repayment Rates: The Role of For-Profit Colleges," *Research in Higher Education*, 54(1), 1–29.

Primary and Secondary Schooling in the United States

A brief preamble to this section for our non-US readers: American government is highly – but unevenly – decentralized. Some functions, such as defense, are handled mostly or almost exclusively by the national government. Other functions, such as law enforcement, are spread across national, state, and local government. Primary and secondary education is among the most decentralized governmental functions in America, with a mix of local and state authority and funding that varies by state and over time. What is rarely found is the arrangement, common in China, where the national government requires local governments to devote substantial resources to a policy purpose, when the localities vary so greatly in levels of economic development and resources.

More than four million Americans work as primary and secondary school teachers, and state and local governments spend about half a trillion dollars a year on K-12 education.[18] Government does not monopolize American education, but it is the dominant provider. A large majority of primary and secondary students attend tax-funded schools. Most, but not all, of the publicly financed schools are also run directly by the government. The exceptions are charter schools, which will be examined shortly.

It was not always so. When America was young, the government's role in education was limited. The very wealthy or very cultured Americans hired private tutors for their children. Many cities and towns had some form of publicly funded or subsidized school; fewer than half of the children attended with regularity. Religious content abounded, even in schools financed by the government.

In the late 1830s, the situation started to shift. Horace Mann, a pioneer of free, secular, and universal education and the inaugural secretary of the nation's first state board of education in Massachusetts, led the creation of a network of "normal schools" throughout that state.[19] Other states followed with their own variants. By the 1860s, more than half of youngsters aged five to seventeen years were attending school.[20] School enrollment surpassed 77 percent by 1889, with nearly 13 million of the 14.3 million pupils attending public rather than private schools. The age of mass education had arrived. But for most young nineteenth-century Americans, formal schooling still ended with the eighth grade, if not earlier.

---

[18] $668 billion in 2014–2015; https://nces.ed.gov/fastfacts/display.asp?id=66. Employment data are from Occupational Employment Statistics data at www.bls.gov/oes/current/oes_nat.htm #25-0000.

[19] The first of these was established in 1839 in the town of Lexington. The building still stands, across the street from where the first draft of this chapter was written.

[20] Historical Statistics of the United States, Table Bc7-18, "School enrollment and pupil–teacher ratios, by grades K-8 and 9-12 and by public-private control: 1869-1996," accessed July 2015.

After the common school movement, America's next revolution in the production of human capital commenced early in the twentieth century, this time in the Midwest rather than New England: high school for the masses.[21] The number of high school students – never more than a few hundred thousand at any point in the nineteenth century – approached a million by 1910 and burgeoned to nearly seven million by the eve of World War II. While the population overall did increase during this period, the skyrocketing growth in high school attendance was many multiples of the rate of population growth. As with the rise of public primary education around eighty years earlier, this growth challenged the primacy of both elite and religious private high schools. In the late 1880s, before the surge in public high schools, nearly a third of secondary students attended private institutions. The private share of high school students plummeted below 10 percent by 1915 and, with minor and occasional upticks, it has rarely exceeded that benchmark. In 2011, private schools accounted for about 10 percent of K-8 students and about 8 percent of high school students.[22]

In 2011, Hispanics accounted for 16.3 percent of the nation's population but just 8.9 percent of private school students; Blacks were 12.6 percent of the population but 9.8 percent of private school students. Non-Hispanic whites and Asians remain overrepresented. While urban Catholic schools catering to mostly non-Catholic Black students have gained considerable press attention, Black private school students are substantially more likely than their white counterparts to attend non-Catholic religious schools or secular schools rather than Catholic institutions.[23]

The cost of private schooling varies widely. Religious schools often secure financial support from their broader religious communities, as well as from in-kind subsidies from teachers and other staff who work for less compensation than they would earn elsewhere. Some secular schools are mission-driven as well and relatively inexpensive; others (while also committed to their own visions of education) are quite pricey. Yearly private-school tuition in 2011–2012 averaged about 7,000 dollars at Catholic schools, about 9,000 dollars at other religious schools, and about 22,000 dollars at secular schools.[24]

[21] Claudia Goldin and Lawrence Katz, "Human Capital and Social Capital: The Rise of Secondary Schooling in America, 1910 to 1940," NBER Working Paper No. 6439, March 1998.

[22] Digest of Education Statistics Table 2015.10, "Private elementary and secondary school enrollment and private enrollment as a percentage of total enrollment in public and private schools, by region and grade level: Selected years, fall 1995 through fall 2011."

[23] Census Bureau, Census Brief C2011oBR-02, Overview of Race and Hispanic Origin, March 2011, Table 1 and NCES, Table 205.40 "Number and percentage distribution of private elementary and secondary students, teachers, and schools, by orientation of school and selected characteristics: Fall 1999, fall 2009, and fall 2011."

[24] NCES Table 205.50, Private elementary and secondary enrollment, number of schools, and average tuition, by school level, orientation, and tuition: Selected years, 1999–2000 through 2011–2012. High-school tuition almost always exceeds that of lower grades, and in some cases reaches the cost of selective private colleges.

Americans of almost every political stripe are dissatisfied with the performance of their public schools. Some public schools, of course, especially those in affluent suburbs, are competitive with the best institutions, public or private, anywhere in the world. But underfunded rural and small-town schools and most inner-city schools chronically disappoint. Any argument for government-supported education as an antidote to inequality only works when the education is effective. America has been plagued by large and persistent disparities – in test scores, graduation rates, college attendance, and employment prospects – among ethnic and racial minorities. The federal "No Child Left Behind" law passed in 2001 sought to reduce these disparities. It obligated states to test all students at regular intervals, and imposed penalties unless all students – the disadvantaged as well as the affluent, those with and those without special needs – advanced at specified rates. Test scores *did* rise, though not to the levels of some other advanced nations. But they rose across the board. Racial disparities narrowed little or not at all.[25]

Chronically ineffective teachers and administrators, of course, hate high-stakes testing regimes. But involved parents and effective teachers have also objected both to the testing treadmill, which often drains resources from art, music, and other subjects not included in the tests, and to the seemingly capricious sanctions required under the law. For example, some excellent schools where virtually all students tested near the top of the range faced sanctions because there was simply no room to improve performance at the mandated rate.

Public–Private Hybrids: Against this backdrop of general dissatisfaction with conventional public education, various forms of public–private hybrids have been advanced as remedies. There is an undeniable appeal – especially to market-friendly Americans – of the prospect of shoring up the US weak suit of K-12 education through the US strong suit of private-sector initiative. But there are some fundamental concerns as well. Adam Smith famously wrote: "It is not from the benevolence of the butcher, the brewer, or the baker that we expect our dinner, but from their regard to their own interest." He might have added: "But from the preacher or the teacher, a bit of benevolence is welcome indeed." That is because we are much better at judging the quality of our hams, beer, and muffins – items we buy frequently – than we are at judging the value of a higher education program. Sometimes Americans seeking to improve schooling remember that education is a special kind of service – and sometimes not.

A commission assembled by the Reagan administration sounded the opening bell in recent American initiatives to improve education via private involvement. Its report, *A Nation at Risk,* was a high profile and widely

---

[25] Thomas S. Dee and Brian Jacob, 2011, "The Impact of No Child Left Behind on Student Achievement," *Journal of Policy Analysis and Management*, John Wiley & Sons, Ltd., 30(3), 418–446, Summer; M. Wong, T. D. Cook, and P. M. Steiner, 2015, "Adding Design Elements to Improve Time Series Designs: No Child Left Behind as an Example of Causal Pattern-Matching," *Journal of Research on Educational Effectiveness*, 8(2), 245–279.

influential jeremiad against poor performance in public schools. The decades since have seen three related but distinguishable efforts to shore up K-12 education by engaging private institutions and promoting competition. Those efforts involve private management of public schools, a shifting of public-school students into private education, and the use of market-style choice and competition within public education.

Many Americans speculated hopefully in the late twentieth century that the country's strength in private-sector innovation and efficiency might compensate for its weakness in public K-12 education. Why shouldn't the freewheeling market approach that served Americans so well for so many goods and services do the same for primary and secondary schooling? Entrepreneurs developed plans to shrink costs, improve performance, and accelerate innovation by enabling agile private organizations to replace lumbering and encrusted government bureaucracies. Political leaders – especially, but not only, Republicans – cheered the entrepreneurs on and adjusted government policies to accommodate them.

Not surprisingly, for-profit firms, with their characteristic agility and ready access to capital, were the first private entities to enter this educational arena. In 1990, the troubled Dade County, Florida, school district announced one of the first major trial runs for the market-based education movement. It would implement a radically different management model for a newly constructed elementary school. The for-profit Educational Alternatives Incorporated (EAI) would handle virtually every aspect of the school, including selecting staff. EAI expanded rapidly, soon gaining high-profile contracts to run nine schools in Baltimore and the entire woebegone public-school system of Hartford, Connecticut.[26] A few years later, media entrepreneur Chris Whittle unveiled an even more ambitious plan for private for-profit leadership of public schools: The Edison Project. Edison took on high-visibility public-school management contracts in Dallas and Philadelphia, and announced plans to grow aggressively through the 1990s to generate learning for schoolchildren and wealth for shareholders.

For-profit education as exemplified by The Edison Project and EAI proved to be a hot-button issue, with fierce detractors as well as cheerleaders. Public-school teachers and their unions were almost uniformly opposed, as were the majority of scholars in traditional schools of education. Some predicted that the lust for high profit margins would inevitably lead private firms to cut corners on educational quality, given the difficulties with monitoring and accountability for virtually every relevant dimension of school quality. Others felt that, even if quality were somehow maintained or enhanced, the profit motive simply did not belong in public education.[27]

---

[26] Steven A. Holmes, "In Florida, a Private Company Will Operate a Public School," *The New York Times*, December 7, 1990, p. 1.

[27] Representative examples of these critiques can be found in Daniel Tanner, November 2000, "Manufacturing Problems and Selling Solutions: How to Succeed in the Education Business

Many observers were willing to entertain the proposition that some injection of market forces could fix what ailed American schools. But even if bureaucracy and union restrictions on hiring and firing helped explain part of the problem with school performance, they were far from the whole story. Other impediments to educational performance, such as residential and demographic patterns that concentrated disadvantaged students into the same schools, family dysfunction that undercut learning in even the best-run classrooms, and an often-toxic youth culture, were simply not the kinds of problems that for-profit school management could remedy.[28] Furthermore, education – especially for younger people – provides complex, delayed, and diffuse benefits that fit poorly with tidy theories of efficiency through choice and competition.

After more than two decades of efforts in collaborative governance for public education, some results are apparent. The Edison and EAI experiments in for-profit public-school management were not the disasters for students that some critics depicted. Investors fared much worse in many cases. Edison's stock price neared $40 in 2001; a few years later, it bottomed out at 14 cents. The firm went private in 2003; the stock price was around $1.80.[29] Most importantly, the transformational revolution that for-profit education enthusiasts had envisioned to supercharge educational attainment never happened. The RAND Corporation, in a careful study, concluded that for-profits' advertised performance advantages had mostly failed to materialize. The high-profile contracts of Edison and EAI in Dallas, Baltimore, Hartford, and Philadelphia were terminated early or not renewed. Columbia University Professor Henry M. Levin, Head of the Center for the Study of Privatization in Education, summarized the general outcome succinctly: "They have neither destroyed the schools, nor have they made a big difference."[30] By the early 2000s, the for-profit education companies had, for the most part, either disappeared, retreated to conventional private schools, or found niches in the charter-school movement.[31]

Over roughly the same time period as the for-profit school management's boom and bust, publicly funded vouchers for private-school students, another hybrid approach to K-12 education, gained attention. Their appeal reflected the convergence of private-school costliness, the highly uneven level of public-school

without Really Educating," *The Phi Delta Kappan*, 82(3) and January 1999, "The Hazards of Making Public Schooling a Private Business," *Harvard Law Review*, special issue, 112,(3). See discussion in Chapter 2 regarding comparative advantage of different ownership forms when quality has important dimensions that are difficult to monitor and assure.

[28] For example, see Tony Wagner, September 1996, "School Choice: To What End?" *The Phi Delta Kappan*, 78(1), 70–71.

[29] Marc Caputo, "Edison Schools Accepts Buyout," *Miami Herald*, November 13, 2003. If the information was not yet in, the $40 price may have been reasonable. On the modest chance that Edison would succeed, the stock price might have sailed to $200.

[30] Martha Woodall, "Nationally, Hired Firms Have Had Little Effect," *Philadelphia Inquirer*, February 1, 2007, pp. A–10.

[31] See Peter Applebome, "For-Profit Education Venture to Expand," *The New York Times*, June 2, 1997, p. 12 on Edison's shift to charters and Woodall, 2007 on EAI's.

performance, the scandalous inadequacy of public schools in most poor urban areas, and conservative political tides.

The roots of this approach antedated by decades the political fireworks over vouchers in the late twentieth and early twenty-first centuries. In 1955, famed free-market economist Milton Friedman proposed that government subsidize private schooling through vouchers in order to harness competition to raise school quality. The idea's legitimacy was undercut when it was seized upon by some southern opponents of integration looking for a financial boost for white families fleeing to segregated private schools.[32] Court decisions soon scuttled this segregationist stratagem. But the voucher idea eventually gained significant mainstream conservative support, notably from President Ronald Reagan. Vouchers have persisted as a perennial topic of political controversy, with dueling claims and numbers seeking to paint vouchers as either the salvation or the ruination of American education.

Largely because the political forces for and against vouchers are reasonably balanced, the actual scale of voucher initiatives – in individual cities and states, or in the aggregate – has been modest. Wisconsin's legislation enacted a voucher program for Milwaukee in 1989; since then twelve other states plus the District of Columbia have established some form of K-12 vouchers.[33] Yet a strongly pro-voucher organization, striving to celebrate a rising tide of choice and change, could point to a total of only 115,580 K-12 students enrolled in voucher programs in the 2013–2014 school year, less than one-quarter of 1 percent of all enrolled K-12 students.[34] Neither side is likely to triumph soon in the decades-long political trench warfare over vouchers. The conflicting arguments and the inertia of the status quo are just too powerful.

The charter school movement, an alternative approach promoting choice and competition in education, has emerged to sidestep the sterile standoff over vouchers. Charter schools are publicly financed (sometimes primarily, often entirely) but privately run.[35] While some are run for profit, the vast majority are nonprofit organizations. Their defining feature, the charter, is essentially a contract that codifies the educational mission, in most cases rather broadly, and that circumscribes but does not eliminate the freedom of teachers, administrators, and trustees to run the school as they see fit.

---

[32] Paul Peterson, "School Vouchers in the United States: Productivity in the Public and Private Sectors," *Zeitschrift für Erziehungswissenschaft*, 11(2), 2008, p. 2.

[33] National Conference of State Legislatures website at www.ncsl.org/research/education/voucher-law-comparison.aspx, accessed July 2015.

[34] American Federation for Children website at www.federationforchildren.org/ed-choice-101/facts/, accessed July 2015.

[35] The US Department of Education defines charter schools as institutions that "provide free public elementary/secondary education under a charter granted by the state legislature or other appropriate authority." National Center for Education Statistics (NCES) Statistical Analysis Report, *Overview of Public Elementary and Secondary Schools and Districts: School Year 2001-02*, US Department of Education, May 2003, Glossary of Key Terms.

Minnesota became the first state to authorize charter schools in 1991. By 2013, the movement had grown to encompass some 6,000 schools in forty-two states, the District of Columbia, and Puerto Rico. About 2.3 million American children and youths (or roughly 5 percent of the total number of students) then attended a charter school rather than a conventional public school.[36] Charters are primarily funded by their claim on the governmental resources that follow a student who opts for a charter instead of a conventional public school, although many also benefit from private donations and various public and private grants. A number of billionaires support their favorite charter schools. Charter schools give conservatives their treasured attributes of choice and competition. They allow liberals to preserve the principle of education as a collective good, with providers accountable to the public at large. No faction loves every aspect of charters, but everyone finds something to like – and nothing to hate enough to make blocking the movement a first-order political priority.

The charter school record is promising but decidedly mixed. The ideal vision for the charter movement is to produce better outcomes for public schools as well as for charters. Successful models would be replicated, and bad approaches would wither away. Three forces could contribute to this virtuous evolution: public schools and new charter endeavors could replicate successful models; parents choosing where to enroll their children could vote with their children's feet and thus reward what works[37]; and state and local governmental managers, including boards of public schools, could implement policies penalizing weak models and favoring effective ones.

So is this ideal becoming reality? Analysts within academia and beyond have studied charter schools at length. Dozens of studies target different pieces of the puzzle, use different measures of success, employ different analytical strategies, and reflect authors with differing degrees of skill, objectivity, and candor. A published study can be found to support just about any point of view about the merits of charter schools.

Success Academy is a much-heralded charter school with a substantial presence in New York City. It runs forty-five schools enrolling 17,000 students. Students are selected from among applicants by a lottery, as local laws usually require for oversubscribed charter schools. Success Academy's students are mostly poor; 95 percent are minority-group members. These are characteristics of students who traditionally score well below the norm. Nevertheless, they vastly outperform students in traditional public schools on New York State's standardized tests, with 95 percent and 84 percent scoring

---

[36] NCES 2015, Table 216.20, Number and enrollment of public elementary and secondary schools by level, type, and charter and magnet status, Selected years 1990–1991 through 2012–2013, accessed July 2015.

[37] See discussion in D. A. Neal, *Information, Incentives, and Education Policy*, Harvard University Press, 2018.

proficient in math and English versus 41 percent and 38 percent. This overstates accomplishment, to be sure: Actively applying to Success Academy (SA), as opposed to passively attending the assigned public school, tends to indicate capability and dedication. But comparing SA's students with those who lost in the lottery to attend SA eliminates this bias. Losers in the lottery scored proficient 60 percent in math and 44 percent in English, better than those who didn't apply to SA but worse than lottery winners, suggesting that the Academy model truly adds value. The nonprofit SA is heavily supported by wealthy philanthropists, denting somewhat the effort to demonstrate better results with the same funds as conventional public schools. Success Academy defines its educational philosophy as rigorous; critics would call it repressive, with undue emphasis on test performance. Its critics, using our concepts, would say that SA is exercising unjustified preference discretion. Success Academy would counter that it is offering a far superior education.

Looking at charter schools in general, and relying only on the more respectable statistical studies, one conclusion *can* be reached with a fair degree of confidence: There is no large and systematic difference on average between charters and regular schools in the educational results they deliver.[38] If charter schools as a group enjoyed a consistent performance edge over other schools or suffered a consistent performance deficit, we would know by now. There is already too much experience with charters, and too many avid partisans eager to prove the case either way, for a dramatic average difference to remain hidden.

"Average" is the key word in the prior paragraph; its use could obscure the central finding. Extensive evidence indicates that some charters are a great deal better, and others are a great deal worse, than conventional public schools. Some charter schools use their freedom to offer curricula that deliver tremendous performance by the metric of test scores, and even more public value that eludes quantification by standardized testing. Some charter schools, no doubt many, sincerely intend to deliver high educational performance but simply bungle the job. Worse, some charters deploy their discretion opportunistically or cynically, tilting their curricula to collect private benefits at the expense of public value.

America's charter movement has been widely but wrongly characterized as lifting from government's shoulders, and shifting to private actors, the responsibility for creating public value. But it actually represents a reorientation, not abandonment, of government's role. A shift from conventional public schools to charter schools entails different tasks for government, but tasks no less vital. Indeed, this is true of collaborative approaches in general. To maximize the odds that private discretion works to produce public value, government must choose, enable, motivate, and oversee its collaborators. If charter schools, as a group, are failing to deliver the clear-cut performance gains that advocates anticipated, it may not be because observers have overestimated the power of private-sector

---

[38] Bifulco and Bulkley, chapter 24 in H. F. Ladd and E. B. Fiske, eds., *Handbook of Research in Education Finance and Policy*, Routledge, 2012.

innovation or underestimated the performance of conventional public schools, but rather because observers have misconstrued the governance work that needs to be done. This may be the most important lesson China might draw from America's turbulent experiments in rebalancing the public–private mix in primary and secondary education. The general lesson for any effort to harness private capabilities to public purposes is that the government must take on new, often unfamiliar, roles to ensure that public value is maximized.

Postsecondary Education and Training in the United States

Degree-Granting Colleges and Universities: If K-12 education is widely seen as a weak area for the United States, postsecondary education is a heralded strength. About two-thirds of young Americans at least begin higher education after finishing high school. Around 60 percent of students who entered a four-year institution in 2007 graduated within six years, though this average concealed wide variations – from over 92 percent for females attending selective private schools to barely 30 percent for males attending open-enrollment public schools.[39] While far from problem-free, American higher education is a global leader, with world-class institutions ranging from huge state universities to small private liberal-arts colleges. Nearly 900,000 young people from other countries, including about 275,000 from China alone, flocked to the United States for postsecondary schooling in the 2013–2014 academic year.[40]

Higher education presents a richly diverse institutional ecosystem. In 2013, there were 4,724 institutions of higher learning operating in the United States (including branch campuses); about two-thirds of them were four-year colleges and universities, and the rest were a mix of junior colleges, community colleges, and other two-year institutions. There were nearly twice as many private (3,099) as public (1,625) schools. But public institutions are far bigger, on average. The total tally of students enrolled in public institutions was nearly 14.8 million versus 5.6 million at private institutions.[41]

Until quite recently, for-profit schools played an almost negligible role in American higher education. The tally of students demonstrates continued dominance by public colleges and universities, but *within* the private category a shift away from the nonprofit norm. For-profits accounted for well below 2 percent of student enrollment during the twentieth century, but the share has soared since.[42] (See Table 6.4)

---

[39] NCES Table 326.10, Graduation rate from first institution attended for first-time, full-time bachelor's degree-seeking students, 1996 through 2007.

[40] NCES 2015, Table 310.20, Foreign students enrolled in institutions of higher education in the United States, by continent, region, and selected countries of origin.

[41] NCES 317.10 and 303.25.

[42] Calculated from NCES Table 303.25, Total fall enrollment in degree-granting postsecondary institutions, by control and level of institution: 1970 through 2013.

TABLE 6.4 *Student enrollment at degree-granting institutions*

	Public (%)	Private nonprofit (%)	Private for-profit (%)
1970–1979	77.5	22.1	0.4
1980–1989	77.8	20.7	1.4
1990–1999	77.8	20.3	1.9
2000–2009	75.0	19.6	5.4
2010–2013	72.1	18.9	9.0

As a broad generalization, private involvement in higher education has served America exceptionally well. The vast number and wide diversity of educational institutions means that virtually every curricular and cultural theme has one or more institutional providers. Almost any prospective college student can find many schools that offer an excellent fit. However, many involved in the college sector (including the authors of this book) see technology and market forces disrupting the ecology of American colleges and universities. Many schools will not survive the next few decades. But we strongly suspect that private nonprofits will – and should – remain a thriving and vital part of the picture in American higher education.

According to at least *some* theories, for-profit institutions should be at least as great a boon for American higher education as nonprofits. John D. Rockefeller founded the University of Chicago in alliance with a nonprofit with which he had a long and close affiliation: The American Baptist Education Society. Rockefeller and his fellow Baptists took well-justified satisfaction in building a magnificent institution that bolstered postsecondary education in America's Midwest and (at least in its early decades) was an ornament and an advertisement for the Baptist faith. But suppose Rockefeller's affiliate for launching the university had been not the Baptist organization but another private institution with which he was affiliated, the Standard Oil Corporation (or, more plausibly, some educational subsidiary of Standard Oil). Why can't for-profits do everything nonprofits can do – and more – in higher education? The profit motive, after all, turbocharges incentives to optimize, innovate, and reduce costs.

For-profit higher educational institutions have significantly expanded their share of higher education students in recent years. But they have focused their efforts away from traditional higher education, where public and nonprofit institutions had first-mover advantages including established reputations, physical capital, institutional structures and, for some, heavy endowments. For-profit entities expanded rapidly in higher education markets not currently well served, and where nimble movement and ready access to capital – their areas of comparative advantage – would prove beneficial. They capitalized on vaulting progress in information technology. Many for-profit institutions specialize in online education, an area where some established educational institutions lagged well behind until the COVID-19 crisis compelled a rapid round of catch-up.

Indeed, Coursera, a leading online instruction company partnered with major universities such as Stanford, Princeton, and the University of Michigan, as well as universities around the world, is a for-profit organization. It represents a promising model of collaborative governance, where both public and nonprofit universities collaborate in one area of undertaking with a for-profit partner. That area is one where the advantages of for-profit production are relatively great. Interestingly, edX, the Harvard- and MIT-led competitor to Coursera, is a nonprofit. Both entities are doing well. Only time will tell whether one outdistances the other, or if they survive as roughly even competitors.

For-profit entities have also been successful in the two-year college market. That market is relatively weak in most areas of the country for the public and traditional nonprofit sectors, and is one where philanthropy plays a much more modest role than in four-year institutions. For-profit two-year institutions seem to do a much better job of actually graduating their students. Only around a fifth of the students who start at a public two-year program actually earn an associate's degree or a nondegree certificate. At private nonprofits, the rate of successful completion is a little over half, and at for-profits it is closer to 60 percent.[43]

As of 2011–2012, for-profits conferred about 11 percent of all degrees, roughly in line with their share of students. Around half of for-profit degrees were two-year associate degrees rather than bachelor's, master's, or doctoral degrees; the share for all institutions together (public, nonprofit, and for-profit) was about one-quarter associate degrees. For-profits gave an outsized share of their degrees in communications, information technology, homeland security, and law enforcement, no doubt reflecting their ability to move quickly into trendy fields for employment. For-profits conferred disproportionately few degrees in relatively unmarketable skills such as journalism, philosophy, and the humanities generally. By contrast, in public and nonprofit institutions, which offer subsidized education, faculties can exercise preference discretion in pushing students into fields with unpromising employment prospects.

This pattern, where for-profits thrive in particular niches, is characteristic of many realms where collaborative governance is found. In health-care delivery, for example, for-profit providers now play a significant role in testing facilities, dialysis centers, and urgent care clinics, whereas for-profit providers are much

---

[43] NCES Table 326.20, "Graduation rate from first institution attended within 150 percent of normal time for first-time, full-time degree/certificate-seeking students at two-year postsecondary institutions, by race/ethnicity, sex, and control of institution: Selected cohort entry years, 2000 through 2010," accessed July 2015.

rarer for hospitals in general. In medical research, for-profits are the predominant providers in pharmaceutical development, but play virtually no role in basic science or initial clinical research.

Yet for-profit organizations also pose special dangers in higher education, an arena where quality is hard for potential customers to judge, and accomplishments are easy to misrepresent. As the higher education sector surged in the twenty-first century, reports proliferated of gullible or desperate students falling for improbable pitches and mortgaging their futures for credentials with little value – or for no credentials at all.[44] The most famous case is that against Trump University, a for-profit enterprise owned by Donald Trump. It faced multiple lawsuits alleging that it took advantage of thousands of students who wished to learn how to achieve success in the real estate sector. Trump noisily denounced the lawsuits, then quietly settled them for $25 million after he was elected president but before he was inaugurated. A much more consequential case involved the 100-campus Corinthian College network. It was plagued by complaints from reams of disappointed students, and went out of business in 2015. The federal government wrote off more than $3.5 billion in loans taken out by Corinthian alumni.[45] Since data on institutional closures started to be collected in the mid-1990s, for-profits have been twice as likely to fail as have other degree-granting institutions.

The ready availability of federal financial aid for low-income students, generally a welcome boost for upward mobility, clearly creates moral hazard for both students and schools. It assures for-profit colleges and training programs that prospective students need have neither savings nor earnings, nor even know anybody who does, in order to be a reliable font of tuition revenue. In the 2011–2012 school year, 93 percent of full-time students at for-profit institutions received federal financial aid – a share substantially higher than at other postsecondary institutions.[46] By 2015, nearly half of the former students who defaulted on their government-backed loans had attended for-profit institutions.[47] That was roughly five times the for-profits' share of total enrollment.

In some sense, this loan-disaster story represents a failure of collaborative governance. In principle, it made sense for the federal government to subsidize the loans for higher education for students with little to offer as collateral, with the expectation that they would go on to more successful careers, pay higher

---

[44] Recent research using methods to isolate causal effects shows low returns to for-profit enrollment. "Among four-year students, for-profit enrollment leads to more loans, higher loan amounts, an increased likelihood of borrowing, an increased risk of default and worse labor market outcomes." Luis Armona, Rajashri Chakrabarti, and Michael F. Lovenheim, 2018. "How Does For-profit College Attendance Affect Student Loans, Defaults and Labor Market Outcomes?" NBER Working Paper No. 25042.

[45] "Lessons of a For-Profit College Collapse," *The New York Times*, July 9, 2014, p. 24.

[46] NCES Table 331.90 Percentage of full-time and part-time undergraduates receiving federal aid, by aid program and control and level of institution: 2007–2008 and 2011–2012.

[47] Tamar Lewin, "For-Profit Colleges Face a Loan Revolt by Thousands Claiming Trickery," *The New York Times*, May 4, 2015.

taxes, and otherwise contribute more to society than they otherwise would have. It was likewise logical to have the students choose for themselves among providers. The problem lay in providing loans with little ability to verify the value of the education it enabled, or the prospects for repayment. It left out the *assessment* step in the four critical components of the cycle of effective collaborative governance.

Worker Training Outside Formal Higher Education in the United States

Much postsecondary education has a vocational element. Many college students, particularly those from less advantaged groups, work while attending school. Much nondegree training occurs at colleges and universities. But workforce development differs from postsecondary schooling in that it tends to target older people and aims for a more immediate and focused employment payoff. Most workforce training takes place within firms. The payoff tends to be shared by trainees and their employers. This diffusion of benefits in workforce development can both amplify its overall value and make public–private collaboration attractive, and in some cases essential. But it raises the problem of how to structure fair and efficient allocations of cost, risk, and discretion.

Unlike K-12 and postsecondary education, where spending is well-defined even if its benefits are more difficult to measure, workforce development spending and outcomes both present a hazy image. Confusion and controversy about its prevalence and the magnitude of its benefits are rife. A mid-1990s piece in the *Journal of Labor Economics* entitled "How Well Do We Measure Training?" runs to twenty-one pages, but the gist could be simply summarized as "not very well."[48] One well-regarded economic study offers multiple reasons to believe that the returns on human capital investments in general, and worker training in particular, are substantial. But it also catalogs the many reasons why precise measures of the impact and the scale of workforce development are inherently elusive.[49] Another respected study aims to show that even government-sponsored training programs, a frequently scorned component of the whole human capital system, reap a more-than-respectable return on average, though low levels of spending mean that they are a relatively small part of the picture.[50]

The umbrella legislation for federal job training has evolved over recent decades. The Comprehensive Employment and Training Act of the 1970s

---

[48] John M. Barron, Mark C. Berger, and Dan A. Black, July 1997, "How Well Do We Measure Training?" *Journal of Labor Economics*, 15(3), 507–528.

[49] Sandra E. Black and Lisa M. Lynch, May 1996, "Human-Capital Investments and Productivity," *The American Economic Review*, 86(2), 263–267.

[50] Robert J. LaLonde, Spring 1995, "The Promise of Public Sector-Sponsored Training Programs," *The Journal of Economic Perspectives*, 9(2), 149–168.

featured a great deal of direct governmental control and, at times, even direct service delivery. The Job Training Partnership Act of 1982 that followed took a sharp, deliberate jump toward private-sector delivery and authority over the allocation of public-training funds. The Workforce Investment Act of 1998 features a more complex model that distributes discretion among individuals, employers, nonprofits, and various levels of government. In our terminology, workforce development experienced two shifts: first from public discretion to private discretion, and then a move back to shared discretion – the hallmark of collaborative governance.

Formal classroom training represents one major category of workforce development. Such training can occur in colleges and universities, in community colleges or trade schools, or in training programs run by state or local governments. Some institution-based worker training is paid for by the workers themselves, some by employers, and some by the government. As noted earlier, many of the same federal loan and grant programs that finance degree-oriented studies can also be applied to nondegree workforce development.

There are other federal programs that focus more tightly on narrowly defined job training. The effectiveness of these programs, to the extent that it can be convincingly measured, varies widely from one target group (such as youth, dislocated adult workers, ex-offenders, and the disabled) to another, across jurisdictions, over time, and according to the cost and benefit concepts employed. Institutional training, by and large, features relatively straightforward measurement challenges. Private for-profit postsecondary institutions, with their advantages and disadvantages, are even more important in nondegree worker training than in conventional higher education. While for-profits account for roughly 10 percent of degree-seeking students, their share of students in short (less than one year) nondegree programs exceeds one-quarter; in longer nondegree programs, it is more than half.[51] But the complexity of blending public and private players and principles is straightforward compared to that in the other major category of workforce development: on-the-job training.

Almost every job includes some element of training. Even burger-flippers need to learn when to flip. Every teen paid to shovel snow clears the second driveway a little better than the first. On-the-job training is ubiquitous and often highly efficient, due to the information advantages that employers possess. Employers know things that the government does not know and cannot easily learn – about the current skill needs; about the likely trajectory of those needs; and about the strengths, weaknesses, and potential of individual workers.

The human capital that is built through on-the-job training can benefit the worker, the worker's employer, and the broader community as the worker

[51] NCES, Table 320.10 Certificates below the associate's degree level conferred by postsecondary institutions, by length of curriculum, sex of student, institution level and control, and discipline division: 2012–2013.

becomes a better colleague, parent, taxpayer, and citizen. How the benefits are shared depends on crucial details of the training itself. In particular (in a simple but powerful formulation generally attributed to Nobel Prize-winning economist Gary Becker), it depends on where the training lies on a spectrum ranging from skills that are narrowly specific to the employer itself to skills that are broadly useful.

If a worker is equipped with purely firm-specific skills, his wage leverage is limited. He cannot sell those skills elsewhere. When skills are truly useless in any alternative employment, it is both fair and efficient for the employer to pay for their development. Conversely, generally useful skills increase a worker's earning power across the board, allowing the employee to ask for and receive higher wages from any employer, including the current one.[52] Theory suggests that workers securing general skills at employer expense will (quite unfairly) demand a boost in compensation and decamp to use their employer-funded skills elsewhere if higher pay is not forthcoming. So the worker (or, if society puts special weight on employee welfare, the government) should pay for on-the-job training that conveys general skills that are readily deployed beyond the firm.

Reality roughly follows what theory predicts. On-the-job training is mostly paid for by employers. The training is mostly in firm-specific skills, with the bulk of the benefits and the costs accruing to employers.[53] In other ways, the situation is more complicated and less benign. Many economists and human-resource experts believe that employers *do* provide some general on-the-job training (without requiring employees to pay for it through lower wages).[54] In theory, employers should only invest in general skills for those workers who are quite likely to stick around, perhaps because of ties to the area or a lack of competing local employers. Many experts also believe that there is much less on-the-job training overall than its payoffs would warrant.[55] The difficulty of determining and implementing a fair division of costs and benefits in on-the-job training seems to mean that employers do less of it, overall, than would be socially desirable. This is likely an aspect of human capital development where deepening the skill at collaboration – among sectors, and between employers and employees – would improve our collective capacity to create value.

---

[52] Cihan Bilginsoy, October 2003, "The Hazards of Training: Attrition and Retention in Construction Industry Apprenticeship Programs," *Industrial and Labor Relations Review*, 57 (1), 54–67.

[53] John M. Barron, Mark C. Berger and Dan A. Black, Spring 1999, "Do Workers Pay for On-the-Job Training?" *The Journal of Human Resources*, 34(2), 235–252. See also US Departments of Labor, Commerce, Education, and Health and Human Services, "What Works in Job Training? A Synthesis of the Evidence," July 22, 2014, especially pp. 7–8.

[54] Margaret Stevens, October 1994, "A Theoretical Model of On-the-Job Training with Imperfect Competition," *Oxford Economic Papers*, 46(4), 537–562; esp. 537.

[55] Ibid. See also Black and Lynch and the interdepartmental "What Works?" compendium.

CHINA

Human capital development in China, as in many arenas of this diverse, populous, and dynamic country, provides a study in contrasts. On one hand, China increased college enrollment six-fold in a single decade, and every year since 1997 China has graduated more engineers than the United States, Japan and Germany combined. On the other hand, China has been criticized for investing a relatively low share of its GDP in education compared to other middle-income countries. The Development Research Center of the State Council of China and the World Bank argue that China will need to increase public expenditures for education by at least 1–1.5 percentage points of GDP by 2030.[56] Researchers have estimated that to sustain even 3–4 percent economic growth and rising living standards, China will need to improve the quantity and quality of schooling for its citizens. Substantial convergence with global high-income levels of human capital is a target within reach. It could be achieved with investments of less than 1 percent of GDP targeted to needed areas, especially in raising high-school attendance and improving incentives for teachers.[57] (In 2007, only 33 percent of rural students and 68 percent of urban students went on to high school after compulsory schooling – grades 1 through 9 in China.)[58]

Table 6.5 and Figure 6.1 show the increase in enrollments in private schools in China since 2001. From a relatively low base of only 1 or 2 percent, the private share has increased significantly at all levels. By 2016, about 8 percent of primary school students and 12 percent of secondary school students were enrolled in private schools, a significant change in a country where public schools have traditionally been dominant and perceived to be of higher quality.

In higher education (discussed in more detail later), the increase has been even more salient, over a period when overall enrollments expanded dramatically. Almost one in five Chinese college students is enrolled at a private institution, with the private share soaring from just 2 percent in

---

[56] See discussion on p.57 of World Bank and Development Research Center of the State Council, PRC. 2012. *China 2030: Building a Modern, Harmonious, and Creative High-Income Society.* Organized jointly by China's Ministry of Finance (MOF), the Development Research Center of the State Council (DRC), and the World Bank.

[57] Among the many parallels between the educational and health components of human capital that we shall explore in these two chapters is the importance of better incentives, for both public and private providers, such as paying teachers and doctors more for the desired public goal, student learning and patient health outcomes, respectively. On incentives for teachers in China, see P. Loyalka, S. Sylvia, C. F. Liu, J. Chu, and Y. J. Shi, 2019, "Pay by Design: Teacher Performance Pay Design and the Distribution of Student Achievement," *Journal of Labor Economics*, 37(3), 621–662.

[58] Hongbin Li, James Liang, Scott Rozelle and Binzhen Wu, "Human Capital and China's Future: Imperatives, Challenges, and Prospects," chapter 8 in Thomas Fingar and Jean C. Oi, eds. *Fateful Decisions: Choices That Will Shape China's Future*, Stanford University Press, 2020, pp. 200–221; and Hongbin Li, Prashant Loyalka, Scott Rozelle, and Binzhen Wu, 2017, "Human Capital and China's Future Growth," *The Journal of Economic Perspectives*, 31(1), 25–47.

TABLE 6.5 *Private share of school enrollment in China at the primary, secondary, and higher education levels, 2001–2016*

	2001	2002	2003	2004	2005	2006	2007	2008
Primary school enrollment	125,434,667	121,567,086	116,897,395	116,304,200	111,718,300	109,767,000	107,898,700	105,665,928
Private primary school enrollment	1,818,438	2,221,370	2,749,341	3,283,213	3,889,404	4,120,907	4,487,915	4,804,015
Private share of primary school enrollment (%)	1.45	1.83	2.35	2.82	3.48	3.75	4.16	4.55
Middle school enrollment	64,310,539	66,040,609	66,184,186	101,839,200	102,971,500	103,502,400	103,216,000	102,043,595
Private middle school enrollment	1,583,552	2,024,687	2,565,747	6,118,550	7,548,237	8,447,424	NA	9,606,897
Private share of middle school enrollment (%)	2.46	3.07	3.88	6.01	7.33	8.16	NA	9.41
Higher education enrollment	NA	NA	18,372,660	21,273,696	24,068,010	26,940,653	28,756,247	30,933,944
Private higher education enrollment	NA	NA	NA	2,082,954	2,126,281	2,804,982	NA	4,012,486
Private share of higher education enrollment (%)	2	3.80	11	10.40	13.70	10	NA	12.97

TABLE 6.5 (CONT.)

	2009	2010	2011	2012	2013	2014	2015	2016
Primary school enrollment	102,822,860	101,353,616	100,942,847	98,602,286	94,848,050	95,674,926	97,869,989	99,962,809
Private primary school enrollment	5,028,766	5,376,255	5,678,255	5,978,535	6,286,015	6,741,425	7,138,225	7,563,291
Private share of primary school enrollment (%)	4.89	5.30	5.63	6.06	6.63	7.05	7.29	7.57
Middle school enrollment	101,141,675	100,129,290	98,078,540	94,214,196	88,582,754	86,015,438	83,833,441	83,274,403
Private middle school enrollment	NA	9,791,778	9,467,961	9,272,466	9,019,335	9,152,304	9,432,563	9,960,356
Private share of middle school enrollment (%)	NA	9.78	9.65	9.84	10.18	10.64	11.25	11.96
Higher education enrollment	32,832,077	34,168,470	35,592,411	37,658,065	39,443,960	40,766,458	41,395,905	41,814,539
Private higher education enrollment	NA	4,766,845	5,050,687	5,331,770	5,575,218	5,871,547	6,109,013	6,340,556
Private share of higher education enrollment (%)	NA	13.95	14.19	14.16	14.13	14.40	14.76	15.16

Note: Data collected from the China Education Statistical Yearbook, Ministry of Education of the People's Republic of China (PRC).

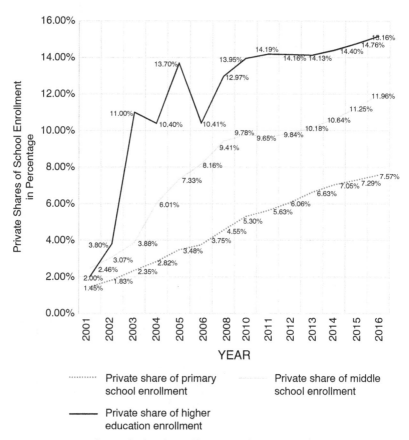

FIGURE 6.1 Private share of school enrollment in China, 2000–2016

2001 (see Table 6.5), although this private share is lower than it had been in 1949 before all private colleges were nationalized,[59] lower than the global average of about 30 percent, and considerably lower than the 50–60 percent private share of China's East Asian neighbors.[60]

China's private sector plays an especially important role in providing care for its citizens at two ends of the lifespan: early childhood education (preschool day care) and long-term care for the elderly (as discussed in Chapter 7). At the

---

[59] About 39 percent of China's higher education enrollment was at private institutions at the founding of the PRC in 1949, according to sources cited in Yuzhuo Cai and Fengqiao Yan, 2011. "Organizational Diversity in Chinese Private Higher Education" in Pedro N. Teixeira and David D. Dill eds. *Public Vices, Private Virtues? Assessing the Effects of Marketization in Higher Education*, pp. 47–66, Rotterdam: Sense Publishers.

[60] Fengqiao Yan and Jing Lin, 2010. "Commercial Civil Society: A Perspective on Private Higher Education in China," *Frontiers of Education in China* 5(4), 558–578.

preschool level, a clear inverse relationship exists between private sector market share and level of economic development, suggesting that improved local finances produce more and better public preschools and less reliance on private preschools. At the high end of the quality spectrum, however, in China's most prosperous regions, private schools are providing services that the public schools do not offer.[61]

In parallel with the US section of this chapter, we discuss primary, secondary, higher education, and worker training in turn.

Primary and Secondary Schooling in China

Responsibility for financing and managing basic education in China rests with local governments, of districts in urban areas, and of counties in rural areas. About two-thirds of education expenditures were dispersed by local governments in 2015.[62] One might suppose that redistribution for human capital development would be vigorous in China, with its vast disparities in living standards between the richest and poorest regions and with its central government controlling public revenue disbursements. However, as most domestic and foreign observers of China point out, the extent of local public services is largely determined by localities' per capita incomes. Consequently, despite central government subsidies, poorer regions struggle to shoulder the fiscal burden of maintaining and upgrading local public services such as schools.

In China, *minban* ("people-run") schools have a long tradition, mostly motivated by governments seeking additional resources for education, what we term "collaboration for resources." First appearing during China's 1927–1937 Civil War, *minban* education spread in the communist-controlled border regions and later in the new republic under Mao Zedong as a way to promote universal education with limited resources.[63] Private education actually dates back much further in Chinese history. Scholars debate about whether the intervening years' civil war and Mao-era central planning completely erased this legacy or whether it still lingers today.[64] Because of the negative ideological connotations of the word "private" in China,

---

[61] Sen Zhou, "Who Is Attending Private Schools in K-12? Evidence from China Institute for Educational Finance Research-Household Survey 2017," in Rong Wang, ed., *Annual Report on New Types of Education Suppliers (2017)*, *Basic Education*, Social Sciences Academic Press, 2018: 72–94.

[62] See discussion in Hongbin Li et al. 2018.

[63] Xiaojiong Ding, 2008, "Policy Metamorphosis in China: A Case Study of Minban Education in Shanghai,"*The China Quarterly*, 195, 656–674.

[64] See for example Zeyu Xu, 2002 "An Overview of Private Education Development in Modern China,"*Education Policy Analysis Archives*, 10(47), http://epaa.asu.edu/epaa/v10n47/), who argues for historical continuity; and Fengqiao Yan and Jing Lin, 2010, "Commercial Civil Society: A Perspective on Private Higher Education in China," *Frontiers of Education in China*, 5(4), 558–578, who argue that the historical legacy was completely severed well before the resurgence of private education in the reform era. It may be worth noting in this context that

nongovernmental schools continue to be referred to as *minban* or "schools run by social forces," terms that sometimes convey a quasi-public meaning in Chinese akin to "private nonprofit" in English, although *minban* schools can be either for-profit or nonprofit.[65]

In Mao-era China, local governments in poverty-stricken rural areas often lacked the funds to deliver education on their own and would elicit villagers' support to house and feed a teacher, and to build a school. As Hannum et al. note, "much of school finance in China during the Cultural Revolution (1966–1976) relied on local community support for *minban*, or people-managed, teachers and schools. ... Education authorities ceded authority over state-managed elementary schools to local production teams or brigades, communes, factories, business enterprises, neighborhood revolutionary committees, etc. ... *Minban* teachers were paid in grain rations and supplementary cash wages."[66] Thus, non-state schools arose as an expedient to supplement government resources in the push toward universal education. Later, many *minban* primary and secondary schools were transformed into public schools, while a second type of *minban* school emerged: private schools filling educational niches for tuition-paying students.[67]

When Chinese government revenues plummeted to 11 percent of GDP in the 1990s, many local governments were unable to pay teachers' salaries on time or in full, leading to low morale, high turnover, and difficulty in guaranteeing a minimum quality of public-school education in poor areas. In response, there was a resurgence of *minban* schools. As Xiaojiong Ding writes, "public education in many localities has been under-funded, and *minban* education has become a way to make up the deficit in public educational finance."[68]

A 1993 official policy encouraged schools run by social groups and individual citizens. Nongovernmental schools grew rapidly, with some local education bureaus sending state-paid teachers to *minban* schools. "Apparently the local education bureau personnel felt that this arrangement was a better use of resources than building a new government school" (Hannum et al. 2008, p. 13). The Chinese central government has never prevented local government agencies from sponsoring *minban* schools.[69] Government appropriations decreased as the source of financing for education from 85 percent in 1991 to 62 percent by 2004 (Hannum et al. 2008, p. 11). This welcoming of the private

---

some of the most elite public universities in China – such as Tsinghua University – started as private missionary-founded colleges over a century ago.

[65] Fengqiao Yan and Xiaoxiao Qu, 2015. "Emergence and Evolution of Private Higher Education in China: Market and Institutional Perspectives," in K. M. Joshi and Saeed Paivandi, eds. *Private Higher Education: A Global Perspective.* B.R. Publishing Corporation, Delhi, India, 2015: 243–270.

[66] P. 217 of E. Hannum, J. Behrman, M. Wang, and J. Liu, 2008, "Education in the Reform Era," *China's Great Economic Transformation*, 215–249.

[67] Xiaojiong Ding. 2008, "Policy Metamorphosis in China: A Case Study of Minban Education in Shanghai," *The China Quarterly*, 195, 656–674.

[68] Ding 2008.   [69] Ibid.

sector in the spirit of "collaboration for resources" is evident even in relatively rich Shanghai, where about 90 percent of *minban* schools have actually been sponsored by local governmental educational agencies. As Xiaojiong Ding has stated, "government sponsorship of *minban* schools is to a great extent a product of local governments' overall spending priority which seeks to stimulate economic growth by saving public funds for industry."[70]

As shown in Table 6.5 earlier, the share of private primary school enrollment increased from less than 2 percent in 2001 to over 7 percent in 2016, but remains in the single digits. The private share of middle-school enrollment rose more, from 2.5 percent in 2001 to 12 percent in 2016. The expansion of private enrollments in China fits well with the "excess demand" hypothesis put forward by James (1993), that is, that the relatively large share of private-school enrollment at the secondary level in developing countries (compared to higher-income countries) stems from limited public spending, which creates excess demand from "people who would prefer to use the public schools but are involuntarily excluded and pushed into the private sector."[71]

The private-sector role in education in China has evolved over time to occupy new niches unfilled by the mainstream public schools. As we shall also see with health care, these niches are not only at the elite end of the spectrum. For example, *minban* schools also have become a prominent means for municipalities to address the dilemma of providing primary and secondary education to the children of migrant workers.

Because the public education system fails to cover migrant children, privately run, tuition-funded, for-profit migrant schools began to spring up in the 1990s, quickly becoming the major venue for the education of migrant children. ... While data do not exist showing exactly what fraction of migrant children are enrolled in migrant schools, estimates are high. For example, in Beijing it is estimated that 70 percent of migrant children attend migrant schools.[72]

Some *minban* schools that are built to absorb the excess demand for public school education mostly coming from migrant children whose parents do not meet the residence registration requirements require neither entrance exams nor residence registration. In addition, these schools can charge tuition levels targeted to their market niches and thus have a degree of flexibility not available in traditional public schools. Their governance involves a range of collaborative arrangements, from relatively clear-cut contracting with a narrow purview, to full collaborative governance with broad private discretion. The

[70] Ibid.
[71] Estelle James, 1993, "Why do different countries choose a different public-private mix of educational services?" *Journal of Human Resources*, 28(3), 571.
[72] P. 69 in Fang Lai, Chengfang Liu, Renfu Luo, Linxiu Zhang, Xiaochen Ma, Yujie Bai, Brian Sharbono, and Scott Rozelle, 2014, "The Education of China's Migrant Children: The Missing Link in China's Education System," *International Journal of Educational Development*, 37, 68–77.

latter arrangement is analogous to that of many charter schools in the United States, but in China, the rationale, even in official documents, has been less about boosting educational value-added than about acquiring additional resources.[73] Moreover, given strict control of national curricula to prepare for the college entrance exams, it is not clear that the diversity of curricula that constitutes one of the strengths of charter schools in the United States is as relevant for *minban* schools in China. These schools account for only a tiny fraction of the students in China, although their total enrollment of over 10 million K-12 students is several times the number of students in all US charter schools combined.

China has promulgated policies to require *minban* schools to declare whether they are for-profit or nonprofit entities, and has gradually expanded administrative provisions to clarify the rights and responsibilities of both types. However, full implementation is ongoing, and rigorous empirical research about that process – or indeed about private primary and secondary schools in China in general – remains limited. Nevertheless, there are a few revealing studies. Zhou (2018) analyzes data from a national survey in 2017, finding that *minban* schools fill two distinct niches: low-cost options for students who fall through the cracks of the system of public schools, such as children of migrant workers (since local long-term residents – with local hukou – have priority for enrollment in local public schools); and a high-tuition option offering a range of educational services not available in public primary and middle schools. Overall, the latter slightly dominates, so that enrollment in and expenditures on attending *minban* schools increases with household income. Chinese households use supplementary tutoring services to complement their option of school, with households spending more on extra-curricular tutoring when the quality of the school is perceived to be below the average of that locality.[74]

Lai et al. (2014) compare academic performance, student backgrounds, and measures of school quality between private schools attended only by migrant children in Beijing (Beijing migrant schools) and rural public schools in Shaanxi

---

[73] The *Law on the Promotion of Non-Public Schools of the People's Republic of China (12.28.2002)* states "the present law shall be applicable to activities conducted by social organizations or individuals, other than the State organs, to utilize nongovernmental financial funds to establish and run schools and other institutions of education which are geared to the need of society. ... The State encourages donations to the establishment and running of schools. The State rewards and commends organizations and individuals that have made outstanding contributions to the development of the undertakings of non-public schools." Peking University Professor Qiren Zhou, who has studied China's voucher system, asserts that [US economist Milton] "Friedman expected that a voucher scheme could promote quality [productivity] of education by introducing more competition on the supply side. In China, we expect such a scheme could promote both quantity [resources] and quality [productivity] of education." (www.ep-china.net/content/academia/c/20040225123637.htm).

[74] Sen Zhou, "Who Is Attending Private Schools in K-12? Evidence from China Institute for Educational Finance Research-Household Survey 2017," in Rong Wang, ed. *Annual Report on New Types of Education Suppliers (2017), Basic Education*. Social Sciences Academic Press, 2018: 72–94.

province.[75] They find that, although migrant students outperform students in Shaanxi's rural public schools when they initially arrive in Beijing, the migrant students' performance deteriorates relative to rural students over time. The main culprits for this relative slide appear to be the poorer school resources and teacher quality in the migrant students' schools. "Additional analysis comparing migrant students in migrant schools to migrant students in Beijing public schools demonstrates that, given access to better educational resources, migrant students may be able to significantly improve their performance" (Lai et al. 2014, p. 68). Of course, it is also difficult to disentangle multiple factors, including time with parents or guardians and selection effects (i.e., parents intent upon children going to high school and college may be less likely to take the children with them when they migrate for work, especially knowing that their children would typically have to return to the rural hometown to take the college entrance exam).

Regulation of *minban* schools illustrates both the universal impulse to rein in exploitative or manipulative behavior (payoff discretion) by "bad apples," and the delicate and shifting balance between government and nongovernment roles in China. Some privately funded schools (such as two schools in Taiyuan described by Wang and Chan 2015)[76] endeavor to provide accountability for quality and garner some autonomy from government oversight by recruiting famous teachers, increasing selectivity of admissions, and achieving outstanding academic results. Some schools utilize links to government to hire teachers with public funds and with public-school job conditions, enabling the recruitment of capable teachers with job stability and fringe benefits.[77]

At the same time, many private schools have pushed the boundaries of profit-making behavior, exploiting loopholes in regulations and enforcement. A significant concern has been inappropriate charging of fees in addition to tuition. Three major strategies have been used to discourage improper fee charging: empowering local governments to "check and approve" tuition and fees of *minban* schools; requiring *minban* schools to publish their fees and standards, along with a method for people to file complaints; and the setting as well as the publicizing of upper limits.[78] However, private schools have found ways to bypass these regulations, sometimes even with the implicit acceptance of local officials. For example, private schools "ask" families for in-kind donations for computers and air conditioners.[79]

---

[75] Fang Lai, Chengfang Liu, Renfu Luo, Linxiu Zhang, Xiaochen Ma, Yujie Bai, Brian Sharbono, and Scott Rozelle, 2014, "The Education of China's Migrant Children: The Missing Link in China's Education System," *International Journal of Educational Development*, 37, 68–77.

[76] Ying Wang and Raymond KH Chan, 2015, "Autonomy and Control: The Struggle of Minban Schools in China," *International Journal of Educational Development*, 45, 89–97.

[77] Ibid.

[78] Xiaojiong Ding, 2008, "Policy Metamorphosis in China: A Case Study of Minban Education in Shanghai," *The China Quarterly*, 195, 656–674.

[79] Ding 2008.

A primary manifestation of the "second-class" role of private schools, and a means to regulate their function, is the practice of limiting the enrollment in *minban* schools. For example, *minban* schools have been forbidden to recruit new students in advance of the recruitment by public schools. Some localities employing this approach, such as Shanghai, have also limited the percentage of *minban* school students in each district to 15 percent of the total student population.[80] These strictly enforced regulations reserve the "primary market" of high-achieving students to the public sector and relegate the "residual market" to the private sector by allowing private schools to take students only after public schools have made their selections. Wealthier parts of China are proud that their public schools outperform any private schools; they even link public schools' competitive edge to broader issues of government credibility.[81]

One arena in which there seems to be great potential for Chinese private firms to collaborate to support human capital development at all levels of China's system is the development of educational technology. In a case echoing Coursera, albeit for compulsory education in China, the for-profit firm CLASS100, an award-winning private online education company, partners with public schools across China to deliver online teaching technology into K-12 students' English classes.[82] Using technology to bring a native English-speaking teacher into real-time classroom instruction alongside one Chinese teacher to assist, the company has expanded rapidly, with over 2,000 foreign teachers involved in collaborative teaching projects with more than 500 top public schools (e.g., Beijing Shijia Primary School, Nanjing Jinling Middle School, Jiangsu Dongtai Middle School, Jiangxi Shaochun Middle School) across ten provinces. Interestingly, the company adopts a "try first, pay later" method that explicitly incorporates a collaborative approach: partner schools are encouraged to employ their services for a month or two for their students with weaker English skills. Then, if the schools are satisfied with the observed results – including the firm's adjustment to the schools' feedback – they enter into an agreement for a longer-term "subscription." The company also incorporates some philanthropy into its operations, waiving payment entirely for some schools in the most remote areas (such as a rural village in Jiangxi). However, challenges persist. One of the major difficulties encountered by the company has been that the governmental education budget does not allow *service* purchase – because this specific type of service procurement remains relatively new in the education sector, administrative procurement regulations

---

[80] Ibid.

[81] As one Shanghai official said, "We always require that public schools never be defeated by *minban* schools. . . . If public schools lost the battle, the citizens would question, 'What are you in government doing?'" Xiaojiong Ding, 2008, "Policy Metamorphosis in China: A Case Study of Minban Education in Shanghai," *The China Quarterly*, 195, 656–674.

[82] See Rong Wang, ed., *Annual Report on New Types of Education Suppliers (2017)*, Basic Education, Social Sciences Academic Press, 2018 [in Chinese].

at first had not adjusted with clear-cut policies, hampering agreements with interested schools and slowing expansion.

Another interesting case involves rural school districts (i.e., county governments) partnering directly with private corporations to provide IT services to their schools. For example, in one county located in western China, in 2016, the local government partnered with three private IT companies to provide local schools with WiFi, computer clusters, cloud databases, multimedia classrooms, video conference rooms, campus monitoring systems, and other related services. The collaborative arrangement includes three parties: the schools, the county financial bureau, and the three technology companies.[83] The agreement is that of a financial lease. In other words, sourcing from the educational budget allocated by the federal, provincial, and overseeing municipality governments, the county will pay the three tech companies an agreed sum of about 70 million RMB over more than a decade. Such arrangements are collaborative in that the IT firms have discretion in actively shaping what services are included following on from discussions with schools about what is working and what latest technologies seem most applicable. Such cases illustrate the potential for collaborative governance to leverage China's burgeoning IT and AI sectors to create public value by bringing appropriate learning technology to students in remote impoverished rural areas. Indeed, the lockdown of millions of Chinese schoolchildren during the COVID-19 pandemic spurred unprecedented development and use of online education – that serendipity amidst crisis will shape the future development of the sector.

China has also seen explosive growth of markets for after-school and weekend supplementary education, primarily for tutoring and exam preparation, but also for extracurricular development of a wide range of youth interests in arts, sports, and hobbies. Much of this market is supplied by the private sector either through commercial firms or through private tutoring (moonlighting) by public sector teachers. Demand is highest among the more advantaged, with wide disparities across regions and income classes. In 2017, expenditures on supplementary education in urban areas was nine times that in rural areas; and households in the top quartile of income spent six times that of households in the lowest quartile of income.[84]

The rise of private international schools also suggests foundational changes for China's educational system, even though the total number of students attending international schools at the primary and secondary levels is quite limited. It represents an important case of *minban* schools fulfilling unmet demand niches in education.[85] More and more Chinese students are also electing to go abroad for studies, starting at earlier ages, and from middle-

[83] See Rong Wang, ed., *Annual Report on New Types of Education Suppliers (2017)*, *Basic Education*. Social Sciences Academic Press, 2018 [in Chinese].
[84] Rong Wang 2018, p. 10.   [85] Ibid.

class families rather than only the wealthy. International schools often aim to serve the market of families targeting college abroad.

In contrast to American students, Chinese students get heavily "tracked" from an early age into either college-preparatory or vocational pathways. Thus, it is important to discuss the distinctive, significant, but arguably underdeveloped role of private actors in vocational education, as we do in the next section.

Vocational Secondary Education in China

Private-sector expertise may be especially important in developing human capital in technical skills at both the secondary and postsecondary levels. Chinese entrepreneurs have complained that the educational system neglects practical skills and innovation, and focuses too much on rote-learning. However, lingering stigma is associated with vocational training in China. Hongbin Li et al. (2012) estimate the returns to education in China using data on twins, showing that one year of schooling increases an individual's earnings about 4 percent. This is a relatively low return by international standards, supporting the criticism that China's academic high school system serves more to select college students than to develop overall human capital.[86]

Despite generally meeting government-set standards,[87] the actual learning outcomes in China's vocational schools appear to be highly heterogeneous and of arguably mediocre quality regardless of ownership form, doing little to decrease the stigma associated with them. Dropout rates from China's senior-secondary technical and vocational education, and from training programs, are high (20 to 30 percent) in many provinces, especially in poorer inland areas, and average more than one in ten nationally.[88]

One contributing factor is limited financial aid.[89] Indeed, using longitudinal data on more than 10,000 vocational and academic high-school students in China and accounting for selection, Loyalka et al. (2015) provide empirical evidence that attending a vocational rather than an academic high school makes

---

[86] H. Li, P. W. Liu, and J. Zhang, 2012, "Estimating Returns to Education Using Twins in Urban China," *Journal of Development Economics*, 97(2), 494–504.

[87] H. Yi, L. Zhang, C. Liu, J. Chu, P. Loyalka, M. Maani, and J. Wei, 2013, "How Are Secondary Vocational Schools in China Measuring up to Government Benchmarks?" *China & World Economy*, 21(3), 98–120.

[88] H. Yi, L. Zhang, Y. Yao, A. Wang, Y. Ma, Y. Shi, J. Chu, P. Loyalka, S. Rozelle, 2015, "Exploring the Dropout Rates and Causes of Dropout in Upper-Secondary Technical and Vocational Education and Training (TVET) Schools in China," *International Journal of Educational Development*, 42, 115–123.

[89] H. Yi, L. Zhang, C. Liu, J. Chu, P. Loyalka, M. Maani, and J. Wei, 2013, "How Are Secondary Vocational Schools in China Measuring up to Government Benchmarks?" *China & World Economy*, 21(3), 98–120.

it more likely that a student will drop out. The dropout rates are much higher for disadvantaged (low-income or low-ability) students.[90]

The government does subsidize disadvantaged students: Starting in 2012, the central government stipulated that the tuition for vocational high school would be waived for students from rural regions and low-income families, and some students would receive additional stipends. Thus, policies have tried to promote employment opportunities for students from rural areas by easing the path through vocational high schools rather than regular public high schools.

"Collaboration for information" provides an advantage when private-sector firms contribute workplace-honed technical expertise and job-market relevance of skills taught. For example, Johnston et al. analyzed data on more than 1,000 vocational students in eastern China (using student fixed effects) to document that a teacher's enterprise experience substantially and positively impacts students' technical skills. These beneficial effects were most salient for high-achieving students.[91]

There is a great deal of room for similar performance improvements. Unfortunately, vocational education in China is marked by lapses in quality and accountability. Li et al. argue that even China's "model" vocational high schools underperform despite receiving higher per-student resources. Using representative data from a survey of approximately 12,000 Chinese students, their analyses suggest that, "there are no significant benefits of attending model vocational high schools on cognitive or non-cognitive student outcomes."[92] The failure of additional resources alone to yield improved outcomes suggests that resources need to be combined with an effective contracting, management, and accountability framework aligning public and private actors with policy goals. To this end, improved strategies of engaging the private sector with accountability could yield significant social benefits. With many more private vocational schools emerging, vocational education, in general, seems especially ripe for innovation in collaborative approaches that harness private sector ingenuity and resources under a transformed government role.

[90] P. Loyalka, X. Huang, L. Zhang, J. Wei, H. Yi, Y. Song, and J. Chu (2015). "The Impact of Vocational Schooling on Human Capital Development in Developing Countries: Evidence from China," *World Bank Economic Review*, 30(1), 143–170; H. M. Yi, G. R. Li, L. Y. Li, P. Loyalka, L. X. Zhang, J. J. Xu, E. Kardanova, H. Shi, and J. Chu, 2018, "Assessing the Quality of Upper-Secondary Vocational Education and Training: Evidence from China," *Comparative Education Review*, 62(2), 199–230.

[91] J. Johnston, P. Loyalka, J. Chu, Y. Song, H. Yi, and X. Huang, 2016, "The Impact of Vocational Teachers on Student Learning in Developing Countries: Does Enterprise Experience Matter?" *Comparative Education Review*, 60(1), 131–150.

[92] G. Li, L. Li, N. Johnson, H. Yi, J. Chu, E. Kardanova, and P. Loyalka (n.d.). "Do Resources Matter? The Impacts of Attending Model Vocational Schools on Student Outcomes in China," *REAP Working Paper*.

Postsecondary Education and Training in China

China has dramatically expanded access to higher education since the late 1990s. Its approach to this expansion – through non-elite, often private institutions – is familiar. Many developing countries have taken a broadly similar approach,[93] and the BRIC (Brazil, Russia, India and China) countries, in particular, have significantly expanded higher education enrollment since 2000 in this way.[94] The primary motivation was in the spirit of collaboration for resources, with government eager to fill expectations for educational access without the commensurate expansion of government financing that purely government-run schools would have entailed. "Private higher education emerged after China's educational reform was launched and as a result of a lack of resources for public higher education. ... individual citizens and organizations were permitted and encouraged to take part in setting up schools privately," Fengqiao Yan and Jing Lin wrote.[95] However, egregious inequalities of higher-education access still remain. For example, Hongbin Li et al. studied all students who took the college entrance exam in 2003; they found that urban youth, as compared to poor rural youth, were seven times more likely to access any college and eleven times more likely to access elite colleges.[96]

Yan and Qu (2015) categorize the historic development of China's private higher education into five stages: recovery and development (1978–1985); adjustment (1986–1992); rapid development (1993–1997); expansion and transition (1998–2006); and stable development (2007–present).[97] In the earliest period, private schools sprang up to teach specific vocational skills or to provide remedial education for students trying to pass the College Entrance Exam.[98] The expansion of private colleges at the dawn of the twenty-first century took place during a period of expanding four-year (*Ben Ke*) and three-year (*Da Zhuan*) institutions through mergers to take advantage of economies of scale. The private colleges were on average smaller than traditional four-year institutions. Many private vocational higher educational institutions expanded

[93] Estelle James, 1993, "Why Do Different Countries Choose a Different Public-Private Mix of Educational Services?" *Journal of Human Resources*, 28(3), 571–592.

[94] M. Carnoy, P. Loyalka, M. Dobryakova, R. Dossani, I. Froumin, K. Kuhns, J. B. G. Tilak, and R. Wang, *University expansion in a changing global economy: Triumph of the BRICs?* Stanford, CA: Stanford University Press, 2013.

[95] Fengqiao Yan and Jing Lin, 2010, "Commercial Civil Society: A Perspective on Private Higher Education in China," *Frontiers of Education in China*, 5(4), 558–578.

[96] H. Li, P. Loyalka, S. Rozelle, B. Wu, and J. Xie, 2015, "Unequal Access to College in China: How Far Have Poor, Rural Students Been Left Behind?" *The China Quarterly*, 221, 185–207.

[97] Fengqiao Yan and Xiaoxiao Qu, "Emergence and Evolution of Private Higher Education in China: Market and Institutional Perspectives," in K. M. Joshi and Saeed Paivandi, eds., *Private Higher Education: A Global Perspective*. B.R. Publishing Corporation, Delhi, India, 2015: 243–270.

[98] Yan and Qu 2015.

by upgrading vocational high schools.[99] Two important legal frameworks went into effect in 2002 and 2004, respectively.[100]

While the market share of the private sector has grown, public universities retain the commanding heights as the elite universities in China, by design. China's private colleges and universities are officially categorized into different types; only a minority is authorized to issue diplomas independently.[101] Recent government investments in key public universities have fostered a growing gap in both per-student spending and various metrics of quality. For example, according to Carnoy et al. (2013), China's elite institutions spent an average of about $10,000 per student in 2010, compared to only approximately $4,000 at non-elite colleges, an increase in about one decade from 1.5:1 to 2.5:1.[102] Private colleges usually rank below the non-elite public colleges in China, and like private hospitals, often hire their professional staff from among new graduates or retirees from public institutions. Furthermore, regulations clearly differentiating the roles and responsibilities of not-for-profit schools are still developing, and many regulations virtually equate private ownership with for-profit and/or vocational education. For example, "Setting Benchmarks on Higher Vocational Education" (2003) replaced the "Temporary Regulations on Privately Run Schools" (1993) as the standard for the private higher education institutions.[103]

Several factors suggest that the government intends to retain the elite level for public universities, while relaxing restrictions and even encouraging the private sector to fill gaps such as mass, non-elite college enrollment, and vocational education opportunities. The government has recently restricted the further expansion of public universities and exerted pressure instead for international recognition in quality and research, while the private sector is expected to provide the rapid scale-up of enrollment slots that society expects.[104] Since private four-year university tuition rates are about twice those of public four-year colleges and the availability of financial aid is much more limited compared to the public universities, only students from wealthy families generally can afford to enroll. Nevertheless, the public and private sectors continue to develop in a largely symbiotic fashion.[105]

---

[99] We thank Professor Lei Zhang for input into this paragraph.   [100] Yan and Qu, 2015.

[101] Fengqiao Yan and Jing Lin, 2010, "Commercial Civil Society: A Perspective on Private Higher Education in China," *Frontiers of Education in China*, 5(4), 558–578.

[102] M. Carnoy, P. Loyalka, M. Dobryakova, R. Dossani, I. Froumin, K. Kuhns, J. B. G. Tilak, and R. Wang, *University Expansion in a Changing Global Economy: Triumph of the BRICs?* Stanford, CA: Stanford University Press, 2013.

[103] Yan and Qu, 2015. The Ministry of Education and the State Planning Commission jointly also emphasized the role of the private sector in the "Implementation of the New Management of Technical-Vocational Education."

[104] Yan and Qu, 2015.

[105] Yuzhuo Cai and Fengqiao Yan, 2011, "Organizational Diversity in Chinese Private Higher Education" in Pedro N. Teixeira and David D. Dill eds., *Public Vices, Private Virtues? Assessing the Effects of Marketization in Higher Education*, Rotterdam: Sense Publishers, 2011: 47–66.

The institutional ecology of China's colleges and universities differs considerably from that in the United States. The "National Outline for Long-term Education Reform and Development (2010–2020)" calls for a distinction between nonprofit private educational institutions and for-profit private educational institutions; however, there is little operational difference between them. In practice, both forms earn net revenue and largely rely on tuition financing; most focus on practical or vocational programs for which there is significant demand, such as business management, accounting, and finance.[106] The "Law of the PRC on the Promotion of Privately Run Schools" stipulates that the fund providers may obtain "a reasonable amount of return" from the cash surplus of the school.[107] This ability to earn revenue has attracted ownership hybrids to channel additional funds to public universities, which can establish an affiliated college in cooperation with a private partner or partners. Such colleges were originally called "second-tier colleges" and later "independent colleges." Their formal governance structures include representatives from both the public and private sides according to their contributions or negotiated capital shares.[108] Different regional forms have developed, such as the "Zhejiang Model" (dominated by government-affiliated "independent colleges") and the "Shaanxi Model" (dominated by "pure private" colleges).[109]

In fact, not only are distinctions between private for-profit and private nonprofit schools hazy, but (as elsewhere in China) the lines between private and public ownership often get somewhat blurred as well. Many of the sponsors of private colleges are public universities; the former benefit from reputation and personnel, while the latter benefit from additional revenue. Sometimes called "pseudo-private" colleges, these ownership hybrids, like joint ventures in other sectors, combine the government-owned partner's land, infrastructure, and reputation with the resources, flexibility, and revenue-generating opportunities of a private partner. The pioneer was the City College of Zhejiang University, jointly owned by Zhejiang University (providing administrators and teachers), the Postal University of Hangzhou (providing its campus), and the local government (providing one-third of the funding).[110] Moreover, because in practice substantial complications arise when forming legal partnerships between public universities and for-profit enterprises, many independent colleges are totally owned and run by public universities through partnership with their monopolized or dominantly shared companies or foundations.[111]

---

[106] Yan and Qu, 2015.   [107] Ibid.   [108] Yuzhuo Cai and Fengqiao Yan, 2011.

[109] Yuzhuo Cai and Fengqiao Yan, 2011, "Organizational Diversity in Chinese Private Higher Education" in Pedro N. Teixeira and David D. Dill eds., *Public Vices, Private Virtues? Assessing the Effects of Marketization in Higher Education*, Rotterdam: Sense Publishers, 2011: 47–66.

[110] Lin, Jing, 2004, "Private Higher Education in China: A Contested Terrain," *International Higher Education*, 36, 17–18.

[111] Yuzhuo Cai and Fengqiao Yan, 2011.

China's private colleges rarely obtain revenues from donations or any government subsidies. Cai and Yan (2011) draw on the theory of isomorphic processes by DiMaggio and Powell (1983) to argue that coercive, mimetic, and normative processes in China to date have largely reinforced the propensity of private colleges to act as for-profit institutions.[112] Examining the income and expenditures of three prominent private colleges, Yan and Lin report that all relied on tuition for 90 percent or more of revenue.[113] Moreover, their active strategies for recruiting high ability to pay students, and other behaviors, are similar to those noted earlier for US for-profit universities; they further reinforce the image of China's private colleges as profit-oriented organizations. In fact, some analysts have argued that the term "commercial" should be added to the concept of "civil society" in analyzing the characteristics of China's private higher-education system.[114]

However, Chinese entrepreneurs of higher education have also developed hybrid models where collaborative approaches aim to compete with elite public universities in specific sectors. For example, Westlake University in Hangzhou, approved by the Ministry of Education in April 2018, represents the first private research university in China. Similar to New York-based Rockefeller University, Westlake University focuses only on postgraduate education in specific scientific fields. It involves a total investment of 3.68 billion yuan ($585 million) and a 99.6-acre campus.[115] Consistent with the aforementioned "Zhejiang model," Westlake University actually represents a collaborative model, with vital inputs – such as the campus land – provided by the local government (the Westlake District government and the Hangzhou Municipal government) as well as the Zhejiang provincial government. As noted by prominent academics involved, this experiment in collaborative approaches to postgraduate education in China will take years to develop but has great potential.

The role of the private sector may also be especially important in education and training programs designed to foster productive and innovative business leadership, given the limits of China's more state- and corporate-led innovation model.[116]

---

[112] Ibid. In essence, DiMaggio and Powell show that institutions, whether public or private, adopt the behaviors of the predominant form in their market. DiMaggio, Paul J., and Walter W. Powell, 1983, "The Iron Cage Revisited: Institutional Isomorphism and Collective Rationality in Organizational Fields," *American Sociological Review*, 48(2), 147–160.

[113] Fengqiao Yan and Jing Lin, 2010, "Commercial Civil Society: A Perspective on Private Higher Education in China," *Frontiers of Education in China*, 5(4), 558–578.

[114] Ibid.

[115] Ma Zhenhuan, 2018, "Westlake University is dream come true for academic," ChinaDaily .com.cn. www.chinadaily.com.cn/a/201804/03/WS5ac36d09a3105cdcf65160c6.html.

[116] See C. Eesley, J. B. Li, and D. Yang, 2016, "Does Institutional Change in Universities Influence High-Tech Entrepreneurship?: Evidence from China's Project 985." *Organization Science*, 27 (2), 446–461.

Worker Training Outside Formal Higher Education in China

Given that even in the "free-market" US job training has in the past featured direct governmental service delivery, it is perhaps not surprising that China's large programs for worker retraining during the transition from a planned to a market economy were heavily governmental. Recent years have seen experiments with a more collaborative form, but little empirical evidence supports either the rosy reports of advocates or the worst condemnations of detractors.

Effective collaboration requires effective government leadership. The primary government authorities overseeing training programs include not only the Ministry of Education and the Ministry of Labor and Social Security, but also powerful PRC ministerial-level agencies such as the Ministry of Personnel and the National Development and Reform Commission. Other important participants are private firms, trade unions, NGOs, and other institutions that provide training and certificates. The huge transformation of China's economy in the 1990s entailed a massive reemployment program for laid-off workers from former "iron rice bowl" jobs at state-owned enterprises. Government policy stipulated that laid-off workers be paid three years of basic living subsidies and benefits. The approach of the "Re-employment Project" included some elements of collaboration for resources, since laid-off (*xiagang*) workers retained formal affiliation with firms, which contributed funds to support programs and help maintain social stability. Decreases in labor force participation were most pronounced for individuals approaching mandatory retirement age,[117] increasing the challenge of retraining. The "Ten Million in Three Years" program[118] organized by the Ministry of Labor and Social Security in 1998 to provide employment counseling and training for 10 million unemployed workers (and additional vocational skills and entrepreneurship training services for 6 million) worked with technical and vocational schools affiliated with the ministry, as well as with colleges and private training organizations accredited by the ministry.[119] Official statistics from the Ministry of Labor and Social Security claim that, by the end of 2003, a total of 21.6 million laid-off workers had been reemployed.[120]

Beginning in 1995, in Beijing, the "Warmth Project" provided training not only for laid-off workers but also for rural migrants and former inmates who had been released from jail. This initiative differed from many others in that it

---

[117] John Giles, Albert Park, and Fang Cai, 2006, "How Has Economic Restructuring Affected China's Urban Workers?" *The China Quarterly*, 185, 61–95.

[118] See C. Dahlman, D. Z. Zeng, and S. Wang, 2007, "Enhancing China's Competitiveness Through Lifelong Learning", p. 220.

[119] C. Dahlman, D. Z. Zeng, and S. Wang, 2007, Enhancing China's Competitiveness through Lifelong Learning. DOI:10.1596/978-0-8213-6943-2.

[120] China Ministry of Culture, The Reemployment Project in China, www.chinaculture.org /cnstatic/doc/photo/zjye.doc.

was organized by an NGO, the National Association of Vocational Education of China, with funding from donations and charitable organizations. According to the association, the program has been very effective in helping workers gain employment.

Some cases of successful training programs with a collaborative flavor have been highlighted in World Bank reports. The "National Training Program for Migrant Farmers: 2003–2010" was jointly initiated by several ministries to provide vocational and technical training opportunities for China's over 200 million migrant farmers. Under the program, special funds were allotted by both the central government and local governments and used, in part, for incentives to employers to improve training for migrant workers. A total of 1.5 percent of workers' salaries was earmarked for training expenses, deductible from taxable income. Migrant farmers who joined the program were subsidized and could earn certification through it. Any qualified providers could apply for the migrant farmer-training fund.[121]

Shanghai has pioneered many such programs dating back to the 1990s. Examples include the "4050" Project (that addressed the needs of redundant female workers in their 40s and males in their 50s), and an experiment with contracting out in 1997 that awarded training contracts through a competitive-bidding process and assessed training providers according to the number of workers who were reemployed after training. Other provinces implemented their own distinctive approaches. In Jiangsu, for example, emphasis was placed on community employment-training programs.[122] National programs trained millions of workers.[123] Whether these programs have reached their potential is debated, but the trend does suggest far greater future public–private collaboration in worker training in China.[124]

In this arena of human capital development – as in many other public undertakings – there are important similarities in the paths the United States and China have taken, but striking differences. One disconcerting

[121] DFID & WBG. The Education and Training of China's Rural Migrants. UK Department of International Development (DFID) and the World Bank (WBG) Study.

[122] Dahlman, Zeng, and Wang, Enhancing China's Competitiveness through Lifelong Learning.

[123] H. Huang, 2013, China Vocational Training: Current Status, Objectives and Policies, *Ministry of Labour and Social Security, P.R.China.*

[124] See for example U. Jürgens, and M. Krzywdzinski, 2015, "Competence Development on the Shop Floor and Industrial Upgrading: Case Studies of Auto makers in China," *The International Journal of Human Resource Management*, 26(9), 1204–1225; M. Warner, *How Chinese Managers Learn: Management and Industrial Training in China.* Springer, 2016; V. Stewart, 2015, "Made in China: Challenge and Innovation in China's Vocational Education and Training System. International Comparative Study of Leading Vocational Education Systems," *National Center on Education and the Economy*; Koo, A., (2016), "Expansion of Vocational Education in Neoliberal China: Hope and Despair among Rural Youth," *Journal of Education Policy*, 31(1), 46–59; M. Ling, 2015, "'Bad Students Go to Vocational Schools!': Education, Social Reproduction and Migrant Youth in Urban China," *The China Journal*, (73), 108–131.

similarity is that both nations have lessons to be learned about the need for accountable contracting and collaboration.

GRADUATION

In both the United States and China, the overarching objective of government policies should be to improve citizens' lives. Following that doctrine, few policy tasks are more important than developing human capital. Both countries, appropriately, have undertaken this task on a collaborative basis, but each has done so in a manner that leaves much room for improvement in bolstering quality and securing better value for money in their collaborative projects for education and job training.

Effectively harnessing private-sector contributions to human capital development requires government to take on new, often unfamiliar, roles to assure that public value is maximized. This task requires a continuous cycle of "analyze, assign, design, and assess," as we first discussed in Chapter 2. Government agents must analyze the benefits and costs of different delivery models; assign responsibility to the right private agents; and design the array of tasks, rewards, management and monitoring arrangements, and so on. Finally, government must assess the performance of its private agents to determine whether the contract or collaboration is functioning as intended. In these areas, especially for local governments in China, pilot experiments and early efforts at collaboration should be valued not only for the results they produce, but also for the learning they impart in the art of collaboration.

The future will offer much opportunity but also immense challenges for human capital development. Past decades have seen American and Chinese workers shift massively from agricultural production to factory work and more recently to service industries. The shift in China came later and was much swifter. These transformations in *what* is produced – from crops to goods to services – have required workers with new skills, and accordingly different education and training.

The future will witness a transformation in how outputs are produced. Robotic production, still a minor force (with sales representing roughly one hundredth of 1 percent of GNP in the United States), is expected to play a major role in both economies. China has designated robotics as a key industry. Its share of world robotics sales has grown from 0.4 percent in 2000 to 29.6 percent by 2016, and its stock of operational robots now represents 19 percent of the global total, more than any other country.[125] Artificial intelligence is at a more nascent stage than robotics, but it has the potential to be more transformative according to studies by academics and industry. These technologies, still more science fiction than major economic forces, will come to

---

[125] P.73 of Hong Cheng, Ruixue Jia, Dandan Li, and Hongbin Li, 2019, "The Rise of Robots in China," *Journal of Economic Perspectives*, 33(2), 71–88.

dramatically influence what workers do and do not do in the tomorrows of the United States and China. Human capital development will have to transform apace.

The successful nation of the coming decades will be a nation that effectively puts all its resources to work in a collaborative fashion to enable its citizens to thrive in this brave new world.

7

Show Me Where It Hurts

State and Market in Health Care

Few, if any, areas of endeavor show a more complicated, and more consequential, tangle of publicness and privateness than health care. It is a prominent, but for the most part, poorly performing arena of public–private interaction in the United States.[1] The governance of this vital sector of the economy – more than one-sixth of GDP – is collaborative; public funds pay for roughly half of medical services (with most of the private spending subsidized through tax preferences), while the vast majority of providers are private. America's public leaders often fail to recognize the dynamic of shared discretion at the heart of the health-care system, and this failure contributes to the private sector delivering care that is less effective, affordable, and accessible than it should be.

Health outcomes for Americans – shaped by a plethora of social factors that are often more important than medical care[2] – are no better and are frequently worse than for citizens in most of its peer nations in levels of economic development. The United States suffers from large disparities in health outcomes by race and ethnicity,[3] tragically laid bare by the COVID-19 pandemic; and even health outcomes of white non-Hispanic Americans compare unfavorably

[1] Donahue and Zeckhauser 2011.

[2] V. R. Fuchs, *Who Shall Live? Health, Economics and Social Choice*. World Scientific, 2011.

[3] In 2016, US life expectancy at birth was 78.6 years, having declined 0.3 years since 2014; life expectancy was highest among Asian Americans [who out-live whites by about 8 years] and Hispanics, and lower among non-Hispanic Black persons, compared to whites. National Center for Health Statistics. Health, United States, 2017: With special feature on mortality. Hyattsville, MD. 2018, www.cdc.gov/nchs/data/hus/hus17.pdf. Racial differences also shape clinical encounters and use of preventive services (M. Alsan, O. Garrick, and G. C. Graziani, *Does Diversity Matter for Health? Experimental Evidence from Oakland* (No. w24787). National Bureau of Economic Research, 2018). On the historical legacy of racial injustice, see, for example M. Alsan, and M. Wanamaker, 2017, "Tuskegee and the Health of Black Men," *The Quarterly Journal of Economics*, 133(1), 407–455.

to those of most European countries.[4] It is the only high-income country without universal health coverage, and most analysts consider a large share of health spending to be wasteful. At 17.9 percent of GDP and $10,739 per capita in 2017,[5] US health-care spending vastly outpaces that of other high-income countries (see Table 7.1 and Figure 7.1). Indeed, the public half of US health spending alone surpasses *total* health spending in almost every other country, much less public spending (which averages about 70 percent of health spending in Organization for Economic Co-operation and Development (OECD) countries). Moreover, the disastrous handling of the coronavirus pandemic revealed how the weaknesses of its health system and the relative underfunding of public health interacted with broader issues of political polarization. The combination undermined science and constrained governance capabilities. Indeed, as Fareed Zakaria has noted, "COVID-19 should be a wake-up call. The United States needs to rebuild its government capacity. The goal is not a big state or a small state but a smart state. For now, what we have is stupid."[6] No informed observer, of any political persuasion, would describe the status quo of the US health system as ideal.

The institutions put in place by the Obama administration's Affordable Care Act (ACA) of 2010, commonly referred to as Obamacare, represent the latest measures – and boldest in decades – to grapple with these inadequacies, enacted when the same party controlled the executive and both legislative houses. When Trump came to office, when he also controlled both houses, he tried to undermine the ACA. His second and more modest attempt, the so-called skinny repeal, lost by two votes in the Senate. The ACA remains an intense flashpoint between Republicans and Democrats, even though it does not transgress the long-standing bipartisan truce that allows government to pay for, but not to deliver, health care, except to veterans.

The Chinese government must also assure that its citizens receive health care, but it can escape most partisan battles, and can and has acted swiftly (including in response to COVID-19, despite initial missteps). In China, overall life expectancy has increased greatly since the founding of the PRC seventy years ago, and according to the World Health Organization (WHO), healthy life expectancy now exceeds that of the much richer United States. Wide regional and urban – rural disparities remain in China. The richest four provinces have average income about three times the average of the poorest four provinces, and their average life

---

[4] A. Case, and A. Deaton, 2015, "Rising Morbidity and Mortality in Midlife among White non-Hispanic Americans in the 21st Century," *Proceedings of the National Academy of Sciences*, 112(49), 15078–15083.

[5] A. B. Martin, M. Hartman, B. Washington, A. Catlin, and National Health Expenditure Accounts Team, 2018, National Health Care Spending In 2017: Growth Slows To Post–Great Recession Rates; Share Of GDP Stabilizes. *Health Affairs*, 10–1377. https://doi.org/10.1377/hlthaff.2018.05085.

[6] Fareed Zakaria, "Smart countries have the edge in fighting Covid-19. The United States isn't one of them." July 9, 2020 https://www.washingtonpost.com/opinions/global-opinions/smart-states-have-the-edge-in-fighting-covid-19-the-united-states-isnt-one-of-them/2020/07/09/8b82ce3e-c21d-11ea-9fdd-b7ac6b051dc8_story.html [accessed August 7, 2020]; *OECD Health Statistics 2018*.

TABLE 7.1 *Life expectancy and health-care spending in the United States, other OECD countries, and emerging market economies, 2017 or latest available year*

Countries	Life expectancy at birth for total population	Health expenditure per capita in PPP dollars	Health expenditures as % GDP
Australia	82.5	4,543	9.1
Austria	81.7	5,440	10.3
Belgium	81.5	4,774	10
Canada	81.9	4,826	10.4
Chile	79.9	1,914	8.1
Czech Republic	79.1	2,629	7.1
Denmark	80.9	5,182	10.2
Estonia	77.8	2,125	6.7
Finland	81.5	4,175	9.2
France	82.4	4,902	11.5
Germany	81.1	5,728	11.4
Greece	81.5	2,324	8.4
Hungary	76.2	2,044	7.2
Iceland	82.3	4,580	8.5
Ireland	81.8	5,446	7.1
Israel	82.5	2,833	7.4
Italy	83.3	3,541	8.9
Japan	84.1	4,717	10.7
Korea	82.4	2,897	7.6
Luxembourg	82.8	7,048	6.1
Mexico	75.4	1,034	5.4
Netherlands	81.6	5,385	10.1
New Zealand	81.7	3,682	9
Norway	82.5	6,351	10.4
Poland	78.0	1,955	6.7
Portugal	81.2	2,888	9
Slovakia	77.3	2,268	7.1
Slovenia	81.3	2,884	8.3
Spain	83.4	3,370	8.8
Sweden	82.4	5,510	10.9
Switzerland	83.7	8,009	12.3
Turkey	78.0	1,193	4.2

(*continued*)

TABLE 7.1 *(continued)*

Countries	Life expectancy at birth for total population	Health expenditure per capita in PPP dollars	Health expend-itures as % GDP
United Kingdom	81.2	4,264	9.7
USA	78.6	10,739	17.9
OECD average	79.0	3,729	8.6
Brazil	74.8	1,401	8.9
China	76.0	762	5.6
India	68.4	238	3.9
Russia	71.8	1,304	5.3
South Africa	57.4	1,090	8.2
Singapore	83.0	4,047	4.9

Note: Data for Canada is from 2011. Ireland and UK life expectancies are estimated values from the OECD Health Database. US numbers adjusted slightly upward to reflect US National Health Expenditure Accounts.
Sources: OECD Health Database 2018; World Health Organization Global Health Expenditure Database, World Bank Data, Singapore Ministry of Health Website for Singapore data; Martin et al. 2018.

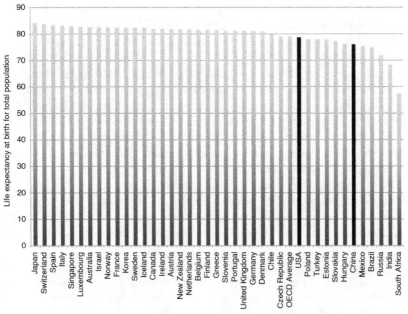

FIGURE 7.1a Life expectancy at birth in the United States, other OECD countries, and emerging market economies, 2017

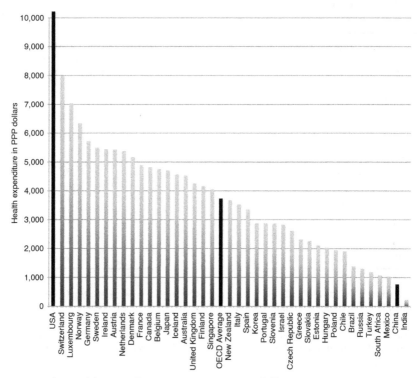

FIGURE 7.1b Health expenditures per capita in PPP dollars, 2017

expectancy is ten years longer.[7] To be sure, most of China's dramatic increase is due to standard of living gains, not health care itself. Nevertheless, China's health-care institutions have been transformed, and its expenditures have vastly escalated.

China's government once completely dominated health-care financing and service delivery. But China's contemporary health sector, like that of the United States, is a realm of collaborative governance in important respects. Although *total income* per capita ($8,827) is less than US *health-care* spending per capita, a similar share of health spending – about half – is public, in the form of direct government fiscal outlays supporting government providers and subsidies for health insurance for the rural and non-employed population.

Private out-of-pocket spending had increased during the 1980s and 1990s, reaching 60 percent of total health spending by the turn of the century. This made access to care difficult for those who were credit-constrained or poor, and it exacerbated regional and urban/rural disparities. The severe acute respiratory

---

[7] Karen Eggleston, 2019, "Healing One-fifth of Humanity: Progress and Challenges for China's Health System," Stanford Asia Health Policy Program working paper (https://aparc .fsi.stanford.edu/asiahealthpolicy/research/asia_health_policy_program_working_paper_series) and *Milken Institute Review* companion piece.

syndrome (SARS) crisis and a series of other events in the early twenty-first century spurred reforms focusing on renewed government financing and establishing universal coverage through social insurance. The approach relied on monopolistic, publicly managed, basic health insurance schemes in each locality. Subsidies from central and local governments support basic voluntary health insurance in rural areas (the New Cooperative Medical Scheme (NCMS)), and a similar voluntary subsidized program for urban residents not covered by employee insurance (Urban Residents Basic Medical Insurance (URBMI)). Increasingly, localities have merged these two programs into larger risk pools. These programs, alongside the compulsory and more comprehensive insurance scheme for urban formal sector workers (Urban Employees Basic Medical Insurance (UEBMI)) and renewed investment in governmental providers, reduced private out-of-pocket spending and achieved universal health coverage, now consolidated under the National Healthcare Security Administration.

An increasingly diverse array of providers delivers health care in China. By 2018, more than one in four hospital beds were in a private hospital, with a higher private share in some nonhospital health services. In addition, health-care reforms expanded the basic public health services funded by per capita government budget allocations, with a higher central government subsidy for lower income provinces (similar to Medicaid in the United States).

Large increases in access and utilization followed these national reforms. By 2017, a higher percentage of Chinese accessed hospital admissions than the average high-income (OECD) country.[8] According to one metric covering 2000 to 2016, China achieved the greatest improvement in health-care access and quality among 195 countries; and China's performance in 2016 was the highest among all countries with same or lower medical spending per capita (see Figure 7.2).[9]

Universal coverage and China's series of other health sector reforms that have occasionally embraced collaborative approaches have not, however, stopped patients from voicing their formerly ubiquitous complaint of *"kanbing nan, kanbing gui"* (obtaining health care is difficult and expensive). Stark regional and urban–rural disparities in health care persist. Indeed, according to the same aforementioned study, the gap in health care access and quality between the

---

[8] Qingyue Meng, Anne Mills, Longde Wang, and Qide Han., 2019, "What Can We Learn from China's Health System Reform?" *BMJ*, 365, l2349. For an overview of China's health sector, see other articles in the June 2019 special collection of articles in BMJ; L. R. Burns and G. G. Liu, eds. *China's Healthcare System and Reform*. Cambridge University Press, 2017.

[9] The Healthcare Access and Quality (HAQ) Index proposed by the Global Burden of Disease 2016 Healthcare Access and Quality Collaborators (2018) is based on measuring premature mortality from causes that should not occur if the individual had access to high-quality healthcare. GBD 2016 Healthcare Access and Quality Collaborators, 2018, "Measuring Performance on the Healthcare Access and Quality Index for 195 Countries and Territories and Selected Subnational Locations: A Systematic Analysis from the Global Burden of Disease Study 2016," *Lancet*, 391(10136), 2236–2271.

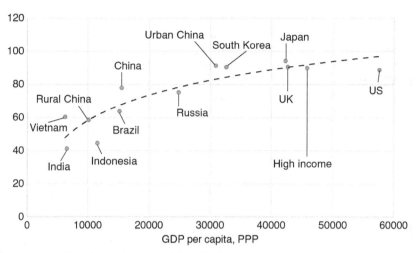

FIGURE 7.2a Healthcare Access and Quality Index, 2016
Note: The proxy for rural China is the mean for Tibet, Xinjiang, Qinghai, and Guizhou; for urban China, it is the mean for Shanghai, Beijing, Tianjin, and Zhejiang.
Sources: Global Burden of Disease 2016 Healthcare Access and Quality Collaborators, Fullman, N., et al. 2018; and World Bank Development Indicators.

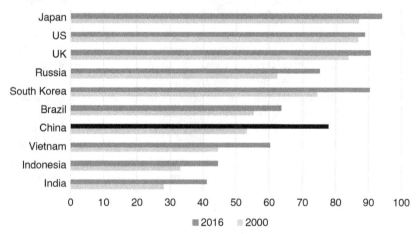

FIGURE 7.2b Change in the Healthcare Access and Quality Index, 2000–2016

lowest- and highest-scoring regions within China is equivalent to the difference between Iceland (the highest in the world) and North Korea.[10]

As we stressed in Chapter 2, collaborative governance calls for a continuous cycle of assessment and refinement (the AADA cycle), tailored to the local governance challenge. For health care in the United States, this cycle turns slowly

---

[10] Eggleston 2019.

and jerkily due to the strong inertial powers that central players – physicians and other health-care professionals, insurance companies, hospital administrators, pharmaceutical and device developers, medical schools, employers as constituents and stakeholders in employment-based insurance, patient advocacy groups and others – exert on the health-care sector. Those forces are reinforced by the complexities of reform in a democratic system. Political ideology, even within America's two parties, is particularly intense in the health-care arena. Dispassionate discussion is rare; consensus almost nonexistent. Given such intensity, the 2017 failure of Trump's administration to deliver on his prime campaign promise to replace Obamacare, despite the Republican control of both houses of Congress, is hardly surprising. The frequent triumph of ideology over analysis renders elusive any conclusive diagnosis of what ails American health care. Health care is assuredly *not* a policy arena where China should seek to follow the American path, but it should take caution from the path America has taken, particularly on matters of expenditure.

China's percentage of GDP spent on health care is one-third that of the United States, roughly equivalent to the United States in the 1960s when large social health insurance programs got underway. But China's health spending has increased at a rate higher than GDP growth and seems poised to significantly increase further, given its extreme boost in per capita income, rising expectations, and its rapidly aging population. As China's health-care system continues to develop, we hope and expect it will pursue better ways to blend public and private responsibilities. Indeed, collaboration for information and productivity with private entities seems unavoidable if some of China's articulated goals are to be met – such as meeting increasing demand for high-end services while constraining government spending, and achieving the health-care portion of its ambitious national plan to make China a global leader in artificial intelligence (AI) by 2030. Yet scandals, such as that of summer 2018 about faulty vaccines produced by a privatized SOE, highlight the risks of collaborative approaches when oversight institutions are weak and patients cannot effectively monitor safety and quality.

This chapter seeks dispassion. It is likely that, in two decades, collaborative governance will still aptly describe the health sectors in each of the two nations. Indeed, health care tends to display an especially intense version of collaborative governance. The public and private sectors both contribute substantial resources, influence how health care functions, and exercise considerable discretion. And thus, collaborative production can yield benefits in productive efficiency, access to information, resources, and legitimacy. A downbeat observation of this chapter, however, is that public and private assets can sometimes work at cross-purposes. Roles may clash. Discretion shared may sometimes be discretion discordant, with the whole worth less than the sum of its parts.

The COVID-19 pandemic underscores these themes in the context of what can be forgotten in normal times: a high-functioning health system, including public-private engagement (and more or less resilient civil society) is of vital social and economic importance. An effective response to COVID-19 required regulatory and scientific collaboration on the development of testing methods, vaccines, and therapies, and community-oriented policies to mitigate the social and economic impact on the most vulnerable (e.g., sick leave, healthcare access, unemployment support). In China, after initial complacency and cover-up,[11] unprecedented measures were undertaken to contain the virus. The health system was much better prepared than it was during SARS 17 years ago. Indeed that previous crisis spurred China to reach universal health coverage.

Vaccine development epitomized "collaborative governance, Chinese-style": a centrally-led effort through SOEs, complemented by global scientific collaboration among entities with multiple ownership forms. The "Joint Prevention and Control Mechanism" (*lianfang liankong jizhi*) directly under the State Council,[12] with its associated science and technology task team (*keyan gongguanzu*), orchestrated multi-pronged vaccine development. The Ministry of Science and Technology, in conjunction with the National Health Commission, the National Development and Reform Commission, and the Ministry of Education, launched the "COVID-19 Technological Response Program," and the State-owned Assets Supervision and Administration Commission urged SOEs like Sinopharm to accelerate the development and production of COVID-19 drugs and vaccines.[13] China's leading vaccine development teams include three collaborations between private for-profit firms and government-controlled non-profit organizations (*shiye danwei*): Abogen and Walvax with the Academy of Military Medical Sciences; CanSino with the Academy of Military Medical Sciences; and Zhifei Longcom with the Chinese Academy of Medical Sciences. Others include a joint venture of domestic and overseas for-profit firms (e.g. Fosun Pharma and BioNtech); a domestic private firm Sinovac receiving "tremendous support" from the Beijing Municipal Government; and collaboration of Clover Biopharmaceuticals with the international foundation Coalition for Epidemic Preparedness Innovations.

In the United States, one of the few promising aspects of a generally fumbled coronavirus response was the collaboration for accelerated vaccine development. One partnership leveraged the expertise of NIH's National Institute of Allergy and

---

[11] Bao Zhiming, Qin Jianhang, Gao Yu, Xiao Hui, and Timmy Shen, "Wuhan Doctors Say Colleagues Died in Vain Amid Official Coverup," March 10, 2020, *Caixin Global*, www.caixinglobal.com/2020–03-10/wuhan-doctors-say-colleagues-died-in-vain-amid-official-coverup-101526650.html [accessed 10 March 2020].

[12] Wang, Binyang, "National Health Commission and Relevant Departments Establish Joint Prevention and Control Mechanism to Confront the COVID-19 Epidemic [guojia weisheng jiankang wei huitong xiangguan bumen lianfang liankong quanli yingdui xinxing guanzhuang bingdu ganran de feiyan yiqing]" *Xinhuanet*, last modified January 22, 2020, http://www.xinhuanet.com/politics/2020-01/22/c_1125491587.htm.

[13] "SASAC: Quick Deployment and Expanded Production of Medical Supplies; Full Promotion of Drug and Vaccine Research [Guoziwei: xunsu anpai bushu yiliao wuzi zhuanchan kuochan quanli tuijin yaowu yimiao keyan gongguan]," *State-owned Assets Supervision and Administration Commission of the State Council* online, February 18, 2020, http://www.sasac.gov.cn/n2588025/n2588119/c13830323/content.html.

Infectious Diseases and the biotechnology company Moderna.[14] A multi-agency collaboration led by the Department of Health and Human Services – dubbed Operation Warp Speed – aimed to deliver 300 million doses of a vaccine for COVID-19 by January 2021.[15] Another vaccine included in the U.S. operation, among the first to enter Phase 3 trials, was the product of a public-private collaboration between the University of Oxford and AstraZeneca.[16] From the world's standpoint, the prospect of many vaccines, relying on different principles, all racing to the market, promises a better outcome than could have been expected without a collaborative approach.

Looking beyond the COVID-19 crisis, health care in both China and the United States is entering an era of continuing upheaval. Technological revolutions in "precision health" and "personalized medicine," with world-leading biotechnology in both countries, will coexist alongside massive demands in care for the elderly and tenacious disparities in health and access. New production modes drawing heavily on collaborative approaches will be needed to meet demands and dampen disparities. Yet collaboration can cut in either direction. To meet their citizens' expectations for safe, quality, innovative, yet affordable health services, both countries will need to attend carefully so as to strengthen their collaborative governance in this sector.

This chapter continues with a brief discussion of conceptual issues important for understanding the collaborative challenges in both countries' health systems, and then discusses the United States and China in turn.

WHAT MAKES HEALTH SYSTEMS INHERENTLY COLLABORATIVE?

Health and medical care involve a prominent government role for many reasons: health complements education as fundamental to human capital and citizens' wellbeing; control of infectious disease involves strong externalities; basic research in mechanisms of disease constitutes a public good; regulation is vital to assure safety and quality, and to avoid market failures in insurance; basic medical care is usually considered a merit good; and assisting the poor with access to health care complements other efforts to counteract the ill effects of income inequality and achieve goals of redistribution, to name a few of the most salient.

In the health sector, multiple organizational forms almost always interact with each other in various realms. Government, with its power to regulate, has primary

---

[14] Andrea Kane. "The first Phase 3 coronavirus trial in the US is expected to begin next week," CNN Health, 27 July 2020, https://www.cnn.com/2020/07/24/health/moderna-vaccine-barney-graham-gupta/index.html.

[15] Fact Sheet: Explaining Operation Warp Speed. HHS, 7 August 2020, https://www.hhs.gov/about/news/2020/08/07/fact-sheet-explaining-operation-warp-speed.html.

[16] Matthew Herper. Studies provide glimpse at efficacy of Covid-19 vaccines from Oxford-AstraZeneca and CanSino, Stat, 20 July 2020. https://www.statnews.com/2020/07/20/study-provides-first-glimpse-of-efficacy-of-oxford-astrazeneca-covid-19-vaccine/.

responsibility for setting the rules of the game and curbing payoff and preference discretion. But it is rare that one form is fully in charge. Form G may pay, but form N may deliver. Form P may be managing at the center, but form N may pick the staff and the responsibilities. In both China and the United States, for-profit private firms play a role within this mixture of organizational forms, ranging from pharmaceutical and medical device manufacturers to pharmacy owners and individual providers. In short, we observe a mixture of discretion amidst a mixture of forms. To shepherd that mixture toward public value rather than an opioid epidemic or proliferating waste, effective government oversight and regulation are crucial.

Before delving deeper into the structure of the health sector in either the United States or China, we remark on two favorite activities of health critics, both on the Left and on the Right. First, they often propose radical solutions to the system's problems, solutions whose prospects for selection and survival are often nil in a sector where inertia prevents root-and-branch changes. In the United States, this often takes a particular form of ritual debate. The Left proposes a single-payer system. The Right celebrates the magic of the market.[17] Second, these critics on both Left and Right identify some other nation that employs their preferred system, as if that makes the case that the United States or China can (or should) follow suit.

To illustrate a system that douses the hopes of most such critics, consider that of Singapore. Health care absorbs less than 5 percent of gross national product (GNP) while helping to underpin the city-state's extremely high life expectancy. The Left would object to the Singapore way because services, though subsidized, are never free at point of use, and because health savings accounts play a major role. The Right would be distressed by the Government of Singapore's heavy involvement in setting rates and objectives, forcing individuals to save and generally directing the system, and because three quarters of that nation's population receives its care through the public system. However, fans of collaborative governance find much to admire. Singapore shows that an effective mixture of public and private efforts can deliver quality care on an efficient and thrifty basis, albeit in a small nation with high government salaries and a limited need to cater to the political whims of the electorate. Chinese leaders have found much to admire in the Singapore model.[18] There is no evidence that many American leaders are familiar with it.

---

[17] High-deductible health plans have increased enrollment in the United States, and there is evidence that they reduce spending, but little evidence of consumers learning to price shop or distinguish wasteful care from valuable care. See, for example, Z. C. Brot-Goldberg, A. Chandra, B. R. Handel, and J. T. Kolstad, 2017, "What Does a Deductible Do? The Impact of Cost-Sharing on Health Care Prices, Quantities, and Spending Dynamics," *The Quarterly Journal of Economics*, 132(3), 1261–1318.

[18] For example, China's approach to affordable housing also borrows from the Singapore Central Provident Fund experience. (See Chapter 4.) For more on the Singapore health system and its approach to public and private roles, see Lim, Meng-Kin, 2004, "Shifting the Burden of Health Care Finance: A Case Study of Public–Private Partnership in Singapore," *Health Policy*, 69(1),

HEALTH SERVICE DELIVERY

A cross-sectoral mosaic in health-care delivery is a pattern found in both the United States and China, although the paths to this pattern differ radically. It is hardly surprising that China, an authoritarian state led by a single, communist party, started with an overwhelmingly government-run health-care system before evolving toward a mixed-ownership system. Government health care encompassed everything from the "barefoot doctors" of the Mao era to the "commanding heights" of modern hospitals that boast the most high-tech equipment, the most skilled physicians, and the most sterling reputations for quality.

In the United States, a mixed ecology of public and private involvement has been an abiding feature of health-care delivery since the middle of the nineteenth century. Over long stretches, species roughly held their own. Thus, of 371,000 short-term general hospital beds in 1928, 16 percent were for-profit, 53 percent private nonprofit, and 31 percent government-owned.[19] By 2012, of 800,566 community hospital beds, 17 percent were for-profit, 68 percent private nonprofit, and 15 percent government-owned.[20] Over an eight-decade period, the one major development in the delivery of hospital services was a loss of half of the government's share; that share went to the nonprofit sector.

Not every feature of American health care is rational or even close to rational; but this gradual tilt away from direct governmental provision broadly makes sense, in light of the many handicaps and constraints government in-house delivery entails. Critics of government-run hospitals and clinics lament inefficiency, lack of capital-market monitoring, soft budget constraints, imprecise or multiple objectives, and politicized resource allocation. Government providers appear to be especially vulnerable to political pressures, averse to unfavorable publicity, and constrained by rules regarding procurement and management compensation, which are not always sensible.

83–92; and Pauly, Mark V., 2001, "Commentary: Medical Savings Accounts in Singapore: What Can We Know?" *Journal of Health Politics, Policy and Law*, 26(4), 727–731.

[19] Rorem, C. Rufus, 1930. *The Public's Investment in Hospitals*. Chicago: University of Chicago Press, p. 14.

[20] Centers for Disease Control and Prevention (CDC) National Center for Health Statistics, www .cdc.gov/nchs/data/hus/2014/098.pdf. We use the term *government-owned* here rather than the more common *public* for several reasons. *Public* is variously used to denote a *private for-profit* entity such as a public corporation, or *public* health vs. personal health care services, or *public* goods. Moreover, in some countries, a *public* hospital refers to any hospital that accepts all patients regardless of income. For example, Boychuk (1999), reviewing the history of hospital policy in the United States and Canada, notes that in Canada "voluntary and municipal institutions both carried the legal designation *public hospital*, meaning open to all without respect to social or economic status" (p. 20, italics in original). Consider the potential confusion between *public* and *private* inherent in the following: "The public hospital system mostly consisted of voluntary [private nonprofit] hospitals" (p. 41). Even in the United States, members of the National Association of Public Hospitals and Health Systems include several private nonprofit corporations (such as the Boston Medical Center or the University of Chicago Hospitals and Health System).

Delivering care in the health-care sector requires the services of many intelligent and highly skilled individuals. These are precisely the kinds of people who tend to earn far more in the private than in the public sector. Public employers generally overpay at the low end of the skills spectrum and underpay at the high end. This is so for a wealth of reasons that are largely unintended but nonetheless durable.[21] That pattern is especially true in health care. For example, there is evidence that government health-care providers in the United States accept lower pay than their private-sector counterparts; they secure greater job security in return.[22] This pattern gives the private sector an edge in the delivery of quality health care, and it will retain that edge in the United States, barring an improbable tectonic shift in its alignment of cultural and political forces. The pattern differs in China, where the incumbent government providers frequently have a reputational and institutional advantage in attracting much of the clinical talent, whereas private providers, especially in primary care or remote areas, must rely on recent graduates or retirees.

Given the major role that nongovernment nonprofits play in the health sector in many countries, especially in the United States and increasingly by government encouragement in China, considerable scholarly and political debate surrounds the motivations and proper roles of for-profit and nonprofit organizations.[23] Theories frequently posit that nonprofits have distinctive sets of objectives. Hypothesized nonprofit goals include quality, quantity, or prestige[24] instead of, or in addition to, net revenue[25]; helping to fulfill demand for local public services[26] or meeting unmet needs in the community[27]; or maximizing the well-being of specific constituencies, such as

---

[21] See *The Warping of Government Work*, John D. Donahue, Harvard University Press, 2008.

[22] For example, the Government Accountability Office (GAO) analysis of CEO compensation collected from a survey of 368 hospitals in the early 1990s found that government hospitals paid 9 percent less than nonprofit hospitals (controlling for size, teaching status, location, and other characteristics) and that for-profit hospitals paid executives about 12 percent more than similar nonprofits. The GAO report suggests that job security is one factor that can explain this compensation pattern (GAO 1994). Zeckhauser, Patel, and Needleman (1995: 106) found that (nonteaching) public hospitals had the lowest compensation per full-time employee, compared to for-profit and nonprofit private hospitals.

[23] K. J. Arrow, 1963, "Uncertainty and the Welfare Economics of Medical Care," *The American Economic Review*, 53(5), 941–973.

[24] J. P. Newhouse, 1970, "Toward a Theory of Nonprofit Institutions: An Economic Model of a Hospital," *The American Economic Review*, 60(1), 64–74. Later mathematical formalizations of Newhouse's model include Sloan and Steinwald (1980) and Phelps (1997).

[25] D. Lakdawalla, and T. Philipson, 1998, *Nonprofit Production and Competition* (No. w6377). National Bureau of Economic Research.

[26] Weisbrod 1975; B. A. Weisbrod, 1997, "The Future of the Nonprofit Sector: Its Entwining with Private Enterprise and Government," *Journal of Policy Analysis and Management*, 16(4), 541–555; J. P. Ballou, and B. A. Weisbrod, 2003, "Managerial Rewards and the Behavior of For-Profit, Governmental, and Nonprofit Organizations: Evidence from the Hospital Industry," *Journal of Public Economics*, 87(9–10), 1895–1920.

[27] R. G. Frank, and D. S. Salkever, 1991, "The Supply of Charity Services by Nonprofit Hospitals: Motives and Market Structure," *The Rand Journal of Economics*, 22(3), 430–445.

the medical staff[28] or the consumers.[29] Conversely, the goals of for-profit firms, and the advantages that they bring, are well understood. Some theoretical frameworks emphasize the importance of regulation and tax policies, positing that firms differ in their ability to benefit from a given ownership form.[30]

Do these different motivations explain behavior? China's government hospitals have no stockholders clamoring for net revenues. They nonetheless can act very much like profit maximizers, as we will discuss in more detail later. That irony shrinks when you learn that nonprofit hospitals in the United States, which also have no clamoring shareholders, often produce revenues that well exceed their costs – quantities in other contexts that would be termed *profits*. In fact, seven of the ten most "profitable" hospitals in the United States in 2013 were nonprofit, earning net revenues ranging from $163.5 million to over $302 million.[31] With profits verboten, these surpluses went to other purposes. The nonprofits' CEOs, for example, often receive salaries that are quite large, though not as lofty as those of their for-profit counterparts.[32]

But what orchestrators of collaborative approaches need to know, when choosing among ownership forms for specific health sector goals, is if these patterns of behavior matter for performance. For example, does the quality of hospital care differ systematically by the organizational form of the hospital? The evidence is murky. The bulk of empirical studies rely on data from the United States, one of the few countries where all three ownership forms directly compete for patients. One meta-analysis found that the majority of studies

---

[28] M. Pauly, and M. Redisch, 1973, "The Not-for-profit Hospital as a Physicians' Cooperative," *The American Economic Review*, 63(1), 87–99.

[29] A. Ben-Ner, and B. Gui, *The Nonprofit Sector in the Mixed Economy*. University of Michigan Press, 1993. Some theories of nonprofits emphasize meeting the expectations of donors (Rose-Ackerman 1987; Lakdawalla and Philipson 1998 and 2001; and Glaeser and Shleifer 2001). As Sloan (2000) and Malani, Philipson, and David (2003) point out, since donations are a very minor source of revenue for nonprofit hospitals, assuming that a donor is the key organizational decision maker (Lakdawalla and Philipson 1998 and 2001) is highly questionable for hospitals.

[30] David (2009) models private nonprofits and for-profits without any assumption of different objectives. Lakdawalla and Philipson (1998) consider firms that have different objectives, but there is not necessarily a one-to-one correspondence between objectives and choice of ownership status. See G. David, 2009, "The Convergence between For-profit and Nonprofit Hospitals in the United States," *International Journal of Health Care Finance and Economics*, 9(4), 403–428; A. Malani, T. Philipson, and G. David, 2003 Theories of firm behavior in the nonprofit sector. A synthesis and empirical evaluation. In *The governance of not-for-profit organizations* (pp. 181–216). University of Chicago Press.

[31] "Non-profit Hospitals Earn Substantial Profits." Johns Hopkins Bloomberg School of Public Health. N.p., May 2, 2016. Web. August 10, 2016.

[32] A study covering 98 percent of private nonprofit hospitals in the United States found that CEO compensation varies widely; the mean compensation was $595,781 (median, $404,938) in 2009, with far higher pay to those managing large urban hospitals. CEO compensation was found to be positively associated with patient satisfaction but not with the hospital's care protocols, patient outcomes, or community benefit (uncompensated care). Joynt, Karen E. et al. 2014, "Compensation of Chief Executive Officers at Non-profit US Hospitals," *JAMA Internal Medicine*, 174(1), 61–67.

reported no statistically significant difference between for-profit and nonprofit hospitals in mortality or other adverse events. Another set of studies, however, pointed to higher adverse event rates in for-profit hospitals than in private nonprofit hospitals. Many studies that compared nonprofit hospitals to government hospitals found that government hospitals provided lower quality. But studies that found that ownership status affected quality of care were influenced by their differences across regions, markets, and eras. Overall, the *true* effect of ownership appears to depend greatly on context.[33]

What *does* appear consistently to differ is the array of services provided. Analyses of US data have shown that government hospitals are most likely to supply the unprofitable services that are disproportionately needed by the poor; for-profits are likely to supply the most profitable services; and nonprofits operate mostly in the broad middle ground.[34]

Thus, motivations and characteristic behaviors among governmental, nonprofit, and for-profit health-care providers differ significantly. It is possible that each of the three forms should be favored, at least provisionally, in some contexts and discouraged in others, as suggested by our discussion of comparative advantage in Chapter 2.

But the actual landscape is often much more mixed than theory would indicate. What forces led to the tangle of different institutional forms in the United States, for example, and why does it not evolve into something conceptually tidier? Is this mixed ecology of government, private nonprofit and for-profit ownership socially desirable? And if not, how can it be changed for the better?

There are two primary explanations for the survival of institutions over long periods of time. Their fitness may earn them their longevity. Or the causal arrow could go in the other direction; longevity itself might confer advantages. Consider the major US nonprofit hospitals of the twenty-first century. Many of them are massive institutions, which have built significant endowments over time, a major competitive advantage, and a direct and indirect source of prestige. They fill their boards with powerful and generous citizens, enabling them to collect further resources and to influence policies. In the organizational world, new forms have to have a much bigger edge to be able to usurp entrenched incumbents.

More generally, nonprofit hospitals – mostly private in the United States, mostly government-owned and managed in China – will usually have survival advantages within a collaborative health-care system for multiple reasons:

- Bureaucracy and politics broadly defer to the status quo.
- These hospitals enjoy resources and prestige that confer direct advantages as well as political and policy influence.

[33] Karen Eggleston, Yu-Chu Shen, Joseph Lau, Christopher H. Schmid, and Jia Chan, 2008, "Hospital Ownership and Quality of Care: What Explains the Different Results?" *Health Economics*, 17(12), 1345–1362.

[34] Horwitz, Jill R., 2005, "Making Profits and Providing Care: Comparing Nonprofit, For-profit, and Government Hospitals," *Health Affairs*, 24(3), 790–801.

- In allocating resources, they can function almost like for-profit hospitals. As the saying goes, "No margin, no mission." To the extent that for-profits have efficiency advantages, nonprofits could be significantly handicapped; therefore, some nonprofit hospitals, especially in the United States, now hire for-profit companies to serve as their managers.
- The expectation, and at times requirement, that nonprofits would provide significant charity and subsidized care is dramatically reduced under widespread insurance – such as the ACA in the United States, and China's universal coverage through local government-run programs – which significantly decreases the need for such care.

REGULATION AND COMPETITION

Most health systems impose a series of regulatory restrictions on private providers that seek to align their activities with the creation of public value. For example in the United States, among the most salient of these are laws leveraging public purchasing to require private providers to serve vulnerable populations, and rules on nonprofits that require community benefits (such as charity care, care for public-program beneficiaries, community services, including 24-hour trauma centers, and programs for special-needs populations) in order to maintain their tax-exempt status. Although admittedly imperfect, these regulatory structures do provide a useful framework for demonstrating that private providers can be harnessed to serve specific populations. We will explore examples in both China and the United States.

The role of competition in health care is more controversial and differs in the spheres of insurance and delivery of services.[35] Should insurance systems be designed to promote competition, as does the ACA or Obamacare in the United States, or should there be a single insurer so as to avoid problems of adverse selection and the strategic maneuvers by insurers to avoid it? The simple answer to that monumental question is: "It all depends."

A full discussion lies outside the scope of this chapter, but it is worth noting that ownership and competition are distinct and can be combined in multiple ways. For example, reliance on private insurance by no means ensures competition. For decades after WWII, Blue Cross-Blue Shield was the predominant health insurer in important regions of the United States, though other insurers could have entered. Conversely, a government-run insurance program can constitute one choice among a menu of coverage options. China has chosen the monopolist route for its insurance provision, with governments in each locality managing "social" (i.e., tax-subsidized or compulsory) health insurance programs for specific populations. Competition is relegated to the supplementary insurance market, and to the delivery system.

---

[35] Martin Gaynor and Robert J. Town, 2011, "Competition in Health Care Markets," chapter 9 in M. Pauly, T. Mcguire, P. Barros, eds., *Handbook of Health Economics*, 2, Elsevier, 499–637.

On the service delivery side, relatively robust evidence suggests that patient choice of health service provider (provider competition), when well regulated, can improve quality.[36] Indeed, a famous paper in this literature is entitled: "Death by market power," showing that lack of provider competition can lead to higher mortality.[37] Thus, policymakers, in orchestrating collaboration, should be cautious of local monopoly care organizations – whether public or private – that claim their dominant position can better coordinate care and improve outcomes while controlling spending. Social value emerges when patients can "vote with their feet," even if that means some providers focus on patient-observable dimensions of care as opposed to its technical quality. Evidence also links competition for patients to hospital management quality.[38] When integrated networks or primary care providers must compete to attract patients with the services they provide, this offers a counterbalance to under-provision, and gives policymakers a key feedback loop for monitoring whether providers are truly meeting people's needs.

On the other hand, health care differs significantly from restaurants and other services for which feet-voting clearly spurs efficiency. Competition among providers can lead to selection of profitable patients and – especially in combination with fee-for-service payment – spur a "medical arms race" of overinvestment in high technologies or other inefficient behaviors. Thus, competition, incentives, and accountability all are important tools for creating public value in collaborative arrangements, applied according to the comparative advantage of each combination; contracting and competition among for-profit providers may work well for most aspects of dental care or pharmaceutical development, but fail entirely for care for individuals with severe cognitive impairment or mental illness.

Health Care in the United States

The US health-care system produces a mediocre outcome at extraordinary expense. Analysts trace this high spending to several features of the US system, from higher prices for physician services, pharmaceuticals, and other inputs, to a more expensive mix of services and higher administrative costs.[39] US health-care

---

[36] See, for example, Cooper, Zack, Stephen Gibbons, Simon Jones, and Alistair McGuire, 2011, "Does Hospital Competition Save Lives? Evidence from the English NHS Patient Choice Reforms," *The Economic Journal*, 121(554), F228–F260; and Gaynor, Martin, Carol Propper, and Stephan Seiler. 2016, "Free to Choose? Reform, Choice, and Consideration Sets in the English National Health Service," *American Economic Review*, 106(11), 3521–3557.

[37] Gaynor, Martin, Rodrigo Moreno-Serra, and Carol Propper, 2013, "Death by Market Power: Reform, Competition, and Patient Outcomes in the National Health Service," *American Economic Journal: Economic Policy*, 5(4), 134–66.

[38] Bloom, Nicholas, et al., 2015, "The Impact of Competition on Management Quality: Evidence from Public Hospitals," *The Review of Economic Studies*, 82(2), 457–489.

[39] See for example Victor R. Fuchs, *Health Economics and Policy: Selected Writings by Victor Fuchs*. Singapore: World Scientific, 2018.

institutions supporting these features differ significantly from those other high-income democracies, in large part because the United States embraces a more collaborative approach, stemming from distrust of a strong government role in regulatory power, insurance provision, and medical care delivery.[40] To explore the genesis of the current system, we start with the history of public and private health service providers.

History of Mixed Ownership in the US Health Sector

We illustrate the historical dynamics of mixed ownership in the United States with hospitals, which developed "from places of dreaded impurity and exiled human wreckage into awesome citadels of science and bureaucratic order" (Starr 1982: 145). Some industries that are now as important or large as health care did not even exist as such a century ago, but hospitals (or their asylum and almshouse predecessors) did. Health care has experienced breathtaking technological transformation over the past century but perhaps a surprising degree of organizational stasis. Of 6,852 hospitals providing care in the United States in 1928, fifteen had been founded before 1800.

In the United States, from early days, a division of roles by ownership structure prevailed, with government-owned institutions as providers of last resort. Government provision and private provision to some extent were complements, not substitutes. The governance of the sector did not at first involve the collaboration that is the subject of this book, but rather a kind of symbiosis between two different "species" in the same ecosystem. Government-funded care was delivered directly through government-owned providers, whereas private care was mostly provided by charitable, philanthropic organizations. As Rosemary Stevens notes in her account of American hospitals in the twentieth century,

[One] attribute of the tradition of private benevolence ... was the assumption by trustees and associates of the charitable hospital that local governments, rather than themselves, were the appropriate and essential residual caregivers. Governments, not hospitals, were to be charged with services to the 'unworthy' and unwanted, that is, to social failures, such as the down-and-out, the incurable, and the chronically sick. ... It was taken for granted that local-government hospitals in major cities should support the role of the charitable (and incidentally the proprietary) hospitals by taking patients these hospitals were not prepared to admit. ... Since government hospitals provided a necessary support structure for the success of private charity in major cities, the number of local-government hospitals did not diminish when other hospitals opened, as one might intuitively expect. Instead, in tandem, government's role became even more important. ... The two sets of institutions were interdependent.[41]

---

[40] "In other high-income democracies, strong egalitarian pressures plus a willingness to use government to require participation result in universal coverage [and lower spending]. In the United States, weaker support for redistribution and a desire to limit the role of government has prevented this result." Fuchs 2018, *Health Economics and Policy*, p. 289.

[41] Stevens, Rosemary, *In Sickness and in Wealth: American Hospitals in the Twentieth Century*. New York: Basic Books, 1989, 27–28.

Indeed, government and private inpatient bed capacity grew in tandem in the early twentieth century. New York City illustrates this symbiosis. Between 1910 and 1934, the total number of general hospital beds in New York increased by 76 percent (from 20,437 to 36,056), while the percentage of beds in government hospitals remained constant, at 41 percent.[42]

Government hospitals were commonly viewed (often correctly) as of lower quality, particularly in the early twentieth century, when they had only recently evolved from almshouses. The Depression provides an interesting case study of the government role as provider of last resort; it illustrates the susceptibility of private (particularly investor-owned) providers to closure during unprofitable times. In 1928, on the eve of the Depression, 2,435 US hospitals of 6,852 were proprietary and mainly small (two thirds with fewer than twenty-five beds).[43] Between 1928 and 1935, 43 percent of proprietary hospitals closed, compared to only 11 percent of church-owned hospitals, 17 percent of hospitals owned by corporations (both nonprofit and for-profit), and 19 percent of government hospitals.[44] During those same years, total capital investment in proprietary hospitals plummeted by 46 percent, whereas investment in nonprofits and government general hospitals increased by 12 percent and 51 percent, respectively.[45]

In the last third of the twentieth century, Medicare expanded the "we-pay, you-deliver" feature that remains the defining characteristic of America's collaborative health-care delivery. But government's role in paying for aspects of the health system goes back further, and is much broader. It proceeded piecemeal, rather than from some grand vision of how government should support health care. Today, beyond subsidizing care at the time of delivery, either directly or indirectly, the public sector subsidizes the training of personnel including physicians, funds research, and enables tax-exempt bonds to fund the construction of facilities. This construction support got launched in major fashion in 1946 when the Hill–Burton program of hospital construction was established. That program

... inspired a commercial transformation of the public sector. Local-government hospitals constructed under Hill-Burton typically served the entire population of their surrounding communities, not just the poor. ... By 1961, public hospitals obtained more than one-half of their aggregate income from paying patients, a stunning departure from prewar times.[46]

Despite resounding success in its goal to spur hospital construction, the Hill–Burton Act provides a cautionary tale of the risks associated with collaborative governance. In the lavishly subsidized nineteenth-century expansion of America's railroads (discussed in Chapter 3), public and private interests were broadly well-aligned. More miles of track quite reliably generated significant public benefits

---

[42] Boychuk, Terry, *The Making and Meaning of Hospital Policy in the United States and Canada.* Ann Arbor, Michigan: The University of Michigan Press, 1999, 75, Table 3.3.
[43] Rorem 1930.   [44] Stevens 1989: 147, table 6.2.   [45] Ibid.: 152, table 6.4.
[46] Boychuk 1999: 152.

alongside corporate profits. Hill–Burton was justified not merely on the diffuse social benefits of hospital construction, but also on a quid pro quo: hospitals built with governmental money incurred a special duty to provide care even to those too poor to pay for it.[47] However, the Act lacked a robust system of monitoring, enforcement, or penalties for hospitals not complying with this duty. In fact, this uncompensated care expectation was not even explicitly defined until 1972. So the quo of collective financing lost its quid of collective payoff. Audits in the 1970s revealed widespread noncompliance – around 70 percent of Hill–Burton hospitals failed to meet the uncompensated care provisions – and little capacity in state agencies to enforce compliance.[48] Recently, some states have sought to enforce uncompensated care provisions as related to nonprofits' tax benefits rather than to long-ago construction funds, by insisting on much more detailed record keeping about whether the cost of such care is at least equal to the foregone real estate taxes that nonprofit hospitals enjoy.[49] Under the ACA, uncompensated care has become far less important than it was earlier.

The first half of the twentieth century saw the rise of private nonprofits from a little over half of the nation's bed capacity to 70 percent, where it has generally remained. The government share declined gently as the for-profit share rose, with each converging to about 15 percent by 2000. Although the government-owned share of US community hospital capacity declined, public ownership still looms large among facilities that serve vulnerable patient groups, such as the severely and chronically mentally ill.[50]

As government retreated as a provider, it stepped boldly forward as a payer. The US system of collaborative governance in health care took shape over roughly the final third of the twentieth century. Publicly financed insurance programs, predominantly Medicare for those aged sixty-five and above and Medicaid for the poor and disabled, came to cover more and more of the nation's health bill, helping to meet several public purposes. For example, evidence shows that the adoption of Medicare increased utilization and improved risk protection (reduced out-of-pocket spending) for the elderly, while also spurring technology adoption

---

[47] One might speculate as to why the United States chose to subsidize private hospitals but land-grant public universities when expanding health care and higher education, respectively. Victor Fuchs suggests one important reason may have been physicians' greater influence, and opposition to government control, compared to that of professors. Another might have been that what we term "preference discretion" appeared less likely in medical care than in educational curricula.

[48] See discussion in Dowell, Michael A., 1987, "Hill-Burton: The Unfulfilled Promise," *Journal of Health Politics, Policy and Law*, 12(1), 153–176; and Rose, Marilyn G., 1975, "Federal Regulation of Services to the Poor Under the Hill-Burton Act: Realities and Pitfalls," *Nw. UL Rev.* 70, 168.

[49] Given that prices in the health-care system rarely reflect the resources involved due to the heavy level of subsidies and cross-subsidies that permeate the system, nonprofit hospitals have considerable ability to manipulate these cost numbers upward.

[50] As noted by Frank and McGuire (2000: 936), "direct public services for the most seriously [mentally] ill persons is a common feature of health systems" despite widely differing approaches to care for the broader populations.

and per capita medical spending;[51] there is no evidence it increased survival benefits or pharmaceutical innovation.[52] Regulation of privately provided supplementary insurance ("Medigap") and contracting with private health maintenance organizations for some programs (e.g., Medicare Advantage, Medicaid managed care) has long been a feature of these US social health insurance programs. And when the United States later decided to expand Medicare coverage to prescription drugs, it chose contracting out through private insurance plans in Medicare Part D.[53] Evidence accumulates that private plans do behave differently from public plans (e.g., systematically setting higher consumer cost sharing for drugs with more elastic demand),[54] although debate continues about whether private insurance plans increase efficiency and whether consumers can effectively exercise choice.[55]

These social insurance programs purchased services from a transformed delivery system. That system features a very large share of private providers. It also includes a remnant of government-owned providers that now often are apt to repudiate their conventional role as providers of last resort for the most vulnerable in order to compete instead for a broader patient clientele.

An overall scorecard for the American health care system would show *overpriced and underperforming*. But aggregate assessments tell little about the performance of parts. These parts are diverse, complex, and display an intricate blend of public and private components. Some parts perform very badly, and some quite well, with no simple alignment between quality and organizational form. There is one prominent area where government pays for *and* delivers care – the vast network of veterans' hospitals run by the Department of Veterans' Affairs. In recent years, these hospitals have been fiercely criticized for delivering low-quality care, often after substantial waits.[56]

But the complex health-care sector defies simple generalization, such as one of governmental ham-handedness. Health research, for example, offers a contrasting

---

[51] A. Finkelstein, 2007, "The Aggregate Effects of Health Insurance: Evidence from the Introduction of Medicare," *The Quarterly Journal of Economics*, 122(1), 1–37.
[52] Finkelstein, Amy, and Robin McKnight, 2008, "What did Medicare do? The Initial Impact of Medicare on Mortality and Out of Pocket Medical Spending," *Journal of Public Economics*, 92 (7), 1644–1668; D. Acemoglu, D. Cutler, A. Finkelstein, and J. Linn, 2006, "Did Medicare Induce Pharmaceutical Innovation?" *American Economic Review*, 96(2), 103–107.
[53] J. Gruber, 2017, "Delivering Public Health Insurance through Private Plan Choice in the United States," *Journal of Economic Perspectives*, 31(4), 3–22.
[54] L. Einav, A. Finkelstein, and M. Polyakova, 2018, "Private Provision of Social Insurance: Drug-specific Price Elasticities and Cost Sharing in Medicare Part D," *American Economic Journal: Economic Policy*, 10(3), 122–53.
[55] See for example J. Abaluck, and J. Gruber, 2011, "Choice Inconsistencies among the Elderly: Evidence from Plan Choice in the Medicare Part D Program," *American Economic Review*, 101 (4), 1180–1210.
[56] The scandal surfaced in April 2014; see Bloche, M. Gregg, 2016, "Scandal as a Sentinel Event – Recognizing Hidden Cost–Quality Trade-offs," *New England Journal of Medicine*, 374(11), 1001–1003; Kizer, Kenneth W., and Ashish K. Jha, 2014, "Restoring Trust in VA Health Care," *New England Journal of Medicine*, 371(4), 295–297.

tale. The intramural research program at the National Institutes of Health (NIH), paid for and run by the federal government, is highly regarded, as is the NIH role in addressing market failures and funding innovation.[57] US firms are also well-recognized globally for innovation in devices, pharmaceuticals and biotechnology, and in AI for a range of medical technologies. Government has partnered to leverage these private strengths for certain public goals, such as the FDA's monitoring drug safety through the Sentinel Initiative, or harnessing the power of big data analytics to strengthen regulation in the Information Exchange and Data Transformation (INFORMED) initiative's "incubator for collaborative oncology regulatory science."[58] In service delivery, another bright spot, both quite large and classically collaborative, is the nation's network of community health centers.

The Case of Community Health Centers
Community Health Centers (CHCs) form the largest primary care system in the United States, serving about 23 million patients a year in more than 9,000 economically disadvantaged locations. Community, migrant, homeless, and public-housing health centers are nonprofit, community-directed providers, also known as Federally Qualified Health Centers (FQHCs); they are located in high-need areas (based on metrics such as high poverty rate, higher than average infant mortality, and few private physicians). By law, patients constitute at least 51 percent of the governing boards of FQHCs, and the centers serve patients regardless of insurance status or ability to pay.

The CHC system was implemented against the 1960s backdrop of the "War on Poverty" and the civil rights movement. Although vilified originally as "socialized medicine," the vast majority of the CHCs are private nonprofits, not governmental health agencies. That status is reinforced by the legal

---

[57] "Research based on unproven ideas is risky and prone to failure. That makes such research difficult to fund and to attract the critical mass of scientists needed to develop an idea. The U.S. National Institutes of Health plays an important role in addressing this failure in the market for scientific research. With a $37 billion annual budget, NIH is the world's largest funder of biomedical research. ... [and the] NIH funded edge science at a higher rate than it funded less-innovative science" albeit less so in the most recent decade. Jay Bhattacharya and Mikko Packalen, "Encouraging Edge Science through NIH Funding Practices," Stanford Institute for Economic Policy Research Policy Brief, November 2018, https://siepr.stanford.edu/research/publications/encouraging-edge-science-through-nih-funding-practices [accessed 30 December 2018]. See also Collins, Francis, MD, PhD. "NIH in the 21st Century: The Director's Perspective." ASL. U.S. Department of Health and Human Services, June 15, 2010. Web. September 3, 2016. Since its start in 1887, the NIH has now grown to support researchers in all 50 states and almost 100 other countries, and more than 130 researchers funded under the NIH have gone on to win Nobel Prizes.

[58] See www.hhs.gov/idealab/projects-item/information-exchange-and-data-transformation-informed-initiative; Khozin, Sean, Geoffrey Kim, and Richard Pazdur. 2017, "Regulatory Watch: From Big Data to Smart Data: FDA's INFORMED Initiative," *Nature Reviews Drug Discovery*, 16, 306; and Sentinel Initiative: http://www.fda.gov/Safety/ FDAsSentinelInitiative/ucm2007250.htm; Steven Findlay, "The FDA's Sentinel Initiative," Health Affairs Health Policy Brief, June 4, 2015. DOI: 10.1377/hpb20150604.936915.

requirement that its board have a majority of "active consumers" such as patients and community members.[59] Legal stipulations also specify that a CHC board limit the representation of those without aligned objectives, a strategy that curbs potential payoff and preference discretion.[60]

Community Health Centers receive funding from multiple federal sources, including Medicare and Medicaid as well as Public Health Service grants.[61] Community Health Centers charge on a "pay-as-you-can" sliding scale for services and medications (with subsidized rates at in-house pharmacies); they also often offer home visits and transportation to appointments.[62] Expansion of insurance since the ACA has bolstered their finances somewhat, although the accompanying surge in demand for services has also strained CHCs and their limited clinical staff. That strain was exacerbated by trying to achieve high metrics for quality when serving disadvantaged populations who face barriers to adherence. There have been reports of reductions in workplace satisfaction[63] and mixed results from quality improvement efforts to become "medical homes."[64]

The National Association of Community Health Centers cites studies that the work done by CHCs would be far costlier if delivered by emergency rooms, conventional hospitals, or specialized facilities, and that it yields aggregate

[59] An FQHC is a public or private nonprofit, charitable, tax-exempt organization that receives funding under Section 330 of the Public Health Service Act, or is determined by the Department of Health and Human Services (DHHS) to meet requirements to receive funding without actually receiving a grant (that is, an FQHC "look-alike"). See Section 1861(aa)(4) of the Social Security Act. National Association of Community Health Centers, "Partnerships between Federally Qualified Health Centers and Local Health Departments for Engaging in the Development of a Community-Based System of Care," 2010, available at www.nachc.com/client/PartnershipsBetweenFederallyQualifiedHealthCentersAndLocalHealth DepartmentsforEngagingInTheDevelopmentOfACommunityBasedSystemOfCareNACHCOct-ober2010.pdf [accessed November 20, 2015].

[60] Within the nonconsumer minority, no more than half of the members may be people who "derive more than ten percent of their annual income from the health care industry." National Association of Community Health Centers, "Partnerships between Federally Qualified Health Centers and Local Health Departments for Engaging in the Development of a Community-Based System of Care," 2010, p. 18.

[61] www.nachc.com/client/documents/12.14%20NACHC%20Comments%20on%20OIG% 20Safe%20Harbors1.pdf.

[62] Bailey, Martha J., and Andrew Goodman-Bacon, 2015, "The War on Poverty's Experiment in Public Medicine: Community Health Centers and the Mortality of Older Americans," *American Economic Review*, 105(3), 1067–1104.

[63] M. W. Friedberg, R. O. Reid, J. W. Timbie, C. Setodji, A. Kofner, B. Weidmer, and K. Kahn, August 1, 2017, "Federally Qualified Health Center Clinicians and Staff Increasingly Dissatisfied with Workplace Conditions," *Health Affairs*, 36(8), 1469–1475.

[64] J. W. Timbie, C. M. Setodji, A. Kress, T. A. Lavelle, M. W. Friedberg, P. J. Mendel, E. K. Chen, B. A. Weidmer, C. Buttorff, R. Malsberger, and M. Kommareddi, July 20, 2017, "Implementation of Medical Homes in Federally Qualified Health Centers," *New England Journal of Medicine*, 377(3), 246–256.

annual savings of $24 billion.[65] Surely, more than one factor explains the CHCs' relative success. One consideration is likely the general efficiency of any primary care network, compared to hospital-based services. Additionally, management frequently complements basic medical care with critical support services such as language interpreting and transportation.

The contracting model used for FQHCs has been reviewed and refined over time, following our prescriptions in Chapter 2 long before they were written. The value of the CHC model is manifest in its bipartisan support and expansion under the latest round of national health reforms.[66] The ACA included $11 billion in funding over 5 years for CHCs, $1.5 billion for the National Health Service Corps, and $230 million for graduate medical education with the purpose of increasing the number of staff at CHCs. The ACA also required that private plans sold in the health insurance exchanges offer a contract to at least one CHC in every county that they cover. After the enactment of the ACA, CHCs were active in assisting patients to gain coverage; more than 80 percent of CHCs provided help with Medicaid applications, and 90 percent provided help with private plan enrollment through the exchanges.[67] Community Health Centers also have been an active part of local collaborative approaches to better health, working with county governments, local private insurers, or integrated care providers, and civil society partners representing specific subpopulations.[68]

Regulations That Guide Collaborative Governance

As noted in the previous section, the US health system, like that of most high-income market-based economies, imposes a series of regulatory restrictions on private providers to align their activities with the creation of public value. Adjustment of such regulations shows that applying the four-step process of analysis, assignment, design, and assessment to refine collaborative governance has the potential to create better performance. For example, one analysis explored the consequences when the charity-care requirements imposed on private hospitals by the Hill–Burton Act expired.[69] This study found that once for-profits were off the Hill–Burton hook, they quickly cut back on charity care, diverting poor

---

[65] United States Health Center Fact Sheet, National Association of Community Health Centers, available at www.nachc.com/client//United_States_FS_2014.pdf.

[66] *The New York Times* editorial, "Help from the Obama Administration for Community Health Centers," www.nytimes.com/2015/08/19/opinion/help-from-the-obama-administration-for-community-health-centers.html.

[67] Peter Shin, "The Health Safety Net: Community Health Centers' Vital Role." National Institutes of Health Care Management Foundation: Transforming Health Care through Evidence July 2016.

[68] For one such example, see A. Fremont, A. Y. Kim, K. Bailey, H. R. Hanley, C. Thorne, R. J. Dudl, R. M. Kaplan, S. M. Shortell, and A. N. DeMaria, September 1, 2018, "One In Five Fewer Heart Attacks: Impact, Savings, And Sustainability In San Diego County Collaborative," *Health Affairs*, 37 (9), 1457–1465.

[69] Almond, Douglas, Janet Currie, and Emilia Simeonova, 2011, "Public vs. Private Provision of Charity Care? Evidence from the Expiration of Hill–Burton Requirements in Florida," *Journal of Health Economics*, 30(1), 189–199.

patients to public hospitals. The fact that providers' behavior changed when rules were dropped shows that regulations have a function.

Another arena of regulation to constrain the most egregious forms of payoff discretion is that of physician self-referral legislation. Between 2004 and 2010, the growth rate of self-referred services outpaced non-self-referred counterparts by a 7:1 margin for magnetic resonance imaging and a 3.5:1 margin for computed tomography.[70] While some of the discrepancy might be attributable to high-use providers self-selecting into ownership of diagnostic facilities rather than to pernicious overuse, this discrepancy in growth rates nevertheless highlights the challenge that orchestrators of collaborative approaches must confront. They must balance legitimate discretion that may improve coordination, quality, and patient convenience, against more venal forms of self-serving behavior.

The Affordable Care Act

The 2010 ACA, often called Obamacare, was the most significant health-care legislation in decades. Most of its provisions embraced the existing US model of public financing, private delivery, and private health insurers, a fundamentally collaborative approach that requires ongoing refinement.[71] The ACA employed several strategies to increase insurance coverage, a salient goal. It required uninsured individuals to purchase in the marketplaces (formerly called exchanges), penalizing those who failed to do so; significantly subsidized the purchase of insurance by lower-income individuals; expanded Medicaid; allowed young adults through age twenty-six years to stay on their parents' health plan; and continued group coverage through employers or by direct enrollment with insurers. New national standards proscribed insurers from excluding patients with preexisting conditions.

The ACA's combination of government subsidy, required purchase, and penalty otherwise, bolstered the existing system of private insurance coverage. Fourteen states and the District of Columbia chose to run insurance exchanges themselves in 2014. The remaining states left this task to the federal government. The ACA also substantially expanded eligibility for Medicaid, though a 2012 Supreme Court decision rendered state participation in the law's expansion optional. The District of Columbia and twenty-eight states chose to implement Medicaid expansion.[72] In states choosing otherwise, people with incomes at or above the federal poverty level can apply for subsidies for private plans in the marketplaces, but the estimated 5 million people living below the poverty level

---

[70] Adashi, Eli Y., and Robert P. Kocher, 2015, "Physician Self-referral: Regulation by Exceptions," *JAMA*, 313(5), 457–458; www.gao.gov/assets/660/655443.pdf.

[71] See discussion in D. M. Cutler, 2015, "From the Affordable Care Act to Affordable Care," *JAMA*, 314(4), 337–338. DOI:10.1001/jama.2015.7683; and Wilensky GR, 2015, "Improving and Refining the Affordable Care Act," JAMA, 314(4), 339–340. DOI:10.1001/jama.2015.5468.

[72] Blumenthal, David, and Sara R. Collins, 2014, "Health Care coverage under the Affordable Care Act—a Progress Report," *New England Journal of Medicine*, 371(3), 275–281.

cannot (since lawmakers had assumed that they would be covered by Medicaid). As a result of these political differences on the propriety of a collaborative governance approach to expanding coverage, expansion of coverage for low-income adults has depended on whether they resided in states that did or did not choose to expand Medicaid.[73] Where coverage expanded, it helped protect Americans from the risk of catastrophic spending, and perhaps enhanced prevention.[74] However, and not unexpectedly, expenditure continues to increase, as does the debate about how to enhance the value of that spending.

The ACA could be bold because the Democrats controlled the presidency and the legislature. Nevertheless, as is the norm in the United States, it was constrained by the interests of major players in place. For example, it specified as follows: no government insurer may directly compete with private insurance plans in the exchanges; comparative effectiveness but not cost-effectiveness may guide policies; and Medicare cannot bargain for reduced pharmaceutical prices. The ACA reforms build upon the existing system of multiple insurance plans. That system enables competition, but layers on administrative costs[75] and adds the governance challenge of managing adverse selection and risk selection in insurance markets. What is feasible can be far from optimal. Some consider the ACA the best that could be achieved in a complex political environment; others hold that a more coherent deal could have been struck.

Accountable Care Organizations and Payment Reforms

The promotion of innovation in payment and delivery systems is one cornerstone of US health reforms. For example, Accountable Care Organizations (ACOs) aim to employ organizational innovations, such as capitation linked to integrated care initiatives, to improve the accountability for quality and cost in the US health system. An ACO is a collection of health-care organizations that agree to accept responsibility for a population of beneficiaries. It remains to be seen if ACOs can overcome the same barriers confronted by integrated-care organizations such as Health Maintenance Organizations in the 1990s.[76] The heterogeneity of ACOs bears some resemblance to charter schools in the education field. Their

[73] B. D. Sommers, M. Z. Gunja, K. Finegold, and T. Musco, 2015, "Changes in Self-reported Insurance Coverage, Access to Care, and Health Under the Affordable Care Act," *JAMA*, 314 (4), 366–374. DOI:10.1001/jama.2015.8421.

[74] Kaufman, Harvey W., Zhen Chen, Vivian A. Fonseca, and Michael J. McPhaul, 2015, "Surge in Newly Identified Diabetes among Medicaid Patients in 2014 within Medicaid Expansion States under the Affordable Care Act," *Diabetes Care*, 38(5), 833–837.

[75] Cutler, David, Elizabeth Wikler, and Peter Basch. 2012, "Reducing Administrative Costs and Improving the Health Care System," *New England Journal of Medicine*, 367(20), 1875–1878.

[76] Burns, Lawton R., and Mark V. Pauly, 2012, "Accountable Care Organizations may have Difficulty Avoiding the Failures of Integrated Delivery Networks of the 1990s," *Health Affairs*, 31(11), 2407–2416.

performance to date varies from dreadful to stellar.[77] If policymakers could scale up or replicate the successful cases and weed out the worst performers, we could have an excellent collaborative system.[78] The words come easily; the accomplishment would be much harder.

A critical tool of collaborative design is systematic evaluation and recrafting of the incentives used to align the behavior of private purchasers and providers with public value. The ACOs and the legislation with bipartisan support introducing physician payment reforms – the Medicare Access and CHIP Reauthorization Act of 2015 (MACRA) – suggest that policymakers across the ideological spectrum see the promise of alternative payment models to reward quality and constrain costs. Government purchasers of any service should craft meaningful monitoring and well-tailored incentives to promote good behavior and discourage bad. Payoff discretion is a vampire sucking resources from health care. Payment systems that reward high-quality cost-effective care are the garlic that wards them off.

The ACO and MACRA innovations provide explicit rewards for serving public needs at private cost – a hallmark of good collaborative governance. However, only time will tell if they live up to their potential. Sometimes "public value" is extraordinarily difficult to assess because its multiple objectives (quality, access, *and* cost) develop over time and at all times are challenging to measure.

Overall, the United States' record in the health sector (including, most recently, the COVID-19 response) is sobering. Nevertheless, it can take pride in trying to improve – occasionally undertaking patient and persistent analytical and managerial work of the AADA cycle – despite the political inhibitions of trying to reform such a significant sector of the economy. Such political inhibitions may be weaker in China. Yet, China too has a health system that was severely strained by the COVID-19 pandemic. Its system also has underlying entrenched interests, and those interests are likely to grow in power as the Chinese sector expands. It is to China's experience that we now turn.

Health Care in China

China's health system, as with most features of this rapidly developing nation, has undergone much faster evolution over recent decades than America's. China announced national health-care reforms in spring 2009, continuing probably the largest expansion of health insurance in the world after the 2003 SARS crisis. In a sequence recalling the trajectory of other universal care campaigns, China focused first on expanding coverage through greater public health-care financing, without any dramatic changes in the delivery system. The public–private mix had been trending toward the reverse of the US system, tilted toward private financing

---

[77] McWilliams J. M., Hatfield L. A., Landon B. E., Hamed P, and Chernew M.E., "Medicare Spending after 3 Years of the Medicare Shared Savings Program," *New England Journal of Medicine*, 379(12), 1139–1149, September 5, 2018.

[78] Jacob J. A., 2015, "Medicare at 50: Reflections From Former CMS Administrator Donald M. Berwick," *JAMA*, 314(4), 324–326. DOI:10.1001/jama.2015.7842.

(mainly patient out-of-pocket payments) but government delivery. The reforms pushed back against that pattern, infusing a large amount of government funds into the health sector, and welcoming private sector delivery for some services. As noted earlier, China achieved universal coverage through a system of social health insurance. This system is based on two or three different varieties of local monopoly plans: compulsory UEBMI for formal sector employees in urban areas; and subsidized voluntary local monopoly insurance plans for rural residents and urban non-employed – the NCMS and URBMI, respectively, which many localities have merged into a single larger "resident basic insurance" risk pool. Currently, about one billion Chinese are covered by the "Urban-Rural Residents' Basic Medical Insurance," insurance with benefits roughly one-fifth those of the 400 million urban employees under UEBMI. These ongoing disparities in coverage leave those with rural *hukou* and without formal sector employment with much greater risk of illness-induced poverty and poorer health outcomes.[79] Current policy initiatives under *Healthy China 2030* and other directives seek to help close this gap, but it has long-lasting implications.

China's system of universal coverage involves a purchaser–provider split. The government-owned hospitals and clinics come under the National Health Commission, which also oversees the broad range of health and aging policies. The health insurance (purchaser) functions fall under the new National Healthcare Security Administration and its provincial and local branches. Commercial insurance companies' involvement has been mostly in offering supplementary coverage for the wealthy or for specific dread diseases, or in providing administrative services for public health insurance plans.

Total spending has grown rapidly, absorbing an increasing share of the economy – more than 6 percent of China's GDP in 2016 – and continues to grow. With the obvious exception of the extraordinary health system response required for the novel coronavirus pandemic that started in Wuhan in late 2019, China's policies increasingly focus on the service delivery system for acute and chronic disease (rather than infectious disease) and improving the quality, efficiency, and sustainability of the overall health system.

History of Mixed Ownership in the PRC Health Sector

China's health care is largely delivered by government-owned hospitals and clinics. Consistent with the general SOE policy of "grasping the large and letting go of the small," private-sector entry and (limited) privatization have transformed the ownership structure of providers such as clinics, village doctors, and some health centers, all the time keeping key provider organizations under government

---

[79] See discussion in Eggleston (2019), Meng et al. and Hu Shanlian [in Chinese]. 2019, "Review and Expectation of New Healthcare Reform in China–Strategies, Role of Government, Market, and Incentives," *Soft Science of Health*, 33(9), 3–6.

TABLE 7.2 *China's health-care delivery system by ownership type, 2016*

	Public (%)	Nonprofit (%)	For-Profit (%)
Hospital beds	78.3	10.3	11.4
Inpatient admissions	84.2	7.9	7.9
Outpatient hospital visits	87.1	6.5	6.4
Primary health-care facilities[81]	54.3	20.3	25.4

Source: Author's calculations based on data from China's health statistical yearbooks.

ownership.[80] Thus, larger organizations – especially urban secondary and tertiary hospitals, the "commanding heights" of health-care delivery – remain under government control.

Table 7.2 summarizes the 2016 distribution of various health services between government-owned, private for-profit, and private nonprofit providers. Government hospitals represent 78.3 percent of hospital beds. Of the 21.7 percent private share of beds, the growth of private nonprofits has translated into an almost even split between nonprofit and for-profit hospitals. Private providers capture a smaller share of inpatient admissions or visits to hospital outpatient departments, reflecting the continued crowding and higher occupancy rates at government hospitals. The private sector accounts for a much larger share – almost half – of primary care providers, such as community health centers and stations in urban areas, and village clinics in rural areas. Most township health centers remain government-run.

Government hospitals' share of inpatient beds declined to 74 percent by 2018 – still a commanding majority – from 94 percent a decade earlier, despite the almost doubling in the absolute number of government beds. The expansion of the private sector has been promoted by a series of policies.[82] In fact, in a step distinctive among post-socialist economies, China's officials set an explicit target for expanding the share of health delivery supplied through the private sector, although most provinces failed to reach that goal (of private health-care providers accounting for 20 percent of hospital beds and provision of services).[83] Some local officials in Shenzhen interviewed by one of the authors even claimed that, in light of prior

[80] Karen Eggleston, "Demographic Challenges: Healthcare and Elder Care," chapter 6 in Thomas Fingar and Jean C. Oi, eds., *Fateful Decisions: Choices That Will Shape China's Future,* Stanford University Press, 2020, pp. 151–179; and "'*Kan Bing Nan, Kan Bing Gui*': Challenges for China's Healthcare System Thirty Years into Reform," chapter 9 in Jean C. Oi, Scott Rozelle, and Xueguang Zhou, eds., *Growing Pains: Tensions and Opportunities in China's Transformation.* Stanford, CA: Walter H. Shorenstein Asia-Pacific Research Center, 2010, pp. 229–272.

[81] Village clinics, township health centers, community health stations, and community health centers.

[82] See, for example, http://en.nhfpc.gov.cn/2014–06/10/content_17575287.htm, "Opinions on speeding up non-public investment in health development" [accessed November 24, 2015].

[83] The State Council, 2012. The Twelfth Five-Year Plan of Health Care Development.

policies discouraging private institutions at the core of the health-care system, as well as patient leeriness about unfamiliar private options, China's private providers required more than a level playing field; they needed "affirmative action."

What has motivated officials to promote the growth of the private sector? Some appear to espouse "collaboration for resources," while others seek to spur productivity improvement of the existing public delivery system by fostering competition for patients. Unsurprisingly, the former motivation is more common in poorer regions, and the latter in richer regions. In health care and in other spheres in China, collaboration for private resources tends to be embraced by localities with limited GDP per capita, as illustrated in Chapter 6 on education. More affluent regions, if promoting a private sector role at all, do so more to collaborate for information and productivity, as well as to expand supply in new services (such as home services for the elderly). This difference between poor and rich regions leads to an interesting bimodal pattern of private market penetration, with the highest private shares in the poorest and richest province-level cities.

Although China's regions have fostered multiple experiments in ways to harness private resources for health goals, the results have been decidedly mixed. For example, a series of hospital privatizations in the 1990s and 2000s led to government repurchase because of fraud, abuse, or simply disappointing results.[84] When the government privatizes and then quickly reverses course, as has happened in a few localities, something significant has gone wrong.

Patients and the public widely perceive private providers – except for a few elite and high-priced organizations – to be of questionable quality.[85] There is indeed considerable heterogeneity in performance among both public and private providers in China. Some limited evidence is available to buttress this point. One study of hospitals in southern China found little systematic difference in quality between public and private.[86] Another recent study, focusing on primary care, suggests that government-owned and government-managed CHCs "may be able to provide better first-contact care in terms of utilization and coordination of care, and may be better at solving the problem of underutilization of the CHCs as the first-contact point of care, one key problem facing the reforms in China."[87] This finding is not so surprising, in light of the comparative advantages of public and

[84] Qiulin Chen and Wei Zhang, 2015. *To Privatize or Not to Privatize: The Political Economy of Hospital Ownership Conversion in China*, draft manuscript, Renmin University of China and China Academy of Social Sciences.

[85] Interviews of both patients and private providers struggling to establish a reputation lend credence to this statement, although nationally representative data over time is lacking.

[86] Karen Eggleston, Mingshan Lu, Congdong Li, Jian Wang, Zhe Yang, Jing Zhang and Hude Quan, 2010, "Comparing Public and Private Hospitals in China: Evidence from Guangdong," *BMC Health Services Research*, 10, 76. Available at www.biomedcentral.com/1472–6963/10/76.

[87] Wang, Harry H. X., Samuel Y. S. Wong, Martin C. S. Wong, Xiao Lin Wei, Jia Ji Wang, Donald K. T. Li, Jin Ling Tang, Gemma Y. Gao, and Sian M. Griffiths. 2013, "Patients' Experiences in Different Models of Community Health Centers in Southern China," *The Annals of Family Medicine*, 11(6), 517–526.

private providers, and the experience embraced even by conservative American politicians that community health centers serving the most vulnerable should be, and by law must be, nonprofit providers (as discussed in the previous section).

In the realm of insurance, Chinese officials have also embraced a private role in expanding insurance coverage, although most often this takes the form of straightforward contracting with commercial insurance companies for supplementary insurance, without much sharing of discretion. For example, when deciding how best to deepen insurance coverage for the existing basic insurance programs, China's State Council decided to enlist private companies in local-level contracts for catastrophic insurance coverage. Using up to 10 percent of premium funds from basic medical insurance as premiums for catastrophic coverage, such plans provide beneficiaries with additional reimbursement for high medical expenditures above the caps of the basic plan. The insurance company typically receives a performance-based payment after evaluation by the local department of Human Resources and Social Security or a third party of the department's choosing.[88] Some localities have gone further in collaborating with the private sector for information and productivity in insurance administration, such as jointly developing with a private sector firm a system for reviewing medical claims, assessing adherence to clinical and administrative guidelines, avoiding fraud and over-provision of services, and reducing the growth rate of spending through careful oversight.

Although the private sector share continues to grow and diversify its role in insurance and delivery, China is more in a preliminary courtship than in the full embrace of a collaborative approach to health care. Such hesitation, or prudence, may be appropriate in light of the need to develop suitable incentive structures to guide entrepreneurial behavior toward the creation of public value while still motivating innovation and investment. Health care is complicated. Forging accountable collaboration is difficult. Mixing the two too aggressively would be a risky move for a nation still working out the ground rules for public–private interaction in social sectors like health and elder care.

However, for some health sector goals, China has embraced collaborative approaches even more aggressively than the United States, especially for its ambitious national plans for developing biotechnologies and AI in the health sector.

Biotechnology and Health Information Technology
Could the US government quickly decide to allocate several percentage points of GDP to a given industrial policy, as China has for biotech and AI, and then select a single private firm as partner for achieving the near-term goal for each

---

[88] Mao, Wenhui, Zhang, Luying and Chen, Wen, 2017, "Progress and Policy Implication of the Insurance Programs for Catastrophic Diseases in China," *The International Journal of Health Planning and Management*, 32(3). 10.1002/hpm.2431. www.researchgate.net/publication/317849402_Progress_and_policy_implication_of_the_Insurance_Programs_for_Catastrophic_Diseases_in_China.

specific component of that endeavor? China has done so. For example, the Ministry of Science and Technology named the large private firm Tencent Holdings the designated partner of the "national AI team" focusing on computer vision for medical diagnosis.

As China devotes a growing share of GDP to biotech and other cutting-edge technologies, local governments have invested in dozens of "science parks." They are aiming to do for biotech what special economic zones did for economic reform in an earlier era. Government supports private sector innovations through major funds such as the State High-Tech Development Program and the Basic Research Program. Thus, the "we pay-you deliver" model may be less prevalent in China in health-care delivery, but it is thriving in biotech.

Vaccine firms have been important beneficiaries of this investment. Few arenas more clearly epitomize government responsibility than protecting against epidemic disease, as underscored by the COVID-19 pandemic. Yet development of biotechnologies just as strikingly epitomizes private sector comparative advantages. Vaccines illustrate both the potential as well as the risks associated with public–private collaboration for information and productivity in the health sector.

Consider the case of the first WHO-approved vaccine produced in China. Surely this was a saga of government promotion of a private firm to meet local and global public health goals through leveraging China's production skills and scientific expertise to address health challenges in low-income countries? Not so. The Japanese Encephalitis vaccine was manufactured by the Chengdu Institute of Biological Products (a subsidiary of China National Biotec Group, a large SOE), which received substantial support from an international private nonprofit, PATH, and from the Bill and Melinda Gates Foundation. Another successful collaborative case was the Chinese domestic start-up CanSino's successful development of an Ebola vaccine collaboratively with a military research institute. The China FDA approved the vaccine in 2017 for emergency use and for a national stockpile. As explained by the Tianjin-based private company's vice president, Dr. Wang Jing:

"We were not particularly in that area until the Military Medical Sciences team came to us in 2014. The team had conducted research into the Ebola virus for years before the breakout, and it needed a platform that was capable of producing the research prototype into a final vaccine product that can be marketed," said Wang. "And within about two years – we benefitted from the favoring policies from the government – we made it. We believe that it demonstrates not only CanSino's, but also the Chinese biomedicine sector's ability in technological innovation ... [The World Health Organization] approached us a couple times and we are well prepared for mass production if the virus makes a comeback."[89]

[89] Pearl Liu, "China approves Ebola vaccine co-developed by CanSino Biologics and the military," www.bioworld.com/content/china-approves-ebola-vaccine-co-developed-cansino-biologics-and-military [accessed September 20, 2018].

Yet China has repeatedly suffered vaccine scandals, including one in the summer of 2018 that prompted calls for investigation from Xi Jinping himself and led to the removal of dozens of officials. In mid-July, authorities announced that Changsheng Life Sciences Ltd, a privatized SOE, seriously violated quality standards in its rabies vaccine production.[90] The company had produced 3.55 million rabies vaccines the previous year, ranking second in China, even though the company had previously been fined for selling over 250,000 sub-standard DTP vaccines. A series of media reports inflamed public outrage not only over the personal accumulation of wealth by the family controlling that firm, but also other "King(s) of Vaccines," as described in an eponymous article read by millions of Chinese before being banned by the authorities.[91] The scandal undermined faith in the accountability and capacity of Chinese regulatory authorities.[92] Chinese President Xi Jinping called for immediate investigation over the "appalling" scandal, and more than forty officials were removed from their positions, including a vice governor of Jilin Province."[93]

Similarly, in 2020 the problematic initial response to the COVID-19 outbreak led to dismissal of local officials and a concerted effort to control the public narrative. On the positive side, scientists and other public and private actors – in China as well as internationally – collaborated to discover vaccine candidates and find appropriate therapies for the new coronavirus, SARS-CoV-2. Simultaneously, tens of millions of Chinese complied with lockdown to help control its spread. Thus, infectious disease control and vaccine development illustrate both the risks of failure from nontransparent privatizations and payoff discretion when oversight institutions are inadequate, as well as the potential success of collaborative approaches to supplement the Chinese instinct toward an overwhelmingly government-led approach, especially during a crisis.

Navigating collaborative approaches in health care can be a minefield, given questions about ownership of patient data and the basic science underpinning lucrative innovations. World-renowned nonprofit research and provider organizations in the United States have also been caught up in sticky legal and reputational questions regarding for-profit ventures.[94]

Incentives, Integration, and Accountability

For China, as for the United States, a key challenge is shifting from fee-for-service payment toward value-based payment. To date, neither nation's health reforms have effectively addressed the warped incentives that drive excessive spending

[90] http://cnda.cfda.gov.cn/WS04/CL2050/329592.html.   [91] www.letscorp.net/archives/132470
[92] http://news.21so.com/2018/ifeng_0722/170410.html; http://finance.ifeng.com/a/20180723/16397718_0.shtml; https://mp.weixin.qq.com/s/4ReAmWLWoCiKY2CiH5vkPQ.
[93] www.bloomberg.com/news/articles/2018-08-16/china-s-xi-oversees-purge-of-40-cadres-as-vaccine-fallout-widens.
[94] See, for example, Charles Ornstein and Katie Thomas, "Sloan Kettering's Cozy Deal With Start-Up Ignites a New Uproar," *The New York Times*, September 20, 2018, www.nytimes.com/2018/09/20/health/memorial-sloan-kettering-cancer-paige-ai.html [accessed September 20, 2018].

growth and the misallocation of health resources. China faces the profound and unresolved contradiction between the expectation that government hospitals should provide inexpensive, high-quality care for all, and the powerful financial incentives of those hospitals to lure more affluent patients to consume profitable services such as high-tech diagnostics and prescription drugs.

The 2009 Chinese reform plan featured pleas to "reverse the profit-orientated behaviors of public health care institutions and drive them to resume their commonweal nature."[95] Subsequently, beyond encouraging private sector entry and competition, authorities have rolled out policies for payment reforms, separating the prescribing and dispensing of medications, and restructuring government hospitals to improve efficiency, quality, and responsiveness. Social health insurance programs in many localities have adopted case-based payment and global budgets.

A recent tantalizing set of policy experiments in China involves health alliances or local integrated health-care organizations based on formal mergers of local government-owned hospitals and primary care providers. A prominent example is the reform of Luohu district of Shenzhen since 2015. Such integration initiatives may provide health benefits while slowing the rate of expenditure growth, although rigorous evaluation will be needed to see if that is the case. Such integrated care organizations usually unify the drug formulary for different levels of provider, so that patients do not have to go to tertiary hospitals to be prescribed specific medications or renew prescriptions (as had been an unfortunate consequence of the essential medication list policy as implemented in some areas).

One concern is that if not managed carefully, such alliances could acquire large market power and squeeze private providers from the market. Integration of all (government-owned) providers in a given district or county in effect creates a local monopoly. With little regulatory oversight on competition or antitrust, the negative sides of this organizational structure could come to outweigh the benefits. In such a case, allowing patient choice to go outside the district or county is one of the few remaining options for competitive incentives to promote ongoing creation of public value. An integrated provider may excel by streamlining services, better coordinating care and investing in efficiency improvements – such as through centralizing procurement, logistics, human resources, and other operations – as well as promoting the appropriate site of care. However, new monitoring and evaluation systems will need to be put into place to make sure these local monopolies live up to social expectations.

Strict, transparent oversight and regulation can be critical to uphold budget constraints and patient rights as well as to deter malfeasance, but, on the other hand, flexibility and autonomy are needed for institutional innovation, and can be well justified as long as the organization is accountable for results. The success of integrated networks in China will depend on how well policymakers achieve this balance.

---

[95] *Yiyaoweisheng tizhi gaige jinqi zhongdian shishi fang'an 2009-2011nian 2009.*

Moving toward prepayment – such as adopting a global budget and/or capitation – does give incentive for prevention and investment in cost-effective settings for management, such as primary care. Yet there is a need for balance and careful monitoring, because strong incentives to control medical expenditures also have important unintended effects, including risk selection (turning away expensive-to-treat patients) and/or under-provision (stinting on care or withholding innovative treatments even when appropriate). Value-added assessment is feasible with straightforward services such as dental and eye care. To date, it has proved almost impossible for conditions such as cancer and mental health care. Pure outcome measures – much easier to tally – are insufficient, since account must be taken of the original severity of the patient's problem. Reforms toward alternative payment systems and organization forms should be rigorously monitored and evaluated for impact on quality of care and access, especially for the most vulnerable patients.

The next frontier may be in expanding coordination of health services with long-term care services for the elderly and disabled. The private role in long-term care – such as nursing homes and home care assisting with activities of daily living for the frail and disabled – tends to be larger in many countries than the private role in health care. Long-term care has lacked both resources and operational capacity, making it critically important for the Chinese government to create favorable conditions to attract private actors in the development of this sector. China's demographic profile imposes special challenges. The generations in or approaching old age have fewer children to care for their elders than did prior generations, and longevity has substantially increased. The change in age structure has evolved over a short time period compared to the multiple generations of adjustment available to the United States and European countries. China's local jurisdictions have experimented with a range of options for coaxing private investments in long-term care for many tens of millions of elderly people. In addition to fiscal subsidies and other supportive policies, some local governments have partnered with private firms to develop affordable eldercare homes for disabled elderly and those with dementia[96]; other such collaborative approaches are set to expand.

"Collaborative Governance with Chinese Characteristics"?
China's health-care reformers have explored collaborative governance, often boldly. The reforms have included expanded government subsidies for social insurance and direct payments to providers. The expansion of health insurance has been dramatic and largely effective, although benefits remain at a fairly low level except for the urban formal-sector employees (UEBMI). China achieved universal health coverage without making enrollment mandatory (in the rural

---

[96] See "Pilot for Beijing's Elderly; Gonghe Senior Apartments," case written by Kirsten Lundberg for Alan M. Trager, President, PPP Initiative Ltd. (PPPI) and Chief Specialist, International, Tsinghua University Center for Public–Private Partnerships.

NCMS or urban non-employed URBMI programs), nor has it allowed much scope for insurance competition – the two touchstones for the American debate on these issues. Instead, central and provincial government subsidies, along with administrative pressure on local officials, led to robust voluntary enrollment. As in the United States, the government has had to negotiate with an array of different public- and private-sector entities with deeply entrenched interests.

In health service delivery, China has made tremendous strides in opening up some policy space for the private sector, while continuing the reform and upgrade of the existing robust system of public hospitals. Indeed, some of the private-sector complaints about discrimination by social health insurance programs and about its difficulties in accessing human capital have already been addressed in many parts of the country. Scandals and policy reversals illustrate the hazards of payoff discretion and other manipulations when discretion is shared and accountability systems are weak. Perhaps ironically, the path to strengthening the role of the private sector in China may come most cost-effectively from strengthening the capacity of local authorities to monitor and oversee both the private and public sector providers.

The formidable challenges ahead for both financing and delivery echo those confronting the United States and virtually all countries trying to sustain universal health coverage, especially the imperative of a continuing cycle of assessment and adjustment to keep collaborators' incentives aligned with public value. China has broad and rich experience marshaling the private sector for products and services outside of health-care delivery. That experience should be drawn upon, with appropriate adjustments for the sector, to bring about value-enhancing contracting and collaboration in its health system.

Full Recovery

Several broad generalizations can be distilled from this overview of health systems in the two countries:

1. The labels "public," "private" and "nonprofit," on their own, tend to tell us remarkably little about how a health-care provider will behave. In both the United States and China, history, context, and systems of governance matter enormously for the performance of all categories of providers.[97]
2. Ownership form affects the likelihood of certain kinds of behavior. For-profit institutions are more likely, all else remaining equal, to seize opportunities to manipulate patients; governmental institutions are relatively unlikely to innovate. However, variation *within* types is too great to prescribe inflexible rules for matching the types to the tasks.

---

[97] P. J. Dimaggio, and W. W. Powell, 1983, "The Iron Cage Revisited: Institutional Isomorphism and Collective Rationality in Organizational Fields," *American Sociological Review*, 48(2), 147–160.

3. A diverse ecosystem of health-care providers involved in tasks and locales is the norm in both countries. For-profit urgent-care clinics may work brilliantly in both San Diego and Shanghai, yet poorly in both Tulsa and Tianjin.

4. Just as we should expect variety in organizational form within a country or health-care subsector at any one point in time, we should anticipate that the right ownership model for any given task will change occasionally over time. Arrangements that once made sense tend to break down because of a range of internal and external stresses, such as new technologies, new political forces, or just the natural encrustation of institutions that operate in an area over time.

5. For all of these reasons, continuous analysis and adjustment of the governance regime by honest and skilled public officials is the underpinning of effective health system governance. The more the system reflects the relatively complex collaborative model, the greater the importance of this function.

6. Domestic policies usually change incrementally in the United States, with its elaborate system of checks and balances and often divided government. For many decades, health care has remained a prime arena for collaborative governance, with massive programs where the government pays and the private sector delivers. The ACA represented the most significant new policy development since the advent of Medicare and Medicaid, although the seismic 2016 election partially reversed its course.

7. China's leaders have introduced several new policies to its health sector in recent years, achieving universal coverage and striving to improve quality and efficiency. The prime force has been rather dramatic economic and demographic changes that have made the *status quo* untenable. Many of these policies represent experiments with collaborative governance.

For both the United States and China, health care is probably the policy sector that has undergone the most rapid change in the past decade. Of course, as we have stressed throughout, policy innovation has generally been much less rapid in the United States, for a variety of reasons – slower economic growth provided less maneuvering room, and strong forces created political inertia. Both nations have experienced rapidly mounting health-care expenditures, due to expanded services, quality - enhancing technological advance and aging populations. Hence, both nations now eagerly seek solutions that control costs without sacrificing quality.

Most important for our central argument, both nations employ an intricate albeit haphazardly created web of collaborative arrangements to deliver health care. For China and the United States alike, the tangles in the web must be removed and the worst of the tugs and tensions must be eased in order to bolster the physical and fiscal health of their citizens.

PART III

THE PATH FORWARD

8

The Transparency Imperative

"There should be more than one voice in a healthy society."

"If the officials had disclosed information about the epidemic earlier, I think it would have been a lot better. There should be more openness and transparency."
Dr. Li Wenliang (to Caixin and The New York Times, respectively, before his death from COVID-19)[1]

"[I]n America the response to date [3/5/20] has been a shambolic missed opportunity. Shockingly, the worst American bungling has more in common with the catastrophic early stages of the Chinese epidemic – when officials minimised risks and punished truth-tellers, thus letting the disease spread much further and faster than it might have – than with the country's later co-ordinated control efforts."
The Economist[2]

Early in this book, we describe the cycle that successful collaboration requires: analyze, assign, design, and assess (AADA). The chapters that followed dissected the experiences of China and the United States in using, misusing, or mistakenly *not* using collaborative governance across a broad spectrum of policy areas. Those accounts reveal, for both nations, many successes and more than a few failures. The successes tend to occur when collaborators

---

[1] "Internet Mourns the Death of Wuhan Whistleblower Doctor," www.caixinglobal.com/2020–02-07/caixin-china-biz-roundup-internet-mourns-the-death-of-wuhan-whistleblower-doctor-101512868.html [accessed February 7, 2020]; Chris Buckley, "Chinese Doctor, Silenced After Warning of Outbreak, Dies From Coronavirus," www.nytimes.com/2020/02/06/world/asia/chinese-doctor-Li-Wenliang-coronavirus.html [accessed February 7, 2020].

[2] What the world has learned about facing COVID-19. www.economist.com/briefing/2020/03/05/what-the-world-has-learned-about-facing-covid-19 [accessed March 6, 2020] COVID-19: New World Curriculum. Also see "U.S. Health Workers Responding to Coronavirus Lacked Training and Protective Gear, Whistle-Blower Says," www.nytimes.com/2020/02/27/us/politics/coronavirus-us-whistleblower.html?referringSource=articleShare.

devise by creative effort, or improvise by trial and error, the proper alloy of public and private responsibilities and the proper sharing of discretion. In many cases, reassuringly, initial failure is the overture to later triumph; when one set of arrangements works badly, collaborators try again.

But we fear that progressive revision toward eventual success is not the reliable norm in collaboration nor, indeed, in public policy generally. No process of natural selection inexorably guides a nation, whatever its political system, to the correct policies for creating social value. Indeed, social value can be destroyed if the political system goes awry, as it did in China during the Cultural Revolution, and not a few would argue is the case today in the United States with its uneven electoral engagement and toxic ideological polarization.

Prior chapters should have made clear our conviction that no single approach – purely public, purely private, contractual, philanthropic, or collaborative – is always and everywhere appropriate. The right delivery model is always conditional. Yet each mode of delivery has its true believers who are willing to downplay or disregard conditions, complications, and contingencies. Sometimes their enthusiasm stems from ideological commitments to an abstract view of what is right and proper. Yet there are almost always some advocates, alas, who favor a particular approach not out of an honestly mistaken faith that it is good for the public at large but rather the selfish observation it promises private benefits to them.

Making reform yet more difficult, the status quo often has a built-in advantage because the policy playing field is tilted toward incumbents. There are abundant examples of such tilts in the United States. Teachers' unions provide a political bulwark for conventional public schools and oppose private-school vouchers (and, less uniformly, charter schools). Private players in the health insurance industry (both for-profit and nonprofit[3]) fiercely resist any move toward single-payer universal health care. Where existing arrangements are other than collaborative – whether purely governmental, private-dominated, or conventionally contractual – status quo bias acts as a drag on desirable collaborative initiatives.

Entrenched interests protect their domains in any political system. The Chinese experience provides comparable examples in which powerful, established agents promoted a bias for the status quo. Many SOEs resisted corporatization or competition from private-sector firms. County-level officials resisted village self-rule when village elections were introduced in 1988.[4] Private firms pressured local governments to promote their narrow

---

[3] Interestingly, and little known, Blue Cross is a for-profit company in some states and a nonprofit in others.
[4] See discussions in Li, Lianjiang, and Kevin J. O'Brien, "The Struggle Over Village Elections," in Goldman, Merle, and Roderick MacFarquhar, eds., *The Paradox of China's Post-Mao Reforms*, Vol. 12, Harvard University Press, 1999; and in R. A. Pastor, and Q. Tan, 2000, "The Meaning of China's Village Elections," *The China Quarterly*, 162, 490–512.

agendas regarding local economic development, and local governments have supported specific private firms to further that development as well as their own careers. Some observers claim that contemporary China exemplifies a "special deals" regime, with entrenched interests blocking further reforms.[5] China's central government felt it necessary to set an explicit goal of increasing private provision of health services in order to uproot dug-in interests that protected the market share of government-owned hospitals and clinics. (See Chapter 6). In this final chapter, we make the case for *transparency* as a potent – albeit imperfect – corrective to some of the most important downsides of the collaborative approach to governance, in the United States and China alike, before a brief summary of the book's major themes.

Knowledge, it is often observed, is power. Whether in China or the United States, the broad provision of information on what is being done by, with, or on behalf of the government can help to thwart interests or individuals seeking special benefits at the expense of public welfare. This chapter employs the term transparency to describe such provision. We are not suggesting that transparency is any kind of cure-all. Information can only improve performance if it is accessible, comprehensible, and received by citizens who have the ability to take action. Information alone is rarely sufficient for accountability. But it is almost always necessary.

As we pledged at the start of this book, we continue to sidestep the ideological briar patch concerning the relative virtues and flaws of one-party China and the (imperfectly) democratic United States. But throughout its pages, we have noted some ways that the political fundamentals influence the conduct of collaborative governance.[6] A broad summary might be that a one-party state can take the long view and is mostly spared the need to respond to short-term public sentiment in order to retain power. A competitive democracy – as the United States surely is at the national level – is more likely to have a productive battle of ideas, as we have seen in the American experience with charter schools

---

[5] It is neither our intent nor our expertise to adjudicate the strength of such claims. For evidence, see, for example, Bai Chong-En, Chang-Tai Hsieh, and Zheng Michael Song, 2019. "Special Deals with Chinese Characteristics." NBER Working Paper 25839, National Bureau of Economic Research, Cambridge, MA.

[6] For general discussions of citizen input and its role in the public and private sector, see Hirschman, Albert, 1970, *Exit, Voice, and Loyalty: Responses to Decline in Firms, Organizations, and States*, Cambridge, MA: Harvard University Press; and Fukuyama, Francis, *Political Order and Political Decay: From the Industrial Revolution to the Globalization of Democracy*, New York: Farrar, Straus and Giroux, 2014. For perspectives on the role in China, see Perry, Elizabeth, 2002, *Challenging the Mandate of Heaven: Social Protest and State Power in China*, Armonk, NY, M. E. Sharpe, and J. Fewsmith, *The Logic and Limits of Political Participation in China* (New York: Cambridge University Press, 2013); Chen, Xi, *Social Protest and Contentious Authoritarianism in China*, Cambridge: Cambridge University Press, 2012; Truex, Rory, 2014, "Representation within Bounds," Doctoral dissertation, Yale University; and Tsai, Lily, 2015, "Constructive Noncompliance in Rural China," *Comparative Politics*, 47 (3), 253–279.

or medical care insurance. This is an important advantage when (as we believe is commonly the case) the right policy approach is far from self-evident at the start.

Once the right approach is identified, however, China has two advantages over the United States. First, wrestling policies through the Chinese political process is much less challenging. Not always, but quite often, political forces in American legislatures are so evenly balanced that major moves in any direction are thwarted. Even when one faction holds a meaningful legislative edge, deadlock can still persist if another party controls the executive branch or if the courts impose priorities from a prior political era. Those who stand to lose from change tend to value their prospective losses much more highly than the potential winners would value their gains. So those whose positions are threatened fight harder. Losers also tend to garner more sympathy from outside observers. And the potential losers, already in place and often with close connections to incumbent legislators, tend to be more readily organized for political battle than potential gainers.

China's second major advantage over the United States has been its rapid rate of growth. Policy change is much easier to accomplish when investments and initiatives are expanding briskly rather than merely creeping ahead. Even as China's growth slows, there remains a window of opportunity to put in place institutions to guide productive collaborative governance in the more difficult, slower-growth decades to come. It is easier to try something new when it does not require encroaching upon a going concern. China has encountered tremendous challenges in reinventing the governance institutions inherited from an ancient civilization for use in a modern society, and from a centrally planned economy to the current market-based global powerhouse. Sharp swings in policy were hardly a surprise as China grappled with the sheer economic and managerial work of dismantling central planning and inventing regulatory structures for market allocation and macroeconomic regulation.

China will continue to confront the challenge of uprooting past legacies that impede present performance. Yet China's pace of development has also yielded virtually blank slates for experimentation that contrast with those of the much younger, yet less rapidly changing, United States. Think of the differences in the task of building an entirely new city – a common undertaking in China despite more than two millennia of civilization, and exceedingly rare elsewhere on the planet – versus trying to redevelop some rundown but heavily populated neighborhood within a US city. Even if the American locale was virgin forest a century or two back, and the Chinese locale has been occupied for millennia, today's flexibility edge decidedly rests with China.

It is thus no surprise that China has often taken bolder steps in its collaborative policies than has the United States. It harkens – only if implicitly – to the words of one of America's most interesting presidents, Franklin Delano Roosevelt. He, then just a candidate campaigning in the frightening depths of the Great Depression, gave the 1932 commencement address at Atlanta's Oglethorpe University. In the segment most quoted from that speech, Roosevelt said:

"The country needs and, unless I mistake its temper, the country demands bold, persistent experimentation. It is common sense to take a method and try it: If it fails, admit it frankly and try another. But above all, try something. ... We need enthusiasm, imagination and the ability to face facts, even unpleasant ones, bravely."[7]

Franklin Delano Roosevelt's words remind us that boldness is only a virtue when accompanied by intellectual honesty. Only analysis of what did and did not work, and then candor about the findings, can transform experimentation into progress. This observation supports the central theme of this final chapter: transparency in objectives, arrangements, costs, and accomplishments is a critical ingredient in ensuring the success of collaborative governance. That is true for both China and the United States, and indeed, in any other country. In our opening chapters we discussed two inherent dangers in collaborative arrangements: preference discretion and payoff discretion. In both situations, the private collaborator distorts a public undertaking to serve its own interests. Governmental collaborators, and citizens in general, find it hard to impose accountability unless they can assess performance and measure outcomes. We invoke another favorite American quotation, this one by the famed jurist Louis Brandeis in a 1913 *Harper's Weekly* piece:

"Publicity is justly commended as a remedy for social and industrial diseases. Sunlight is said to be the best of disinfectants; electric light the most efficient policeman."[8]

Brandeis might have continued by pointing out that wrongdoing, and in our particular case the abuse of discretion, breeds best in the shadows.

Transparency has conventionally been seen chiefly as a defense against the defects of direct governmental action. It can reveal, and thereby trigger political resistance to, the public sector's characteristic failings: inefficiency, reluctance to innovate, excessive uniformity, catering to the powerful, sometimes outright corruption. Performance monitoring, outcome metrics, media oversight, financial audits, and other tools of transparency can be powerful broad-spectrum remedies against these tendencies. A few American examples:

- *K-12 Education:* The landmark "No Child Left Behind" legislation hinged on test-based metrics on school performance that families were encouraged to use in their decisions about their children's schooling. While by no means without its flaws (as discussed in Chapter 6), the law and its sequels intended, and to some degree achieved, the empowering of parents with data to insist upon accountability from public schools.

---

[7] May 22, 1932, Address at Oglethorpe University, sourced from The American Presidency Project website, www.presidency.ucsb.edu/ws/?pid=88410, August 2, 2018.

[8] "What Publicity Can Do," *Harper's Weekly* (December 20, 1913).

- *Official Compensation:* To compensate for the lack of market pressure against excessive pay, most governmental jurisdictions in the United States publicize the compensation of many employees.
- *Police Behavior:* "Internal affairs" investigations, body cameras, and a range of other transparency devices have sought to deter abuse and improve citizen trust in the police, with significant (if inevitably incomplete) success.[9]
- *Political campaigns:* Donors to all federal and most other political campaigns in the United States are obliged to disclose their identities and, in many cases, their employment.[10] In the landmark 2010 Supreme Court *Citizens United* case, the justices were bitterly divided on whether there should be limits on corporate and union efforts to influence elections. But eight of the nine justices voted for the transparency requirement that donors to PACs be identified.[11]

Transparency has long been a watchword of governmental reform campaigns in the United States and beyond. A long sequence of legislative mandates for transparency marked the second half of the twentieth century in Washington: the Administrative Procedures Act, the Freedom of Information Act, the Government in the Sunshine Act, the Inspector General Act, and the Government Performance and Results Act, to name just some of the more prominent laws.[12] On his very first day in office, President Barack Obama issued an executive order entitled the Open Government Memorandum, calling for "an unprecedented level of openness in government."[13] In the United Kingdom, a 2000 law required the release of detailed performance information on most aspects of local government.[14]

Such measures are not confined to high-income democratic countries. In fact, the incremental benefit of transparency may be largest in settings lacking long

---

[9] Mason, David, et al., 2014, "Are Informed Citizens More Trusting? Transparency of Performance Data and Trust Towards a British Police Force," *Journal of Business Ethics*, 122 (2), 321–341.

[10] La Raja, Raymond J., 2014, "Political Participation and Civic Courage: The Negative Effect of Transparency on Making Small Campaign Contributions," *Political Behavior*, 36(4), 753–776. Contributors to political action committees (PACs), which are often organized to support particular candidates, need not identify themselves. The major constraint on PACs and on their privilege of contributor anonymity is that PACs cannot directly coordinate with a candidate's campaign.

[11] Newbold, *Public Administration Review*, p. 49.

[12] Stephanie P. Newbold, "Federalist No. 27: Is Transparency Essential for Public Confidence in Government?" *Public Administration Review*, Supplement to Volume 71: The Federalist Papers Revised for Twenty-First-Century Reality (December 2011), pp. S47–S52, at 49. See also Bernardino Benito and Francisco Bastida, 2009, "Budget Transparency, Fiscal Performance, and Political Turnout: An International Approach," *Public Administration Review*, 69(3), 403–417.

[13] Jennifer Shkabatur, Fall 2012, "Transparency With(out) Accountability: Open Government in the United States," *Yale Law and Policy Review*, 31(1), 79–140 at 79.

[14] Alessandro Gavazza and Alessandro Lizzeri, 2007, "The Perils of Transparency in Bureaucracies," *The American Economic Review*, 97(2), 300–305.

traditions of government openness. Studies have shown transparency initiatives can increase government program effectiveness in Indonesia and elsewhere.[15] In China, multiple initiatives – particularly by local governments – have been designed to show responsiveness to citizen input, such as government "office visiting" days, committees devoted to public consultation, and officials' "mailbox" platforms. A 2000 law states that citizens have the right to "participate in legislation through various channels" (Legislation Law of the People's Republic of China: Article 5, 2000). Top leaders call for "democratic centralism" and mandate that party officials take account of citizen input in policy formulation. Some NGOs have used administrative appeal (*xingzheng fuyi*) and administrative litigation (*xingzheng susong*) for policy engagement and advocacy.[16]

Transparency can improve governance, whether collaborative or otherwise, in several related but distinguishable ways.

Empowering Choice: The benefits of transparency are magnified when citizens enjoy some degree of choice. In such cases, government itself can take on some of the features of a well-functioning market. Solid information is one prerequisite for accountability and efficiency. The more citizens know about the performance of a provider and the context of that performance – whether a school, a hospital, a toll road, or a nursing home – the better equipped they will be to select the effective and shun the ineffective. Such choices bring immediate benefits; current clients are better served than they would be without alternatives. But perhaps more importantly, citizen choice confers broader benefits: rejected providers are motivated to improve their performance or surely suffer and possibly perish. Successful providers expand their output. This assumes, of course, that resources follow clients or that being in demand is in some other way rewarded.

At the extreme, informed choice can drive selection and encourage accountability *among* governments. One school of thought has sought to use this logic to render governance essentially a special case of market economics.[17] To the extent that people can move across locales, they can migrate toward those that efficiently provide the right bundle of public services and away from those that operate inefficiently or fail to offer the services that people value most.[18] Towns within a state can compete to offer better services at lower costs.

[15] A. Banerjee, R. Hanna, J. C. Kyle, B. A. Olken, and S. Sumarto, 2015, *The Power of Transparency: Information, Identification Cards and Food Subsidy Programs in Indonesia* (No. w20923), National Bureau of Economic Research.

[16] See Dai, Jingyun, and Anthony J. Spires, 2018, "Advocacy in an Authoritarian State: How Grassroots Environmental NGOs Influence Local Governments in China," *The China Journal*, 79(1), 62–83.

[17] The seminal text here is Charles M. Tiebout, October 1956, "A Pure Theory of Local Expenditures," *Journal of Political Economy*, 64(5), 416–424. Tiebout also welcomed the prospect that different jurisdictions would offer different mixes of services for their particular clients.

[18] During China's rapid urbanization of millions, with tightening labor markets and a shrinking working-age population, competition among municipalities may take on some of this flavor,

States or provinces within a nation can seek to lure desirable people or businesses with attractive tax or policy regimes. China and the United States compete to secure initial public offerings on their financial markets, and many nations compete in providing sound legal procedures so as to be chosen as the locale for the arbitration of commercial contracts written elsewhere. In practice, there are severe limits to this market metaphor for government in general.[19] But for limited, albeit important, areas of public service, there are large and obvious advantages to transparency-empowered choice.

Informing Behavior: Even in the market-infatuated United States, it is the exception, not the norm, for citizens to be able to choose among multiple alternative suppliers of publicly funded services. There is only one US Department of State or Social Security Administration. Cities, even big ones, usually have just one police force or fire department. But rich, reliable data can still be invaluable in informing citizens' interactions with governmental entities. Choosing *when* to begin receiving Social Security can make the difference between a comfortable and a pinched retirement. So it is worth celebrating the Social Security Administration's array of tools that makes it easier to understand the implications of alternative timing decisions. Similarly, tourists can benefit from State Department security alerts. Citizens likewise are better off with access to police department records regarding criminal activity in various areas.

Enabling Responsible Criticism: Transparency about government's performance enables citizens to praise what works and protest what does not. This is not a bad thing, from the perspective of an enlightened government, whatever the nature of the political system. Well-informed, responsible feedback is something all public officials should welcome. One universal lesson from the whole sweep of human history is this: People will gripe. Their complaints can be diverted, deflected, rebutted and, in the short run, ignored. But no kind of leadership has ever been able to stifle all criticism. In the current age of instantaneous electronic connection, silencing complaint is especially difficult. Whether in a free-wheeling democracy or in a one-party state, governmental performance can improve when criticism is well-informed. Do citizens suspect that their taxes mostly go not for services that benefit the people but rather to support the lavish lifestyle of top bureaucrats? Solid data on officials' compensation and on the share of governmental resources devoted to valued public services can put those suspicions to rest. Demagoguery about rising crime or prices can be countered by transparency about current rates and historical trends. Keeping citizens in ignorance does not eliminate criticism.

---

although China's current household registration (*hukou*) system and local initiatives for granting urban *hukou* do not actively encourage such competition for residents.

[19] John D. Donahue, Autumn, 1997, "Tiebout? Or Not Tiebout? The Market Metaphor and America's Devolution Debate," *The Journal of Economic Perspectives*, 11(4), 73–81.

But it makes that criticism imprecise, error-prone, and ultimately unhelpful to public officials who seek to deliver results.[20]

In China, some local governments have experimented with "participatory budgeting" as part of local "Sunshine Project" or "Sunshine in Government" initiatives,[21] allowing for local resident participation in the allocation of government funding for community projects. In 2011–2012, the central government required each province to select a handful of counties for a transparency initiative meant to provide constituents with information about local government affairs and communication links to express their views on those affairs. According to the "Opinions of the National Government Affairs Openness Leading Group on Implementing the Electronic Platform to Strengthen the Openness of County Government Affairs and the Pilot Work of Administrative Services" and other official documents, two to four counties in each province were required to disclose data and documents on an official website about a wide swath of administrative matters – from public finance and land resources to education, police, and the environment – as well as to create a link that would enable county residents to provide comments, submit requests, and air grievances. Analysis suggests that this transparency initiative reduced corruption and increased public investments in the participating counties, relative to counties that did not implement it.[22]

Transparency initiatives are by no means restricted to government itself but are often aimed at for-profit and nonprofit private actors. A few examples from the United States:

- *Charities:* In the United States and elsewhere, charities are generally obliged to disclose information about their leadership, financing, and expenditures on an annual basis.[23]

---

[20] In March 2020, "well-known author Fang Fang posted a blog on Caixin's Chinese-language website lambasting the 'arrogance' of top government officials in the central city of Wuhan, after they announced plans to roll out so-called gratitude education to make sure local residents properly thank the Communist Party for controlling the coronavirus epidemic that [had at that time] killed nearly 2,500 people in the city, according to official figures. Fang's article argues that rather than soliciting praise from their citizens, Chinese officials should thank the country's medical workers, sickened patients, and bereaved families for their self-sacrifice, restraint, and cooperation amid a grave human tragedy." www.caixinglobal.com/2020-03-12/opinion-thank-the-government-for-controlling-the-virus-no-they-should-be-thanking-us-101527671.html [accessed March 12, 2020].

[21] See, as examples, Wu, Yan, and Wen Wang, 2011, "The Rationalization of Public Budgeting in China: A Reflection on Participatory Budgeting in Wuxi," *Public Finance & Management*, 11 (3), 262–283; and Cabannes, Yves and Zhuang Ming, 2014, "Participatory Budgeting at Scale and Bridging the Rural-Urban Divide in Chengdu," *Environment and Urbanization*, 26(1), 257–275.

[22] Daniel Berkowitz, Yi Lu, and Mingqin Wu, 2019 working paper, "What Makes Local Governments More Accountable? Evidence from a Website Reform." August 25, 2019.

[23] Carolyn Cordery, 2013, "Regulating Small and Medium Charities: Does It Improve Transparency and Accountability?" *Voluntas: International Journal of Voluntary and Nonprofit Organizations*, 24(3), 831–851.

- *Dangerous chemicals:* The Toxic Substances Control Act mandates an "inventory" of all substances deemed dangerous by the Environmental Protection Agency – where they are produced, stored, employed, and disposed of – so that citizens can know when they are being exposed and take informed steps to protect themselves from risk.[24]
- *Nursing Homes:* US nursing homes are required to report on their staffing levels, safety records, and other performance metrics.[25] Unfortunately, this particular effort at transparency is notoriously undermined by chronic misreporting, yielding a mixed record of usefulness in guiding consumers.[26]
- *Hospitals:* Government mandates transparency standards that private agents must meet. An organization called the Joint Commission accredits and certifies nearly 21,000 health-care organizations; several other programs collect and disseminate performance data on hospitals and other healthcare organizations in the United States.[27] Informed critics have asserted that more extensive, readily available, and comprehensible data could help patients choose where to seek care more wisely.[28]
- *Financial Institutions:* In the wake of the 2008 global financial crisis – sparked in large part by ignorance or confusion on the part of investors – dozens of countries adopted or strengthened reporting rules in the hope

---

[24] www.epa.gov/tsca-inventory, accessed August 3, 2018.

[25] The "Nursing Home Compare" data are available at the website www.medicare.gov/nursinghomecompare/search.html, accessed September 19, 2019. For some coverage of the controversies, see, for example, Jordan Rau and Elizabeth Lucas, "Medicare Slashes Star Ratings at 1 out of 11 Nursing Homes," *The New York Times*, July 27, 2018.

[26] R. M. Werner, E. C. Norton, R. T. Konetzka, and D. Polsky, 2012, "Do Consumers Respond to Publicly Reported Quality Information? Evidence from Nursing Homes," *Journal of Health Economics*, 31(1), 50–61; and Johari, Kayla, et al., 2018, "Ratings Game: An Analysis of Nursing Home Compare and Yelp ratings," *BMJ Qual Saf*, 27(8), 619–624.

[27] For the Medicare example of Hospital Compare, see www.medicare.gov/hospitalcompare. For an overview and comparison of national hospital rating systems, see J. M. Austin, A. K. Jha, P. S. Romano, S. J. Singer, T. J. Vogus, R. M. Wachter, and P. J. Pronovost, 2015, "National Hospital Ratings Systems Share Few Common Scores and May Generate Confusion Instead of Clarity," *Health Affairs*, 34(3), 423–430. There is a growing literature documenting the impact of performance data on health plans and nonhospital providers, including individual physicians; see J. T. Kolstad, and M. E. Chernew, 2009, "Quality and Consumer Decision Making in the Market for Health Insurance and Health Care Services," *Medical Care Research and Review*, 66 (1_suppl), 28S–52S; and J. T. Kolstad, 2013, "Information and Quality When Motivation Is Intrinsic: Evidence from Surgeon Report Cards," *American Economic Review*, 103(7), 2875–2910.

[28] Though incomprehensible hospital data can be useless, a 2017 initiative by the Department of Health and Human Services required hospitals to publicize price information – which they did, but in a form that was essentially gibberish to most potential patients. Robert Pear, "Hospitals Must Now Post Prices, But It May Take A Brain Surgeon To Decipher Them," *The New York Times*, January 13, 2019.

that businesses and consumers would take steps to discourage excessive risk-taking on the part of banks and other financial institutions.[29]

- *Labor Abuse:* Frustrated at its inability to deter abusive workplaces – or "sweatshops" – in the apparel industry, the Clinton administration's Labor Department turned to transparency. Its "No Sweat" initiative motivated brand-name labels to police their own supply chains by unsubtly encouraging consumers to shun brands that failed to do so. Similarly, 2010 legislation required the labeling of "conflict diamonds" sourced from – and likely worsening chaos in – war zones.[30]

Transparency can be at once more important and more challenging when private agents are involved than it is when governments act on their own. More important because private entities, especially for-profits, have powerful incentives to depart from a focus on the interests of the broad public – to abuse payoff and preference discretion, in our terms. Government officials, moreover, generally have more opportunity for illegitimate accommodation of private and parochial interests when production is collaborative. Private interest with government accommodation is a potentially toxic brew: favoritism at best, corruption at worst.

Transparency is more challenging in such cases, both because of private players' intense motivations to outwit accountability regimes, and because of the characteristic complexity of collaborative governance. There are, by definition, multiple players, with different organizational designs and objectives. Private-sector discretion is a deliberate feature of the relationship rather than a flaw to be eradicated. As we note elsewhere, it is rarely possible to avoid *all* of the downsides of discretion. The goal instead is to work toward a more favorable ratio of benefits and costs flowing from the allocation of discretion between the government and the private sector. That ratio can be improved by limiting delegation to tasks less prone to such abuse; by selecting agents who are less likely to abuse discretion; and by skill and discipline in structuring relationships with private agents.

A push toward transparency is a complementary tool that can play a significant role in controlling the almost inevitable residual risks of delegation. To the extent information about the performance of private agents entrusted with public tasks is timely, reliable, accessible, and fine-grained:

- government will be better equipped to adjust or end poorly performing collaborations and to expand successful ones;
- where citizens have a choice among providers, as is common in education, health care, and many other areas, they will be able to choose more wisely;

---

[29] J. C. Sharman, 2011, "Testing the Global Financial Transparency Regime," *International Studies Quarterly*, 55(4), 981–1001.

[30] John R. Crook, 2010, "New U.S. Legislation Requires Transparency in Conflict Minerals Trade," *The American Journal of International Law*, 104(4), 668–672.

- the pattern of public–private collaboration will more rapidly and surely evolve to replicate what performs well and to cull what does not.

As we have observed throughout this book, China and the United States are strikingly similar in some ways, but profoundly different in others. Much as we recommend transparency as a complement to collaboration, we recognize that it will – and should – manifest itself in China in distinctive ways. As collaboration expands and matures in China, there are already valuable lessons to be drawn.

The motivations, scope, and effectiveness of Chinese transparency initiatives vary. Some transparency measures aim to control potential payoff and preference discretion and to guide consumer choice while regulating private social actors. For example, as mentioned in Chapter 7, local governments often require *minban* schools to publish their fees and establish a method for people to file complaints, to constrain the less scrupulous private schools from charging exorbitant fees.[31] China's approach toward "social management" also embraces elements of transparency. The Charity Law of 2016 requires that charitable organizations submit annual reports and financial accounting reports that are open to the public.

In other cases, transparency initiatives aim to allow higher levels of government to monitor the performance of lower levels of government, while enabling citizen feedback to smooth implementation of policies and uncover corruption or abuse of power. "Consultative authoritarianism" or other terms have been used for gathering citizen input to enhance governance outcomes in this way.[32] China's initiatives in this regard date back at least to the late 1980s, when village elections were introduced. More recent examples include the adoption of public hearings, deliberative consultations, and community self-governance experiments. Online participation platforms appear to increase citizens' perceptions of governmental effectiveness, albeit unevenly, with the greatest impact on marginalized groups and the less educated.[33]

China's "Open Government Information Ordinance," declared national policy by the State Council in 2007, requires local governments to increase transparency, such as by making budgetary information public, collecting citizen input through government websites, and offering online platforms for submitting questions and comments. Local implementation varies in detail and

---

[31] Xiaojiong Ding, 2008, "Policy Metamorphosis in China: A Case Study of Minban Education in Shanghai," *The China Quarterly*, 195, 656–674.

[32] See A. J. Nathan, 2003, "Authoritarian Resilience," *Journal of Democracy*, 14, 6–17; J. Teets, 2013, "Let Many Civil Societies Bloom: Regional Ideational Variation in China," *The China Quarterly*, 213, 19–28; and J. M. Mbaku, and Z. Yu, 2013, "Information Communication Technologies, Transparency and Governance in China," *International Journal on World Peace*, 30(1), 9–59.

[33] R. Truex, 2017, "Consultative Authoritarianism and Its Limits," *Comparative Political Studies*, 50(3), 329–361.

responsiveness. Most county-level and higher-level governments host such citizen input websites. Chen, Pan, and Xu (2016) found that approximately 85 percent of county government online forums have publicly viewable posts and replies, although posts are reviewed prior to posting. Officials' responsiveness depends on how questions are framed. For example, a randomized experiment demonstrated that local governments are responsive to citizen complaints, especially when there is even a slight hint of possible collective protest.[34]

Chinese local governments collect citizen feedback on governance issues to monitor employees and minimize corruption. Some social support programs (such as the *dibao* basic income program for the poor) must publicly post the names of recipients. But – as is sadly common in both countries – this transparency regime can be manipulated. One study, based on rare access to internal communications between a monitoring agency and upper-level officials, found that "citizen grievances posted publicly online that contain complaints of corruption are systematically concealed from upper-level authorities when they implicate lower-tier officials or associates connected to lower-tier officials through patronage ties."[35] Some localities have introduced citizen-monitoring organizations, such as the Wenzhou municipality's "Civil Monitory Organization" launched in 2010. This citizen monitoring initiative was awarded "The Best Chinese Government Innovation" by Peking University in 2015, part of the self-declared "Wenzhou Model of monitory democracy." However, tensions between citizen input on one hand, and controlled media on the other limit the generalizability and effectiveness of this kind of transparency regime.[36] Survey evidence suggests that 15 percent of urban Chinese have complained to local government, and 37 percent of rural respondents reported making complaints to village authorities.[37] Knowing someone working in government has been shown to lead to greater willingness to voice such complaints, suggesting that trust in the integrity of the process is a function of familiarity with government.[38]

---

[34] Chen, Pan, and Xu (2016) find that, "at baseline, approximately one-third of county-level governments in China respond to citizen demands for government assistance in obtaining social welfare. Demands that include vague threats of collective action and specific threats of tattling to upper levels of government cause county-level governments to be 30 to 35% more responsive," J. Chen, J. Pan, and Y. Xu, 2016, "Sources of Authoritarian Responsiveness: A Field Experiment in China," *American Journal of Political Science*, 60(2), 383–400.

[35] J. Pan, and K. Chen, 2018, "Concealing Corruption: How Chinese Officials Distort Upward Reporting of Online Grievances," *American Political Science Review*, 112(3), 602–620.

[36] Zhuang, Meixi, Xiaoling Zhang, and Stephen L. Morgan, 2018. "Citizen–Media Interaction in China's Local Participatory Reform: A Contingent Participation Model," *Journal of Contemporary China*, 27(109), 120–136.

[37] P. 638-9, Lily L. Tsai and Yiqing Xu, September 2018, "Outspoken Insiders: Political Connections and Citizen Participation in Authoritarian China," *Political Behavior*, 40(3), 629–657.

[38] Tsai and Xu (2018).

China's success in collaborative governance in the decades to come will depend on its skill, discipline, and honesty in the analysis of policy challenges and opportunities; on the assignment of appropriate collaborators; and on the design of collaborative relationships so as to constrain payoff and preference discretion while capitalizing on the production efficiencies that collaboration can bring. The 2018 summer vaccine scandal (see Chapter 7) illustrates how China's regulatory authorities uncovered ghastly private sector payoff discretion that threatened harm to citizens. That scandal also demonstrated that previous regulatory sanctions on the same firms had been neither transparent nor effective. Far greater transparency is imperative for reaping the gains and dodging the pitfalls of the collaborative approach to governance.

There are also disturbing lessons about failures of transparency from the United States. The Trump administration's attempts to label as "fake news" anything uncongenial to its agenda – sometimes echoed by other political players – represent a mortal assault against transparency. Even milder attacks on truth can do profound damage to accountability.

The benefits of transparency do not come without burdens. Most obviously, these include the direct expenses of gathering, verifying, and disseminating information. But those obvious costs are often exceeded by hidden and indirect costs. Tools of investigation are regularly combated with tools of obfuscation. Thus, private agents may take expensive actions to cloud, evade, or manipulate transparency policies.[39] They may propose fine sounding but misleading metrics to judge their performance.

Even when the metrics are appropriate, citizens may misinterpret or otherwise misuse them. Examples would include moving away in panic because of some newly revealed waste dump with scary-sounding chemicals that, in fact, present minimal risk; moving *to* a school district whose lofty scores are largely due to student demographics rather than to educational quality; or responding to terms like "FDA approved" with little understanding of what they mean. Unintended consequences abound. The requirement to reveal political contributions can, and does, deter privacy-loving citizens from political activity.[40] Agency leaders may not *want* the surge in demand produced by soaring performance metrics if they know that it will not be accompanied by an increase in resources.[41]

Even if metrics are cheap and accurate, there remain some activities where transparency brings more harm than good. Top-level personnel decisions frequently fall into this category. Final candidates to head a state university

---

[39] George Loewenstein et al., 2011, "The Limits of Transparency: Pitfalls and Potential of Disclosing Conflicts of Interest," *The American Economic Review*, 101(3), 423–428.

[40] See, La Raja.

[41] Gavazza and Lizzeri, See also Andrea Prat, 2005, "The Wrong Kind of Transparency," *The American Economic Review*, 95(3), 862–877. For a brief and only partly tongue-in-cheek commentary, see John D. Donahue, "Seeing through Transparency," *Governing the States and Localities*, February 3, 2010, www.governing.com/columns/mgmt-insights/Seeing-Through-Transparency.html.

system – not infrequently individuals drawn from other universities or government service – often do not want their identities revealed. To do so might be harmful to them and their current institution if they are not chosen. Hence, where candidates will be announced, strong applicants shrink from applying. To reveal collaborative relationships designed to curtail criminal activities such as cyber hacking may make such relationships less effective. But most of the situations where transparency will be detrimental are readily identified. "Too much" transparency can happen but is relatively rare. "Too little" transparency is all too common. So we urge officials in both countries to tilt toward more rather than less transparency.

"COLLABORATIVE GOVERNANCE, CHINESE-STYLE"

As our book approaches its end, it is worth reinforcing the point that China's approach to collaborative governance will be distinctive, just as its political system, its economy and its culture are distinctive.[42] One critical feature where China differs from the United States – at least in degree if not in kind – is the importance and the heterogeneity of local-level government. Across China, local government leaders vary greatly in skills and experience, as well as in the socioeconomic development of their jurisdictions and the severity of the fiscal constraints they face. This marked heterogeneity leads to wide variation in approaches and levels of performance. It also has a pragmatic implication: The appropriate choice of delivery model will depend directly on the broader incentive system that local bureaucrats face. Even in relatively large municipalities, local public servants are agents for multiple principals, and must confront the "multiple logics" of Chinese bureaucracy.[43] To return to Zhou et al.'s prior metaphor, such public servants are like acrobats inching along a high wire. As acrobats, local Chinese officials must "muddle through" or, as others might phrase it, "balance carefully," as they face forces pulling in many directions, such as residents' expectations, central government's unfunded mandates, and sometimes conflicting administrative directives from provincial and central bureaucracies.[44]

For example, Jennifer Pan (2020) shows the inherent contradictions with the transparency initiative that is part of China's means-tested, non-conditional cash transfer program, the *dibao* welfare program. Local officials attempt to fulfill two different mandates from higher-level officials: equitably distribute cash transfers to alleviate poverty; and preserve social stability. Lists of those

[42] As noted in Chapter 1, "Chinese-style" or "with Chinese characteristics" are epithets common in many prominent policy documents and social science discourses on China, illustrating a parallel: both the United States and China consider themselves sui generis.
[43] Zhou, Xueguang, Hong Lian, Leonard Ortolano, and Yinyu Ye. 2013, "A Behavioral Model of 'Muddling through' in the Chinese Bureaucracy: The Case of Environmental Protection," *China Journal*, 70, 120–147.
[44] Ibid.

who receive *dibao* must be posted for local citizens to view. The intention of such a transparency requirement is to avoid corruption and improve program targeting. However, it reveals how *dibao* is also allocated to those "less deserving" (when used to buy off people suspected of protesting), thus arousing perceptions of injustice. Pan uses considerable quantitative and qualitative evidence to show that "it is the pursuit of stability itself that damages the government's programmatic commitments, leading to more protests and to a gently simmering dissatisfaction that has negative consequences for public assessments of government performance and legitimacy."[45]

Motivations for collaborative governance differ across China's local governments, and even for a single locale motives can change as development proceeds. Huge regional and urban–rural disparities in living standards[46] shape China's approach to delegation. In relatively poor localities, contracting or other delegation may take the form of de facto collaboration for resources – even when a conventional service contract seemingly makes more sense. In principle, government should hold tight to control if there is little upside to private discretion. In practice, local officials can lack both the funds and the expertise to specify and enforce a detailed contract for services. In the most developed municipalities, by contrast, sharing of discretion is often deliberate and carefully crafted to promote public value. Motivations may also shift away from resources toward collaboration for information and productivity.

Another key characteristic of China's approach to the embrace of private roles for public goals, highly relevant to the topic of transparency, is the rapidity of change over the past two decades. Consider the contrast between the original railway system and its current high-speed railways (Chapter 3); the shift in approach taken between hosting the 2008 Olympics and those to take place in 2022 (Chapter 5); or Chinese officials' handling of health crises such as the 2003 SARS pandemic versus more recent avian influenza or vaccine scandals (Chapter 7). China's housing policy (Chapter 4) followed a trajectory that touched upon a wide range of delivery models. From direct state provision it evolved to indirect provision through work units – often SOEs with broad mandates to provide welfare to employees, and soft budget constraints to support them – and finally to support for the purchase of privately built housing. This heavily collaborative model coincided, of necessity, with governmental efforts to manage a booming housing market to avoid a bursting bubble that would have profound domestic and global repercussions.[47]

[45] Pan, Jennifer, 2020. *Welfare for Autocrats: How Social Assistance in China Cares for its Rulers.* Oxford University Press p. 24.

[46] Kanbur, Ravi, Yue Wang, and Xiaobo Zhang. *The Great Chinese Inequality Turnaround.* Vol. 1637. Intl Food Policy Res Inst, 2017.

[47] E. Glaeser, W. Huang, Y. Ma, and A. Shleifer, 2017, "A Real Estate Boom with Chinese Characteristics," *The Journal of Economic Perspectives*, 31(1), 93–116; Chang Liu and Wei Xiong, 2018, "China's Real Estate Market," NBER working paper 25297,

The United States could not experience such dramatic shifts, for several relatively obvious reasons: The United States never transitioned from central planning to markets, and its transition from majority agricultural work to a mostly urban, services-based economy stretched over more than a century. Moreover, its messy democratic arrangements are such that the tug and pull of political processes and the power of entrenched interests often dramatically slow the pace of even highly desirable policy change.

In both countries, each in its own way, transparency is critical to the healthy, legitimate growth of collaborative governance. It helps to fend off a vicious cycle of rewarding and attracting into partnerships the kinds of actors who would seek to undermine collective goals and to divert public resources to their own coffers. In the United States, transparency is usually acknowledged with enthusiasm, sometimes verging on reverence. Even if the merits of transparency may be oversold in the United States, it has undeniable potential – also amid undeniable challenges – in China for empowering choice, informing behavior, enabling responsible criticism,[48] and deterring corruption.[49]

LOOKING FORWARD

Any day's headlines provide a crude, profoundly fallible first draft of history. Today's headlines invite the impression that the relationship between China and the United States is fundamentally one of antagonistic symbiosis. The two countries can't live without each other; the economy of each is intimately dependent on the other. And yet they can't live comfortably *with* each other. Their antagonism is highlighted by pandemic recriminations, trade and tariff squabbles, fights over intellectual property, military buildups, episodic near-clashes, and disputes in international forums. We can't dismiss the possibility that one day soon – perhaps even before this book has been published – the headlines will blare out some calamitous flare-up of the smoldering tensions or (less probably but more hopefully) some unexpected détente.

Here we have sought to chronicle a completely different dimension of the relationship, beneath and beyond the daily headlines but perhaps more consequential in the long arc of history. In many of their most important

---

November 2018, prepared for *The Handbook of China's Financial System*, edited by M. Amstad, G. Sun, and W. Xiong.

[48] Chinese with family members in government are more likely to voice complaints and provide feedback, arguably because they have reassurance that their complaints will be viewed as responsible criticism; Tsai and Xu (2018) thus conceptualize political connections as a resource for civic participation.

[49] One interesting case mentioned in Chapter 4 is that of corruption in China's land markets and the effectiveness of Xi Jinping's anti-corruption campaign in reducing some of the inside dealing that allowed politically connected firms to obtain land at discounted prices; see, T. Chen, and J. K. S. Kung, 2018, "Busting the "Princelings": The Campaign against Corruption in China's Primary Land Market," *The Quarterly Journal of Economics*, 134(1), 185–226.

undertakings, from providing health care and education to building transportation infrastructure and housing, neither symbiosis nor antagonism is relevant. In these domains, China and the United States are neither codependent nor grappling for supremacy. They are more like dissimilar siblings engaged in parallel play. There is little opportunity for either toy-sharing or toy-stealing. The United States does not worry that China will take over its public schools. China neither hopes nor fears that the United States will address its looming imbalance between working-age and elderly citizens.

But both countries may learn from the efforts that the other is taking to engage the private sector to advance public goals. This book has sought to distill lessons, both positive and negative, from those efforts. These concluding observations make no attempt at a comprehensive summary of those lessons. To do so would risk either confusingly dense compression or tedious length. But, embracing ourselves the transparency imperative, we find it helpful to explicitly name some recurring themes, lest they get lost in the real-world complexity of our many examples:

- Collaborative governance is an important category of collective action, distinguished by its defining characteristic of shared discretion from simple contracting, voluntarism, or pure governmental responsibility.
- The vivid differences between the United States and China – in history, culture, institutions, values, and governmental structure – should not obscure some fundamental similarities in the historical situations of these two world-leading nations. Both countries have big ambitions *and* big problems.
- The ancient Eastern nation and the relatively young Western one are both in a period of turmoil over the right ways to structure and manage their public responsibilities. It is at once inspiring and sobering to witness leaders' willingness to rethink the fundamentals.
- In part because many collective tasks – an increasing share in complex modern economies – invite or require engaging the private sector, and in part because business is in the blood of both the American and the Chinese people, cross-sectoral collaboration is, and will almost certainly remain, a feature of both countries' governments.
- The nonprofit sector, long a mainstay of collective action in the United States, is only haltingly and unevenly beginning to stir in China. We expect that a decade or two hence nonprofits – with Chinese characteristics, to be sure – will be coming into their own as a major social force.
- Both countries display a gradient in the degree of private engagement. That degree is influenced by the nature of each public task; by each nation's political and ideological fundamentals; and by accidents of history.
- Both nations are flexible and eclectic in the ways they take on public tasks. Yes, China tilts more toward government. Yes, the United States is more ideologically inclined toward markets. Yet ever since Deng Xiaoping

initiated economic reforms in the late 1970s, China – despite being governed by the Communist Party with an official socialist ideology – has shifted away from central planning. It now vests the vast portion of its economy in the private sector. Current rhetoric stresses the goal of building a "moderately prosperous society" based on "market socialism" as part of "socialism with Chinese characteristics for a new era."

- Both countries' leaders aver that the interests that should be served are those of the citizens. Such assertions, we recognize, are at best unevenly sincere, are sometimes coated with a glaze of cynicism, and at times are even glaringly false. Nevertheless, we believe it is impossible to understand public life in either country without granting them a meaningful degree of truth.

Both the United States and China, despite their dominant ideologies, have shown themselves to be highly pragmatic nations. They have both evolved toward collaborative approaches for producing a broad range of goods and services for their citizens. But collaboration should never be the goal in and of itself. The central objective of government, and of public policy more generally, should be the creation of public value. Whenever government structures a role for private actors, it is the citizens' interests that should be served. They should get good value for the resources that they put up for the pursuit of those interests, whether through taxes, fees, or the (implicit or explicit) ceding of power to the government. In China as in the United States, wise and patriotic public officials are experimenting with ways of engaging the private sector to do better by the people than the government could do on its own. The concepts, principles, tools, and examples offered here have one goal: To aid the noble and necessary work of creating public value.

Index